Participation: from tyranny to transformation?

SAMUEL HICKEY AND GILES MOHAN | editors

Participation: from tyranny to transformation?

Exploring new approaches to participation in development

Participation: from tyranny to transformation? Exploring new approaches to participation in development was first published by Zed Books Ltd, 7 Cynthia Street, London N1 9JF, UK and Room 400, 175 Fifth Avenue, New York, NY 10010, USA in 2004.

www.zedbooks.co.uk

Cover designed by Andrew Corbett
Set in FF Arnhem and Futura Bold by Ewan Smith, London
Printed and bound in the UK by Biddles Ltd <www.biddles.co.uk>

Distributed in the USA exclusively by Palgrave Macmillan, a division of St Martin's Press, LLC, 175 Fifth Avenue, New York, NY 10010.

A catalogue record for this book is available from the British Library.
US CIP data are available from the Library of Congress.

ISBN 1 84277 460 3 cased
ISBN 1 84277 461 1 limp
Second Impression, 2005

Contents

Acknowledgements

This book draws directly on papers presented at an international conference in Manchester in February 2003, although the commentary section and one other paper have since been added. For reasons of space, we were unable to include all of the papers presented at what was a vibrant and progressive gathering, although their contributions and those of participants more generally were vital in shaping our thinking around and enthusiasm for this project. Thanks to our respective institutions and also the UK Department for International Development for their financial support of the event and subsequently for funding the circulation of this book to institutions in the South. We are very grateful to Debra Whitehead for pulling the conference together so expertly, and also helping to prepare the final manuscript. For finishing this job and preparing the index, many thanks to Karen Hunt. Zed Books, and our editors Robert Molteno and Anna Hardman, have provided support throughout.

The intellectual debts for this project, which comes not from a specific research project but from a decade or so of engagement with research and teaching on issues of participation, are numerous. However, particular thanks go to Peter Beaney, Tony Bebbington, Jeremy Holland, Uma Kothari, Diana Mitlin, Kristian Stokke and his colleagues in Oslo, and Neil Webster for reading earlier drafts of our chapters and making insightful and critical comments. The IDPM Masters course on 'Decentralization and Participation' provided a pedagogic space through which many of these ideas emerged, and study fellows have more recently acted as insightful adjudicators concerning debates over 'tyranny' and 'transformation'. The contributors to this collection themselves have taken the underlying thinking behind this venture and reshaped, deepened and broadened it in ways we hadn't previously imagined, and have thus provided a very stimulating editorial experience. Finally, working for Village AiD has proved to be a constant source of stimulation and insight into how the politics of participatory development need not always get lost in international development work.

Sam Hickey, Giles Mohan

To Fiona and Katy

ONE | From tyranny to transformation?

1 | Towards participation as transformation: critical themes and challenges

SAM HICKEY AND GILES MOHAN

Setting the scene

The notion and practice of participation in international development stands at an uneasy crossroads, reviled in some academic and practitioner circles, yet as ubiquitous as ever in others. Having moved virtually unchecked from the margins to the mainstream of development since the mid-1980s, the past decade witnessed a growing backlash against the ways in which participation managed to 'tyrannize' development debates without sufficient evidence that participatory approaches were living up to the promise of empowerment and transformative development for marginal peoples. This was vividly captured in a book entitled *Participation: The New Tyranny?* (Cooke and Kothari 2001), which focused explicitly on 'participation' in the form of participatory rural appraisal. Few contributors to the *Tyranny* collection envisaged a positive future for participatory development.

Nevertheless, the evidence so far in the new millennium suggests that participation has actually deepened and extended its role in development, with a new range of approaches to participation emerging across theory, policy and practice (however, although characterized as tyrannical, this mainstreaming and spread are highly uneven). Most significantly, people in developing countries are continually devising new and innovative strategies for expressing their agency in development arenas. What remains to be explored is not only the extent to which the current generation of participatory approaches can offer answers to the critique ranged against participatory development, but can also (re)establish it as a legitimate and genuinely transformative approach to development.

Participation essentially concerns the exercise of popular agency in relation to development, a concern that has been characteristic of post-impasse development studies (e.g. Long and van der Ploeg 1994), and much contemporary development policy is (ostensibly) based on recognizing existing capacities of people as active claims-making agents (e.g. sustainable livelihoods and rights-based approaches). It is not the aim of this collection directly to refute the *Tyranny* critique, but we feel its contribution to understandings of participation as popular agency can be extended in three ways.

First, although the *Tyranny* collection marked the high-point of the backlash against participation, the notion has been subject to a much longer and arguably deeper series of critiques that go beyond narrow interpretations of participation (e.g. Stiefel and Wolfe 1994, Cooke, this volume). It therefore makes little sense to have this as the only source of departure. Second, we agree with the *Tyranny* critique's charge that participatory development has often failed to engage with issues of power and politics and has become a technical approach to development that, in various ways, depoliticizes what should be an explicitly political process. As such, the intention here is to draw out the most salient of these charges, and critically assess contemporary approaches to participation against them.

Finally, the contours of debates over participation have changed in recent years, in ways that matter to both critics and proponents of participation. The importance of participation in development can no longer juxtapose the alleged benefits of bottom-up, people-centred, process-oriented and 'alternative' approaches with top-down, technocratic, blueprint planning of state-led modernization. The mainstreaming of participatory approaches to development – particularly the spread of project-based methodologies like participatory rural appraisal (PRA) from non-governmental organizations to major development agencies, and the scaling up of these approaches into national and international policy-making, through participatory poverty assessments – has helped to blur these neat divisions. Moreover, the recent broadening of the participatory agenda, to encompass institutional issues of governance as well as development policy and practice requires an engagement with wider debates concerning the changing state, in relation to processes of democratization and decentralization. Any claims that participation can challenge the problems of 'uneven development' must be grounded in evidence and theoretically-informed argument rather than in opposition to previously dominant models of development.

The collection is divided into six sections, the first of which reviews contemporary debates and thematic challenges surrounding debates over how participation might be (re)established as a transformative approach to development, while also offering a sceptical note on the dangers of continuing with any participatory project. The second section seeks to rethink the concept of participation through theoretical engagements with space, political capabilities and citizenship. The next three sections analyse case studies of different actors and processes engaged in participation. Section III continues the theoretical debates over participation in relation to the links between participation and popular agency as an embedded practice, and focuses on the complexities of 'indigenous' decision-making. Part IV focuses on civil society and the local state and the synergies and conflicts between them while Part V examines participatory initiatives by international development donors. The final section comprises short reflections by key commentators based both on a selection of chapters from the collection and wider debates on participation.

As will become clear, an underlying theme in all the contributions is that 'politics matters' within international development. We believe, and most contributors confirm, that understanding the ways in which participation relates to existing power structures and political systems provides the basis for moving towards a more transformatory approach to development; one which is rooted in the exercise of a broadly defined citizenship. This chapter seeks to identify the key thematic challenges with which participatory approaches must make a constructive engagement if participation is to be (re)constituted as a viable and transformative approach to development. This requires that we first situate participation within development theory, policy and practice, from both a historical and contemporary perspective.

A brief history of participation in development

Participation has a longer and more varied genealogy in development thinking and practice than is usually acknowledged, and has been periodically regenerated around new schools of thought, institutional agendas and changing political circumstances. This is an important recognition since much of the focus on the mainstreaming of participation over the 1990s, both laudatory and critical, has tended to single out the spread of PRA and treat it as the definitive form of participation. This obscures the diversity of participatory approaches and also overlooks previous debates around alternative approaches.

As Table 1.1 makes apparent, participation has been a central concern for a number of different approaches to development. Each approach has its own trajectory and contextual specificities, and is characterized by particular debates and empirical experiences. Some have continued while others have petered out, and there has been a politics and a political economy surrounding the relative success of each approach, particularly the recent mainstreaming of the 'participation in development' approach. Conversations, both complimentary and critical, can clearly be heard between the different approaches to participation. For example, Chambers (1994) cites Freirean action research as one of several influences on the emergence of PRA, although he is cautious of the more radical Freirean school, restricting talk of power reversals to individuals rather than broader systems of power relations through which people are structurally disempowered (Williams et al. 2003a).

There are at least four ways in which different approaches to partici-

TABLE 1.1 Participation in development theory and practice: a selective history

Era	Approach	Institutional and intellectual influences	Development theory: approach to immanent processes and imminent interventions	Approach to citizenship	Locus/level of engagement
1940s–1950s	Community development (colonial)	United Kingdom Colonial Office 1944 Report on Mass Education in Africa	*Immanent* (Re)produce stable rural communities to counteract processes of urbanization and sociopolitical change, including radical nationalist and leftist movements *Imminent* Development requires participation and self-reliance; cost-sharing. *Animation rurale*, adult literacy and extension education, institution-building, leadership training, development projects	Participation as an obligation of citizenship; citizenship formed in homogeneous communities	Community
1960s–1970s	Community development (post-colonial)	Post-colonial governments (social welfare or specialized departments)	*Immanent* As above; also development of state hegemony, moral economy of state penetration *Imminent* As above; also health, education		
1960s	Political participation	North American political science	*Immanent* Political development dimension of modernization theory. Participation as securing stability, legitimacy for new states and strengthening the political system *Imminent* Voter education; support for political parties	Participation (e.g. voting, campaigning, political party membership) as a right and an obligation of citizenship	Political system and constituent parts; citizens

1960s–1970s	Emancipatory participation (EP)	Radical 'southern' researchers / educationalists. Freire, Fals Borda, Rahman	*Immanent* Analyse and confront 'structures of oppression' within existing forms of economic development, state formation, political rule and social differentiation *Imminent* EP: Participatory action research, conscientization, popular education, support for popular organizations LT: Form base Christian communities, training for transformation, popular education	Participation as a right of citizenship; participatory citizenship as a means of challenging subordination and marginalization	Economic and civic spheres; communities; citizens
	Liberation theology (LT)	2nd Vatican Council, Latin American Catholic priests. Gutierrez, Sobrino			
1970s–1990s	'Alternative development'	Dag Hammarskjold Conference 1974. Development Dialogue, IFAD Dossier. Nerfin, Friedmann	*Immanent* Critique of 'mainstream' development as exclusionary, impoverishing and homogenizing; proposal of alternatives based around territorialism, cultural pluralism and sustainability *Imminent* Popular education; strengthen social movements and self-help groups	Participation as a right of citizenship; citizenship as a key objective of alternative development, to be realized in multi-level political communities	Initially focused on communities and civic society, latterly the state through 'inclusive governance'
1980s–present	Populist / Participation in development	Development professionals, NGOs (e.g. MYRADA, IIED) World Bank Participation Learning Group, UN Agencies. Chambers	*Immanent* Little direct engagement; implicit critique of modernization *Imminent* Failure of top-down projects and planning; participation required to empower people, capture indigenous people's knowledge, ensure sustainability and efficiency of interventions. Participatory: rural/urban appraisal, learning and action, monitoring and evaluation; NGDO projects.	Focus on participation in projects rather than in broader political communities	Development professionals and agencies; local participants

TABLE 1.1 Participation in development theory and practice: a selective history (cont.)

Era	Approach	Institutional and intellectual influences	Development theory: approach to immanent processes and imminent interventions	Approach to citizenship	Locus/level of engagement
Mid-1990s–present	Social capital	World Bank Social Capital and Civil Society Working Group. Putnam, Bourdieu, Narayan	*Immanent* Social capital promoted as a basis for economic growth *Imminent* Local institution building, support participation in networks and associations	Participation as a right and obligation of citizenship	Civic associations
Late 1990s–present	Participatory governance and citizenship participation	Participatory Research and Action (Delhi), Institute for Development Studies, Brighton (Participation Group)	*Immanent* Development requires liberal or social democracy, with a responsive state and strong civil society. Some focus on social justice *Imminent* Convergence of 'social' and 'political' participation, scaling-up of participatory methods, state–civic partnerships, decentralization, participatory budgeting, citizens' hearings, participatory poverty assessments, PRSP consultations	Participation as primarily a right of citizenship	Citizens, civil society, state agencies and institutions

pation can be characterized and compared: the locus and level of engagement, ideological/political project, conception of citizenship, and links to development theory. Analysis along these axes, and particularly the latter two, allows for greater clarity over which form of participation is being discussed and promoted, and for what purpose. The locus of change that participatory approaches seek to engage with might be individual/institutional or micro/macro. For example, a recent criticism has concerned the overly localist approach of many participatory approaches to the exclusion of broader, more structural patterns of injustice (Mohan and Stoke 2000). This level of engagement determines who or what will be the focus of efforts towards empowerment and transformation, or potentially the subject of coercion and control.

Following on from this, the second dimension of comparison concerns the ideological underpinnings of different approaches to participation. What Table 1.1 reveals is that 'participation' has been called on to perform a wide range of functions for differing purposes, ideologies and political projects. It has never been entirely free of charges of being tyrannical. The emancipatory projects of social justice that underpin the 'alternative' approaches of the 1970s can be juxtaposed with the community development movements (colonial and post-independence) where there were clear intentions to control rural populations.

Third, the promotion of 'citizenship' as a normative goal of participation is woven throughout most approaches to participation to date. What has varied has been the different forms and content of citizenship promoted under each approach. It can be asked whether the focus has been on liberal forms of citizenship at the national level (e.g. political participation) or on substantive, communitarian forms (community development), and whether the emphasis is on participation as a right (alternative development) or as an obligation of citizenship (community development). In contemporary terms, the concept and practice of citizenship is increasingly viewed as the means by which to capture both popular agency in a more political sense and the convergence between participatory development and participatory governance (e.g. Gaventa, this volume). We return ourselves to this theme below and in more depth in Chapter 4. Finally, it is important to trace the links between approaches to participation and broader trends within development theory, and it is this neglected dimension that we turn to here.

Participation and development theory

Several approaches to participation emerged in an era of state failure, panic over top-down modernization approaches, proclamations of the end of grand explanations and a measure of post-colonial guilt. As Vincent (this volume) notes, the 'community' has periodically been destroyed by underlying processes of development, only to be resurrected as the proper source of recovery through trustee-led interventions. We are now undergoing a reassessment of development theory, much of it condensed to debates over the respective roles that institutional arenas (public, private and civic) should play (e.g. Brett 2000). The convergence between participatory development and governance can be seen in the context of an increasing interest in the synergies and division of labour between public and civic spheres. However, we would argue also that development theory is far from limited to such institutional debates, and that real contests remain concerning the form that development and democracy, state and civil society can and should take, and concerning how to theorize the role of agency within debates over development and governance. There are good reasons for participation to engage with this broader level of theorizing.

The imminent/immanent divide is of particular utility in setting the terms of this debate (Cowen and Shenton 1996). The relationship between 'development' in the form of specific interventions and 'development' as a historical process of social change is a perennial concern within development studies. Imminent development, led by a belief in the 'makeability' of society, emerged over the past two centuries largely as a means of managing those 'surplus populations' that have either been excluded from or 'adversely incorporated' into processes of immanent development (ibid.). It can be argued that there has been a tendency within contemporary development studies to focus on imminent rather than immanent processes of development, in part due to the strong moral imperative to focus solutions on ongoing problems of impoverishment and exclusion. It is this tendency which Kapoor (2002) describes as inductive and empiricist as opposed to metaphysical and theoretical. More specifically, two recent movements have further consolidated this trend: first, the apparent failure of 'classic' development theory adequately to capture and predict these historical processes (Booth 1994) and, second, the perceived need for development research to become more 'relevant' in terms of directly informing interventions (Edwards 1994). However, to privilege the practices of imminent development risks a further type of 'irrelevance' by distracting from an engagement with the underlying forces of socioeconomic and political change that shape people's livelihoods. The related assertion that development can be wilfully 'managed' through 'the right mixture' of institutional responses has further 'depoliticized' the practice of development in poor countries (Ferguson 1994), rendering it a technocratic process to be administered and planned for by agents of development rather than negotiated with and contested by its subjects.

The mainstream and 'populist' form of 'participation in development' of the 1980s onwards claimed to address these various irrelevancies. It asserted the importance of placing local realities at the heart of development interventions and the need to transform agents of development from being directive 'experts' to 'facilitators' of the collection of local knowledge and the 'enablers' of capabilities. Moreover, the 'power' transformations required between 'uppers' and 'lowers', it was argued, could be achieved through according participatory roles to the subjects of development at each stage of development interventions. It was with this form of participatory development that the critical backlash of the 1990s has been most clearly directed, not least, we argue, because of its failure to engage with underlying processes of development.

Reframing participation: towards citizenship

As we have noted, the populist approach to participation in development came under increasing criticism during the 1990s. It is not our intention to revisit these well-known discussions, but to examine how recent approaches can be read against these critiques. Broadly, the key arguments against participatory development include an obsession with the 'local' as opposed to wider structures of injustice and oppression (Mohan and Stokke 2000); an insufficiently sophisticated understanding of how power operates and is constituted and thus of how empowerment may occur (e.g. Mosse 1994; Kothari 2001); an inadequate understanding of the role of structure and agency in social change (Cleaver 1999); and, partly as a result of the mainstreaming of participation, a tendency for certain agents of participatory development to treat participation as a technical method of project work rather than as a political methodology of empowerment (Carmen 1996; Cleaver 1999; Rahman 1995). Many of these problems, we would argue, have arisen because the populist form of participation that has come to dominate eschewed an engagement with development as an immanent process in favour of a narrow focus on development interventions and experts. This approach tends towards a methodological individualism (Francis 2001) that obscures an analysis of what makes participation difficult for marginal groups in the first place, particularly in relation to processes of state formation, social stratification and political economy.

A characteristic of the most severe critiques has been an explicit focus on the work of Robert Chambers, and, more specifically, the project-based approaches to participation which he has advocated (e.g. PRA) over the past two decades (Cooke and Kothari 2001; Kapoor 2002; Kumar and Corbridge 2002; Williams et al. 2003b). There are at least two problems here. First, the tendency to reduce 'participation' to one particularly visible and mainstreamed variant that fails to appreciate those historical moments and contemporary developments in participation that can offer ways around the failures of populist approaches. Second, and as argued here by Cornwall, and Waddington and Mohan, critics also take Chambers's work at face value and thereby ignore both the strategy that underpins it (namely to fight the economism, 'professionalism' and other biases that pervade mainstream development thinking and research) and the genuine gains that might be had for marginal people from such approaches.

Within this context, at least three contemporary approaches to participation can be read against the contemporary critique of participation. The first response is to claim 'mainstreaming' as a sign of success and focus on both honing the methodologies and ensuring that these are scaled up and diversified across all arenas and levels of decision-making (e.g. participatory poverty assessments, PPAs). The second response confronts the critique against participation by broadening the agenda to capture a more political sense of agency and the recent overlaps with participatory governance, through a reconceptualization of participation. This approach includes work on 'citizenship' and 'rights', 'political space', 'political capabilities', 'political contract' and 'political capital' (see Cornwall, Williams, Vincent and Hickey and Mohan, this volume). The third response rejects 'participation' in its current form and seeks radical alternatives, usually in relation to 'alternative development' thinking (e.g. Carmen 1996).

Our contention, developed in more detail in Chapter 4, is that for participatory approaches to be transformative requires a critical engagement with each of these three approaches. First, participation must be ideologically explicit and tied to a coherent theory of development. Second, the locus of transformation must go beyond the individual and local and involve multi-scaled strategies that encompass the institutional and structural. We argue that a radicalized notion of citizenship – derived in part from alternative development theories of participation – provides the intermediary analytical and strategic basis upon which this project can be pursued.

Citizenship has usually been associated with its liberal incarnation, referring to the legal rights and responsibilities conferred by the state. Alternative and populist approaches saw citizenship in active terms initially related to decision-making at the community level, but later engaging with citizenship in multiple political communities including the state (e.g. Friedmann 1992). The recent move towards participatory governance helps bring together these different political spheres, and holds out the possibilities not only for a more unified notion of citizenship (Gaventa, this volume) but also a radical and transformatory form of citizenship (Mohan and Hickey, this volume). Citizenship also provides a means of linking participation with the emerging 'rights-based' agenda (Holland et al., this volume). Within these twin movements – a coherent ideological and theoretical stance and the reframing of participation as multi-scaled citizenship – we have identified from the chapters gathered here and wider debates a series of thematic priorities – transformation, the temporal and spatial, and representation – with which contemporary approaches to participation must engage in order to (re)constitute participation as a viable and legitimate approach within development.

Transformation

There remains a strong sense in the literature on participatory development that the proper objective of participation is to ensure the 'transformation' of existing development practice and, more radically, the social relations, institutional practices and capacity gaps which cause social exclusion. This is central to many of the approaches to participation outlined in Table 1.1, although efforts to define 'transformation' in terms of the levels at which it takes place, the period over which it occurs, and the ideological underpinnings of transformation are often overlooked. For most mainstream interventions, it is unrealistic to expect participatory projects to transform existing patterns of power relations (e.g. Kumar and Corbridge 2002: 76). Some (e.g. Williams, this volume) argue that it is therefore necessary to alter the basis upon which participation is evaluated. However, it might be argued that a prior move would be to avoid promoting participatory approaches at local levels where there is little pre-existing popular agency of or on behalf of the poorest/most excluded, or where the wider political space is unsupportive of such initiatives (Fox 1997; Kohl 2003).

However, we argue that participatory practice and political action can be directly associated with the types of institutional and structural transformations required to create this form of political space.[1] In such examples, whether NGO programmes of REFLECT or participatory budgeting, it is apparent that the approaches are strongly informed by an engagement with development as an underlying process, rather than a series of technical interventions, and are tied into broader projects of social justice and radical political change. Such a convergence can be worked towards by international development agencies through a close reading of local development processes and partnerships with local organizations, in part through building on existing forms of popular agency (see Hickey 2002, Masaki, Waddington and Mohan, and Mitlin, this volume). To do this requires appreciating the meanings and levels of transformation.

Vincent's chapter reworks the 'localist' problem within participatory approaches, such that interventions at this level will have little impact on broader patterns of exclusion and injustice, noting that 'locals' themselves are well aware of this and are consequently reluctant to commit their agency to such interventions. Some Foucauldians would argue that Marxist and other structuralist accounts of power which see it concentrated in certain spheres (the state, IFIs etc.) potentially ignore the capillarity of power and hence its potential to be used productively. Structuralists would counter that a change in individuals' attitudes does not guarantee the overthrowing of deeper institutional divisions or the forms of governance thrown up by uneven development (cf. Kelly, this volume). By combining structural and post-structural accounts of power it is possible to examine how individuals (re)make rules and (re)constitute institutions and conversely how institutions shape individual actions (Masaki, this volume).

In this vein, the transformative potential of localized participatory approaches are reliant on broader political change. In terms of relations between civil society organizations and the local state, Mitlin (this volume) shows that the eventual successes of federated community-based organizations in securing rights for poor people in terms of land and housing were not simply dependent on securing greater levels of voice for civil society and state responsiveness. Underpinning these changes was a deeper transformation of the power relations between the local state and citizens, as a result of elections, the decreased legitimacy of the central state and the changing needs of local capital.

For Williams et al. (2003a), transformations do not necessarily involve a reversal of power relations but a strengthening of the bargaining power of the poor *within* these relations. Here, local patrons are portrayed as being of great utility to 'lowers', with the former preferring to work through them rather than take their place. Similarly, the work of Village AiD in Ghana (Waddington and Mohan, this volume) showed that mainstream participatory approaches which sought to make transparent and public the processes of decision-making were resisted by many women since it cut down their opportunities for informal politicking through the male elders. Participatory interventions can facilitate this to the extent that they develop the political capabilities of the poor in ways that advance their room for manoeuvre within local power relations, including their capacity to hold patrons to account (Williams, this volume).

Within historical processes of community formation, popular agency has often been co-opted into projects of establishing local ethnic–territorial hegemony, and utilized as the basis upon which local development is pursued. Within the African context, participation forms an element of local citizenship obligations, which are frequently institutionalized within 'hometown associations' (Henry, this volume). Such 'traditions' and associations contain structures of domination which oblige members of clans and ethnic groups to enact 'development' as part of their identity. It is on this understanding of 'participation as obligation' that many local initiatives are based, rather than the 'participation as a right' approach that has been pursued by international development agencies over the past two decades. Where such obligations weigh more heavily on some members of the 'community', participatory interventions may lead both to heightened levels of oppression and (conversely) the emergence of civic virtue (Masaki, this volume).

Overall, it appears that transformations need to reach beyond the local, involving multi-scaled strategies that are operationalized at all levels – individual, structural and institutional – and are linked to a radical development project. This is not to underplay the importance of being cognisant of local sociopolitical structures and practices, but does involve recognizing both the room for manoeuvre within the local, and that not all local elites and power relations are inherently exclusive and subordinating.

The temporal aspects of participation

Development by its very nature is suggestive of change over time whether this is articulated in notions of evolution (Cowen and Shenton 1996), modernity as enlightenment (Pred and Watts 1992), development as class contradiction (Warren 1980) or modernization as involving a series of stages of growth (Rostow 1960). In many senses these are the *longues durées* of immanent development which lie in stark contrast to the rapidity of the project timeframe of imminent interventions or the timeless romanticism of some post-developmental visions. Hence, the temporal dynamics of participation are important in understanding the potential for transformative development. There are three closely related senses in which the temporal is important for participation: understanding histories, overlapping temporalities, and the unfolding of political processes in relation to catalytic participatory interventions and critical moments. Cutting across this discussion is Masaki's warning, drawing on Bourdieu, that analysts and practitioners of social change should avoid imposing a linear and continuous notion of 'calendar time' on to the 'practical time' within which negotiations over power relations operate, and which involve a great variety of rhythms in the different places and for the different actors involved.

The deeper understanding of local sociopolitical dynamics and their relationship to other scales of governance called for above requires an historical analysis of how institutions and agencies evolved over time. In this collection Vincent analyses the historical reasons why people do not offer their agency while the notion of 'political capabilities' developed by Williams seeks to situate the current exercise of popular agency within a longer historical trajectory of collective behaviour.

The second implication of a temporal analysis is in the overlapping of political processes. We discuss in more detail below how spaces of participation may overlap which sometimes reinforce one another and at other times are antagonistic. In the same way political processes can unfold at different 'speeds' and in different 'cycles' which can be beneficial to the poor or work to undermine efforts in different political arenas. For example, several contributors (Florisbelo and Guijt; Mitlin; Masaki) discuss the importance of elections and how these become key moments when participatory processes can either be strengthened and/or manipulated for electoral gain or where manoeuvring in the formal political sector sidelines less formal processes.

The final understanding of time relates to the unfolding of political processes and how the embedding of such practices might allow deeper transformations to take place. Participatory development has been charged with being too rapid and participatory methodologies used cynically to 'prove' a project's participatory credentials. Conversely, Williams et al. (2003b) discuss how long-term political projects are far more promising than one-off transformative events, and require institutional change not just sporadic events. In his analysis of citizenship formation over time regarding the respective rights and roles of migrants and indigenes, Masaki notes that processes of social justice might often be temporally lengthy and grinding rather than explosive. Between these two positions, both Florisbelo and Guijt (regarding coalition-building) and Mitlin (on the construction of federations) note not simply the importance of allowing time for such processes to mature, but also the importance of catalytic moments in starting participatory processes on the road to transformation. As Brigg (2002) notes, seeing power and development as multi-dimensional rather than intentional and mono-causal allows us to incorporate contingency into our analyses. Such moments disrupt notions of smooth political teleologies although they cannot be created artificially by policy.

Space

Political theorists tend to privilege the temporal over the spatial with the former suggesting dynamism and progression. Doreen Massey (1994: 253) summarizes this belief as 'Time Marches On but space is a kind of stasis, where nothing really happens'. She calls for an alternative view of space which is socially constructed with a necessary dialectic between the spatial and social on the one hand, and between the spatial and temporal on the other. The implications of this 'politics of space/time' are numerous with a number of authors beginning to tease out the implications of a spatialized take on participation. We identify three interrelated ways in which this is occurring: spaces as situated practices, spaces as sites of resistance, and spaces as dynamic political fields.

Situated practice A criticism of some approaches to participation is that they tend to romanticize and homogenize the places in which political action occurs. The most prevalent tendency here is to treat the 'local' and 'community' as self-evident and unproblematic social categories. However, if we view places as sites where complex social worlds are situated then we can avoid this tendency and thereby produce less essentialist analyses. Clearly, political practices take place at and across a range of sites which put 'community' back, not in an idealized or abstract sense, but as a living and contested entity. From this we get a more subtle understanding of both political subjects and places. Massey (1995: 286) uses a 'layering' metaphor to evoke ongoing 'rounds' of identity formation so that 'Political subjects are indeed constituted in political practice, but they are not constructed out of nothing'. This observation urges us to take note of the historical construction of place-based identities that is sensitive to the effects of prior processes which are themselves shaped by forces that may not originate within that space.

Place and resistance This emphasis on identity, place and political action has been taken up by a variety of social and political analysts, usually as a means of conceptualizing 'resistance' (Amoore et al. 1997; Peet and Watts 1996). Many of these tend to posit localities as sites of resistance to 'global' forces in which local cultures become the bedrock for various alternatives to development. Two lines of critique have emerged. The first, as we just outlined, is that the local is not a bounded entity; rather it is constructed from overlapping and intersecting flows. These more nuanced engagements with 'local' culture are evidenced in the chapters by Masaki, Henry and Vincent in this volume. Second, this focus on identity can ignore the material basis for identity, exploitation and politics, a theme which Anthony Bebbington and others have recently developed.

Bebbington (2000) argues that the culturalist views of Escobar, while important, tend to underplay those factors that neo-liberals discuss; namely market forces and material well-being. Bebbington is also critical of Escobar and others' insistence on localities as sites of 'resistance', because this fails to understand how people make a living in these increasingly global times, a point further articulated here by Vincent. He argues that rather than seeing places as sites of resistance we need to see them in more complex terms involving production and reproduction. Bebbington characterizes this as 'place-making', because people are not simply detached recipients of external assistance, but active and knowing agents in their own well-being. While this is welcome, Bebbington is also in danger of essentializing place by implying that everybody in a given place is equally committed to its 'making'. This risks treating places as harmonious entities untroubled by inequalities of power and wealth and the political agendas this engenders. To avoid this we need to unpack places and look at the different forms of political action that occur and how these relate to concepts and practices of participation.

Different spaces, different politics Many current approaches to spaces and places of participation are rooted in theoretical approaches informed by French social theory and the awareness that 'Less attention has been paid to what *actually* happens in practice' (Cornwall 2002: 7). This straddles the understandings of space as a social and theoretical construct and spaces as a lived experience. Such approaches examine these spatio-political practices as being initiated either by the marginalized or in some way provided by the powerful (Cornwall, this volume); each with different implications for participatory politics. The difference lies in the power relations and motivations for creating and/or entering spaces. Provided spaces may be the well-worn sites of formal political processes such as council meetings, whereas claimed spaces are more 'organic'.

It would be misleading to see all participatory spaces, provided or claimed, as disempowering simply because they are touched by the 'development machine'. Such analyses of spaces as unequal and disempowering overlook the ways in which wider understandings of political agency can be exercised. To see them as such denies the less powerful any agency when in fact 'beneficiaries ... constitute and manipulate project discourse in managing their own relationships with external patrons and donors' (Mosse 2003). This has two implications. First, that seemingly contrived spaces can still hold the potential for action which is to some degree managed by the marginalized, albeit often in unintended ways. Second, that these different spaces are not discrete or singular but allow a form of political learning where experiences from one space are transported and transformed consciously or unconsciously in different and new spaces. Away from the transformation of micro-social relations, such processes can impact on citizenship whereby invited project spaces engage with formal policy spaces.

Representation

In the light of efforts to overcome the 'localism' of participatory development, it is somewhat surprising that so little has been written about 'representation' within the participatory literature. Representation can mean 'speaking of' – constructing accounts and writing texts – or it can mean 'speaking for' – advocating and mediating. Some participatory learning and action combine the two, believing that by speaking of the subaltern experience they will change the political relations in their favour. Our concern is with the importance of representation and the variety of legitimate modes of political engagement. Some approaches to participation import political processes, like ranking within PRA exercises, that may not be seen as legitimate by the participant, or which could supersede existing political channels.

The character of the institutional channels available within political systems, and of the resources required to participate at ever higher levels (education and time in particular) means that much of what is considered 'participatory' is more a process whereby large numbers of people are *represented* by a relatively small group of participants. As Mitlin's definition of federation among local organizations makes clear, this is primarily about the organized interaction of *leaders* rather than members *per se*.

Debates about representation are increasingly important in recent work on participatory development and governance. Some of this is in recognition of critiques that have been made concerning the costs of participation. For example, Mitlin (this volume) notes that direct participation may be seen as too risky by the poor, who willingly hand over this 'right' to others. Williams et al. (2003a: 177–8) similarly reposition local power brokers as being highly valued by the poor as people who can represent them at higher levels, rather than as the self-seeking entrepreneurs of those who might seek purer forms of participation of the poorest themselves.

It is important to reconsider the potential tensions and synergies between the project that underpins moves towards greater participation and the wider project of democratization, with its primary focus on representative forms of democracy. The rationale for promoting wider participation is often made on the basis that electoral representation offers a particularly limited form of democracy, that party systems often exclude the poor and that procedural democracy lacks the substance of a broader set of participatory engagements (Gaventa and Brown, this volume). In terms of participatory governance, it is apparent that for reforms such as decentralization to be transformative, they need to be promoted by a political party that represents both a substantial section of the disadvantaged and excluded citizenry, within a broader project of social justice (Heller

2001; Schneider and Goldfrank 2002). In this collection, Florisbelo and Guijt describe how the participatory project of unions and NGOs in Brazil failed to move forwards until they secured support from a political party, while for Masaki, democratic politics opened up a space through which a marginal group could begin to renegotiate its status as 'forced labour' in local development efforts.

However, critics also note that participatory approaches to policy-making serve to undermine representative democracy (e.g. Brown). First, the typical outputs of participatory processes (e.g. consultations) could be framed as being more malleable than those of electoral democracy (see Barczak 2001). Second, formal participation may force out more legitimate approaches to securing the agency of marginal groups. For example, the legal codification of the Law of Popular Participation in Bolivia has empowered certain organizations at the expense of those that have historically represented the interests of the poorest (Jeppesen 2002).

This type of analysis – focused on teasing out and unravelling the problem of representation that runs through participatory development and governance – is required to overcome the current lack of understanding within the participatory literature concerning the ideological origins, typologies and problems with representation. If participation is to (re)establish itself as a coherent, viable and transformative approach to development, a more adequate theory of representation, and/or of alternative ways of conceptualizing the ways in which popular agency is legitimately conferred to higher level agents, is required.

Conclusion

We are not best positioned to take stock of where this volume takes the broader field of participation – a task we leave to a panel of authoritative observers (see Part VI). However, what we hope this collection reveals is that there are good reasons for remaining optimistic concerning the potential of participatory approaches to development and governance to effect genuine transformations at a range of levels. This is not in any way to reject the criticisms made of participation over recent years, but to note that the problems of power and politics raised by the critique have in some cases been addressed, most notably through an engagement with a radical political project on the basis of promoting citizenship. Where an engagement with these challenges is not made, then participatory approaches may still have considerable benefits and advantages over other approaches, but cannot be claimed as transformative, and may have to find a new 'gradualist' language with which to extol its virtues (Williams, this volume). Far from being defeated, the eighty-year history of participation within development thinking shows little sign of abating. New and promising ways forward are available. What is required is a greater level of honesty and clarity from both critics and proponents as to what form of participation is being debated; greater conceptual and theoretical coherence on participation; and more considered claims regarding its potential to transform the power relations that underpin exclusion and subordination.

Notes

1 An empirical analysis of these examples can be found in Hickey and Mohan (forthcoming).

2 These include Cornwall (this volume); Jones and SPEECH (2001); Moya Garcia and Way (2003); also Escobar (2000), Gupta and Ferguson (1999), and Kelly (this volume).

References

Amoore, L., et al. (1997) 'Overturning "Globalisation": Resisting the Teleological, Reclaiming the "Political"', *New Political Economy*, 2 (1) 179–95.

Barczak, M. (2001) 'Representation by Consultation? The Rise of Direct Democracy in Latin America', *Latin American Politics and Society*, 43 (3): 37–59.

Bebbington, A. (2000) 'Reencountering Development: Livelihood Transitions and Place Transformations in the Andes', *Annals of the Association of American Geographers*, 90 (3): 495–520.

Booth, D. (1994) 'Rethinking Social Development: An Overview', in D. Booth (ed.), *Rethinking Social Development: Theory, Research and Practice* (Harlow: Longman), pp. 3–41.

Brett, E. A. (2000) 'Development Theory in a Post-Socialist Era: Competing Capitalisms and Emancipatory Alternatives', *Journal of International Development*, 12: 789–802.

Brigg, M. (2002) 'Post-development, Foucault and the Colonisation Metaphor', *Third World Quarterly*, 23 (3): 421–36.

Carmen, R. (1996) *Autonomous Development* (London: Zed Books).

Chambers, R. (1994) 'The Origins and Practice of Participatory Rural Appraisal', *World Development*, 22 (7) 953–69.

— (1995) 'NGOs and Development: The Primacy of the Personal', *IDS Discussion Paper*, 14 (Brighton: Institute of Development Studies).

Cleaver, F. (1999) 'Paradoxes of Participation: Questioning Participatory Approaches to Development', *Journal of International Development*, 11: 597–612.

Cooke, B. (2003) 'A New Continuity with Colonial Administration: Participation in Development Management', *Third World Quarterly*, 24 (1): 47–61.

Cooke, B. and U. Kothari (eds) (2001) *Participation: The New Tyranny?* (London: Zed Books).

Cornwall, A. (2002) 'Making Spaces, Changing Places: Situating Participation in

Development', *IDS Working Paper* 170 (Brighton: Institute of Development Studies).

Cowen, M. and Shenton, R. (1996) *Doctrines of Development* (London: Routledge).

Edwards, M. (1993) 'Does the Doormat Influence the Boot? Critical Thoughts on UK NGOs and International Advocacy', *Development in Practice*, 3: 163–75.

— (1994) 'Rethinking Social Development: The Search For Relevance', in D. Booth (ed.), *Rethinking Social Development: Theory, Research and Practice* (Harlow: Longman), pp. 279–97.

Engberg-Pedersen, L. and N. Webster (2002) 'Introduction to Political Space', in N. Webster and L. Engberg-Pedersen (eds), *In the Name of the Poor: Contesting Political Space for Poverty Reduction* (London: Zed Books), pp. 1–29.

Escobar, A. (2000) 'Culture Sits in Places: Reflections on Globalism and Subaltern Strategies of Localization', *Political Geography*, 20: 139–74.

Ferguson, J. (1994) *The Anti-Politics Machine: 'Development', Depoliticization, and Bureaucratic Power in Lesotho* (Minnesota: University of Minnesota Press).

Fox, J. (1997) 'How Does Civil Society Thicken? The Political Construction of Social Capital in Rural Mexico', in P. Evans (ed.), *State–Society Synergy: Government and Social Capital in Development*, IAS Research Series, 94 (Berkeley: University of California Press), pp. 119–49.

Francis, P. (2001) 'Participatory Development at the World Bank: The Primacy of Process', in B. Cooke and U. Kothari (eds), *Participation: The New Tyranny?* (London: Zed Books), pp. 72–87.

Friedmann, J. (1992) *Empowerment: The Politics of Alternative Development* (Oxford: Blackwell).

Gupta , A. and J. Ferguson (1999) 'Culture, Power and Place: Ethnography at the End of an Era', in A. Gupta and J. Ferguson (eds), *Culture, Power, Place* (Durham, NC and London: Duke University Press), pp. 1–29.

Harper, C. (2001) 'Do the Facts Matter: NGOs, Advocacy and Research?', in M. Edwards and J. Gaventa (eds) *Global Citizen Action* (Boulder, CO: Lynne Rienner), pp. 247–58.

Heller P. (2001) 'Moving the State: The Politics of Democratic Decentralization in Kerala, South Africa, and Porto Alegre', *Politics and Society*, 29 (1): 1–28.

Hickey, S. (2002) 'Transnational NGDOs and Participatory Forms of Rights-based Development: Converging with the Local Politics of Citizenship in Cameroon', *Journal of International Development*, 14 (6): 841–57.

Jeppesen, A. M. E. (2002) 'Reading the Bolivian Landscape of Exclusion and Inclusion: The Law of Popular Participation', in N. Webster and L. Engberg-Pedersen (eds), *In the Name of the Poor: Contesting Political Space for Poverty Reduction* (London: Zed Books), pp. 30–51.

Jones, A. and SPEECH (2001) '"Of other spaces" – Situating Participatory Practices: A Case Study from South India', *IDS Working Paper*, 137 (Brighton: Institute of Development Studies).

Jordan, L. and P. van Tuijl (2000) 'Political Responsibility in Transnational NGO Advocacy', *World Development*, 28 (12): 2051–65.

Kapoor, I. (2002) 'The Devil's in the Theory: A Critical Assessment of Robert Chambers' Work on Participatory Development', *Third World Quarterly*, 23 (1): 101–17.

Kohl, B. (2003) 'Nongovernmental Organizations as Intermediaries for Decentralization in Bolivia', *Environment and Planning*, 21 (3): 317–32.

Kothari, U. (2001) 'Power, Knowledge and Social Control in Participatory Development', in B. Cooke and U. Kothari (eds), *Participation: The New Tyranny?* (London: Zed Books).

Kumar, S. and S. Corbridge (2002) 'Programmed to Fail? Development Projects and the Politics of Participation', *Journal of Development Studies*, 39 (2): 73–103.

Long, N. and J. D. van den Ploeg (1994) 'Heterogeneity, Actor and Structure: Towards a Reconstitution of the Concept of Structure', in D. Booth (ed.), *Rethinking Social Development: Theory, Research and Practice* (Harlow: Longman), pp. 62–89.

Massey, D. (1994) *Space, Place and Gender* (Cambridge: Polity Press).

— (1995) 'Thinking Radical Democracy Spatially', *Environment and Planning D: Society and Space*, 13: 283–8.

Massey, D. (1994) *Space, Place and Gender* (Cambridge: Polity Press).

Mohan, G. and K. Stokke (2000) 'Participatory Development and Empowerment', *Third World Quarterly*, 21 (2): 266–80.

Moser, C. (1993) *Gender Planning and Development: Theory, Practice and Training* (London: Routledge).

Mosse, D. (1994) 'Authority, Gender and Knowledge: Theoretical Reflections on PRA', *Development and Change*, 25 (3): 497–526.

— (2003) 'The Making and Marketing of Participatory Development', in P. van Ufford and A. Giri (eds), *A Moral Critique of Development: In Search of Global Responsibilities* (London and New York: Routledge).

Moya Garcia, X. and S.-A. Way (2003) 'Winning Spaces: Participatory Methodologies in Rural Processes in Mexico', *IDS Working Paper*, 180, (Brighton: Institute of Development Studies).

Peet, R. and M. Watts (1996) 'Liberation Ecology: Development, Sustainability, And Environment in an Age of Market Triumphalism', in R. Peet and M. Watts (eds), *Liberation Ecologies: Environment, Development and Social Movements* (London: Routledge), pp. 1–45.

Pred, A. and M. Watts (1992) *Reworking Modernity: Capitalisms and Symbolic Discontent* (Rutgers, NJ: Rutgers University Press).

Rahman, M. D. A. (1995) 'Participatory Development: Towards Liberation and Co-optation?', in G. Craig and M. Mayo (eds), *Community Empowerment: A Reader in Participation and Development* (London: Zed Books), pp. 24–32.

Rostow, W. (1960) *The Stages of Economic Growth* (Cambridge: Cambridge University Press).

Schneider, A. and B. Goldfrank (2002) 'Budgets and Ballots in Brazil: Participatory Budgeting from the City to the State', *IDS Working Paper*, 149 (Brighton: Institute of Development Studies).

Stiefel, M. and M. Wolfe (1994) *A Voice for the Excluded: Popular Participation in Development* (New York: UNRISD).

Warren, B. (1980) *Imperialism: Pioneer of Capitalism* (London: New Left Books).

Williams, G., R. Véron, M. Srivastava and S. Corbridge (2003a) 'Participation, Poverty and Power: Poor People's Engagement with India's Employment Assurance Scheme', *Development and Change*, 34 (1): 163–92.

Williams, G., M. Srivastava, R. Véron and S. Corbridge (2003b) 'Enhancing Pro-Poor Governance in Eastern India: The Role of Action Research in Institutional Reform', *Progress in Development Studies*, 3 (2): 159–78.

2 | Towards participatory governance: assessing the transformative possibilities

JOHN GAVENTA

For the last twenty years, the concept of 'participation' has been widely used in the discourse of development. For much of this period, the concept has referred to participation in the social arena, in the 'community' or in development projects. Increasingly, however, the concept of participation is being related to rights of citizenship and to democratic governance. Nowhere is the intersection of concepts of community participation and citizenship seen more clearly than in the multitude of programmes for decentralized governance that are found in both southern and northern countries.

Linking citizen participation to the state at this local or grassroots level raises fundamental and normative questions about the nature of democracy and about the skills and strategies for achieving it. The literature is full of debates on the meanings of citizenship and of participation, on the role and relevance of 'the local', especially in the context of globalization, and of course on the problem of governance itself. In this chapter, I pose six challenges which point to the importance and potential for assessing the transformative possibilities of citizen engagement with local governance. In general, I argue that bringing more direct and empowered forms of participation into the local governance sphere can lead to both democracy-building and pro-poor developmental outcomes, but only under certain conditions. Finally, I conclude that simply creating new institutional arrangements for participatory governance will not necessarily be more inclusive or more pro-poor. Rather, much will depend on the nature of the power relations which surround and imbue these new, potentially more democratic, spaces.

Relating people and institutions

> A first key challenge for the 21st century is the construction of new relationships between ordinary people and the institutions – especially those of government – which affect their lives.

Recently, a number of studies have pointed to the growing gap that exists within both North and South between ordinary people, especially the poor, and the institutions which affect their lives, especially government.

For instance, the *Voices of the Poor* report, prepared for the WDR 2000/1, finds that many poor people around the globe perceive large institutions – especially those of the state – to be distant, unaccountable and corrupt. Drawing from participatory research exercises in twenty-three countries, the report details:

> From the perspectives of poor people world wide, there is a crisis in governance. While the range of institutions that play important roles in poor people's lives is vast, poor people are excluded from participation in governance. State institutions are often neither responsive nor accountable to the poor (and they see) little recourse to injustice, criminality, abuse and corruption by institutions, even though they still express their willingness to partner with them under fairer rules. (Narayan et al. 2000: 172)

The *Voices of the Poor* study is not alone in its findings. Another study by the Commonwealth Foundation (1999) in over forty countries also found a growing disillusionment with their governments on the part of citizens, based on their concerns about corruption, lack of responsiveness to the needs of the poor, and the absence of participation or connection to ordinary people.

The empirical evidence on the crisis in the relationship between citizens and their state is not limited to the South. Though for perhaps entirely different reasons, in a number of established democracies, traditional forms of political participation have gone down, and a series of studies show clearly the enormous distrust citizens have of many state institutions. In the UK, for instance, a study sponsored by the Joseph Rowntree Foundation points to the

> need to build a new relationship between local government and local people. There are two reasons for this. The first has to do with alienation and apathy. There is a major issue about the attitudes of the public, as customers or citizens, towards local government ... This is a symptom of a lack of deeper malaise, the weakness or lack of public commitment to local democracy. (Clark and Stewart 1998: 3)

Other data in the United States, most notably the work by Robert Putnam, point as well to the decline in civic participation and the growing distance between citizens and state institutions. More recent work by Skocpol (2003: 11) warns of the emergence of a 'diminished democracy', in which public involvement has lost its link to political life and political engagement has become more the domain of professionalized associations, such that 'early-twenty-first-century Americans live in a diminished democracy, in a much less participatory and more oligarchicly managed civic world'.

Working both sides of the equation

> To rebuild relationships between citizens and their local governments means working both sides of the equation – that is, going beyond 'civil society' or 'state-based' approaches, to focus on their intersection, through new forms of participation, responsiveness and accountability.

As Fung and Wright (2001: 5–6) observe, the right has taken advantage of the decline in legitimacy of public institutions to 'escalate its attack on the affirmative state'. They and of course many others argue that the response to the crisis should focus not on dismantling the state, but on deepening democracy and seeking new forms for its expression. They argue that the 'institutional forms of liberal democracy plus techno-bureaucratic administration – seem increasingly ill suited to the novel problems we face in the twenty-first century'.

However, those who have sought to deepen democratic governance have often been divided on their approach to the problem. On the one hand, attention has been paid to strengthening the processes of citizen *participation* – that is, the ways in which poor people exercise a voice through new forms of inclusion, consultation and/or mobilization designed to inform and to influence larger institutions and policies. On the other hand, growing attention has been paid to how to strengthen the *accountability* and *responsiveness* of these institutions and policies through changes in institutional design, and a focus on the structures for good governance.

Increasingly, however, we are beginning to see the importance of working on both sides of the equation. As participatory approaches are scaled up from projects to policies, they inevitably enter the arena of government, and find that participation can become effective only as it engages with issues of institutional change. And, as concerns about good governance and state responsiveness grow, questions about how citizens engage and make demands on the state also come to the fore.

In both South and North, there is growing consensus that the way forwards is found in a focus on *both* a more active and engaged civil society which can express the demands of the citizenry, *and* a more responsive and effective state which can deliver needed public services. In focus groups around the world, the Commonwealth Foundation (1999), for instance, found that despite their disillusionment with the state as it is, poor people would like to see a strong government which will provide services, facilitate their involvement and promote equal rights and justice. The study argues that at the heart of the new consensus of strong state and strong civil society are the needs to develop both '*participatory democracy* and *responsive government*' (ibid., p. 76): the two are mutually reinforcing and supportive – 'strong, aware, responsible, active and engaged citizens along with strong, caring, inclusive, listening, open and responsive democratic governments' (ibid., p. 82).

Similarly, Heller (2001: 133) discusses the limits of both of the 'technocratic vision', with its emphasis on the technical design of institutions, and of the 'anarcho-communitarian model', with its emphasis on radical grassroots democracy. Rather, he calls for a more balanced view (the 'optimist conflict model') which recognizes the tensions between the need for representative working institutions, *and* the need for mobilized and demand-making civil society. The solution is not found in the separation of the civil society and good governance agendas, but in their interface.

Reconceptualizing participation and citizenship

The call for new forms of engagement between citizens and the state involves a reconceptualization of the meanings of participation and citizenship in relationship to democratic governance.

Traditionally in representative democracies, the assumption has been that citizens express their preferences through electoral politics, and, in turn, it is the job of the elected representatives to make policy and to hold the state accountable. In both North and South, new voice mechanisms are now being explored which argue for more direct connections between the people and the bureaucracies which affect them. In the UK, for instance, the White Paper on Modern Local Government puts an emphasis on more active forms of citizenship, and on the concept of community governance. Critical of the tendency towards passive forms of representative democracy in local authorities, the White Paper argues that 'active conception of representative democracy can be reinforced by participatory democracy – all the more easily in local government because of its local scales and its closeness to the local communities' (quoted in Clark and Stewart 1998).

Similarly, the Commonwealth Foundation (1999: 82) argues that the 'connection' between states and citizens must be based on participation and inclusion rather than on traditional modes of representation through intermediaries and political party members and structures.

Linking participation to the political sphere means rethinking the ways in which participation has often been conceived and carried out, especially in the development context (Gaventa and Valderrama 1999). In the past, within development studies, the drive for '*participatory development*' has focused on the importance of local knowledge and understanding as a basis for local action, and on direct forms of participation throughout the project cycle. A wide range of participatory tools and methodologies has grown from this experience, which emphasize the importance of gathering more pluralistic forms of knowledge in planning and policy processes.

On the other hand, work on political participation growing out of political science and governance debates has often focused on issues largely underplayed by those working on participation in the community or social spheres. These include critical questions dealing with legitimate representation, systems of public accountability, policy advocacy and lobbying, rights education and awareness building, and party formation and political mobilization. Yet, the political participation literature has paid less attention to issues of local knowledge, participatory process, or direct and continuous forms of engagement by marginalized groups.

Each tradition has much to learn from the other. In the development field, they are increasingly being brought together under the concept of '*participatory citizenship*', which links participation in the political, community and social spheres. The concept of 'citizenship' itself has long been a disputed and value-laden one in democratic theory (Jones and Gaventa 2002; Gaventa 2002). On the one hand, citizenship has traditionally been cast in liberal terms, as individual legal equality accompanied by a set of rights and responsibilities and bestowed by a state on its citizens. Newer approaches aim to bridge the gap between citizen and the state by recasting citizenship as practised rather than as given. Placing an emphasis on inclusive participation as the very foundation of democratic practice, these approaches suggest a more active notion of citizenship – one which recognizes the agency of citizens as '*makers and shapers*' rather than as 'users and choosers' of interventions or services designed by others (Cornwall and Gaventa 2000).

Extending the concept of participation to one of citizenship also recasts participation as a right, not simply an invitation offered to beneficiaries of development. As Lister also suggests, 'the right of participation in decision-making in social, economic, cultural and political life should be included in the nexus of basic human rights ... Citizenship as participation can be seen as representing an expression of human agency in the political arena, broadly defined; citizenship as rights enables people to act as agents' (Lister 1998: 228). Increasingly, this idea is invoked in development under the mantle of 'rights-based approaches to development' (DFID 2000; UNDP 2000).

Other arguments extend the idea of 'a right to participation' further, suggesting that if rights and citizenship are attained through agency, not simply bestowed by the state, then the right to participate – e.g. the right to claim rights – is a prior right, necessary for making other rights real. And, while the liberal versions of citizenship have always included notions of political participation as a right, extending this to encompass participation in social and economic life *politicizes* social rights through recasting citizens as their active creators. As Ferguson (1999: 7) asserts, for example, people cannot realize their rights to health if they cannot exercise their democratic rights to participation in decision-making around health service provision. Thus, while T. H. Marshall and others argued that social rights can be seen as positive freedoms in terms of helping citizens to realize their political and civil rights, participation as a right can be seen as a positive freedom which enables them to realize their social rights (Ferguson 1999; DFID 2000; Lister 1997).

New forms of citizen–state engagement

> With the re-conceptualization of participation as a right of citizenship, and with the extension of the rights to participation beyond traditional voting and political rights, comes the search for more participatory approaches to ensuring citizen voices in processes of democratic governance.

Increasingly, around the world, a number of these mechanisms are being explored which can foster more inclusive and deliberative forms of engagement between citizen and state. Goetz and Gaventa (2001) review a number of these mechanisms, arguing that they may be seen along a continuum, ranging from ways of strengthening voices on the one hand, while also strengthening receptivity to voices by institutions on the other. The 'voices' end of the spectrum, we argue, must begin with examining or creating the pre-conditions for voices, through awareness-raising and building the capacity to mobilize – that is, the possibility for engagement cannot be taken as a given, even if mechanisms are created. Then there are a series of strategies through which citizens' voices may be amplified in the governance process, ranging from advocacy research to citizen lobbying for policy change, and citizen monitoring of performance. Then there are increasingly the arenas in which civil society and the state meet: these range from joint management and implementation and management of public services (through various forms of partnership), to legally mandated fora for participatory planning and joint decision-making.

Just as there are a number of mechanisms for amplifying voices, the paper argues, so these must also be strengthened by initiatives that strengthen the receptivity to voices within the state. These range from government-mandated forms of citizen consultation, to setting standards through which citizens may hold government accountable, to various incentives for officials to be responsive to citizen voices, to changes in organizational culture, to legal provisions which in various ways make participation in governance a legal right.

At the intersection of the mechanisms for greater voice and the mechanisms for greater state responsiveness are a number of new legal or constitutional frameworks for participatory governance which incorporate a mix of direct forms of popular participation with more representative forms of democracy. There are numerous examples of this approach, ranging from provisions for participatory planning at the local government level in India and the Philippines, to participatory budgeting and participatory health councils in Brazil, to citizen monitoring committees in Bolivia, to forms of public referenda and citizen consultation in Europe. (For a review of legal frameworks for citizen participation see McGee et al. 2003.) In many cases, the scale of these new fora is enormous. For instance, in Brazil, over 5,000 health councils were created by the 1988 constitution, mandated to bring together representatives of neighbourhoods, social movements and civil society organizations, with service providers and elected representatives to govern health policy at the local level (Coelho et al. 2002). Such innovations go under various labels, ranging from 'participatory governance' to deliberative democracy, to 'empowered participatory governance' (Fung and Wright 2003: 5). Fung and Wright argue that these reforms 'aspire to deepen the ways in which ordinary people can effectively participate in and influence policies which affect their lives ... They are participatory because they rely upon the commitment and capabilities of ordinary people to make sensible decisions through reasoned deliberation and empowered because they attempt to tie action to discussion.' Arguing in a similar vein, Wainwright (2003: x) explores a series of experiments around the world which represent 'a new participatory approach to political power'.

While new innovative mechanisms offer a great deal of possibility for strengthening citizen participation *as a right* in the governance process, their creation alone does not ensure their transformative possibility. Whose voices are really heard in these processes? What about issues of representation and accountability within them? How will various forms of local governance accommodate differing meanings of citizenship that cut across gender, political, cultural and social lines? Does greater participation lead to pro-poor outcomes?

The need for more evidence

While the creation of new spaces for participatory governance holds out the possibility for transformative change, far more needs to be learned about how such spaces work, for whom, and with what social justice outcomes. In general, however, while there is some evidence of both the pro-poor development outcomes and the positive 'democracy'-building outcomes of participatory governance, these exist only under certain conditions.

The promises on behalf of participatory governance, especially in the literature on democratic decentralization, have been great. As Blair (2000: 23) notes: 'the hope is that as government comes closer to the people, more people will participate in politics ... that will give them representation, a key element in empowerment, which can be defined here as significant voice in public policy decisions which affect their futures. These improvements will then reduce poverty and enhance equity among all groups.' However, evidence concerning the degree to which these outcomes have been realized is mixed.

For example, there is evidence that democratic decentralization simply opens up space for the empowerment of local elites, not for consideration of the voices and interests of the more marginalized. Obstacles of power, social exclusion, minimal individual and collective organizational capacity mean that few gains will be made by the poor. As Manor observes, he has 'yet to discover evidence of any case where local elites were more benevolent than those at higher levels' (quoted in Blair 2000).

On the other hand, more recent studies of participatory forms of local governance have begun to point to some more positive outcomes. Blair's own study of democratic local governance in six countries points to some gains in accountability and as well as participation and empowerment goals. Moreover, some improvement may be seen in 'universal services', such as education and healthcare, arguably because these served to benefit the local elites as well. Less success was seen in programmes targeted for the poor themselves, as these were more likely to be 'captured' by local elites. Similarly, Osmani (2001) points to numerous examples of where 'truly participatory decentralisation' has contributed to greater equity and efficiency of local services, due to increased responsiveness. However, such cases have faced obstacles both of the unwillingness of those at the top to give up power and of gaining the involvement of the poor from the bottom.

The case of outcomes of participatory budgeting in Porto Alegre reveals outcomes that went beyond 'administrative rationality and efficiency' to include 'more social justice when allocating public resources' (Navarro 1998: 68). The outcomes of the experiment included a reduction in corruption and administrative malpractice, due to greater transparency; an improvement in the political behaviour of elected and bureaucratic local officials; and, most significantly, a redistribution of resources through higher taxes on the middle class and wealthy sectors, with increased spending towards the priorities of deprived and poor neighbourhoods.

While Navarro suggests some positive pro-poor material outcomes, Heller's (2001: 158) study of democratic experiences in Kerala, Porto Alegre and South Africa focuses more on what might be termed 'democratic process outcomes'. He finds that the synergies created between state and society through participatory reforms in local governance

- create new associational incentive and spaces
- allow for a continuous and dynamic process of learning
- promote deliberation and compromise
- promote innovative solutions to tensions between representation and participation
- bridge the knowledge and authority gaps between technocratic expertise and local involvement

While much is still to be learned about the outcomes of more 'empowered' forms of participatory local governance, the emerging evidence suggests that, at least in some conditions, they can lead to positive pro-poor and pro-democracy outcomes. But they do not always. A further set of questions must be asked about what are the conditions in which such outcomes might occur. This is particularly important, as many of the experiments held up as recent 'success' stories in participatory local governance are limited to a few places in the world, and often reflect contexts and conditions which are not widely found elsewhere. For instance, Heller's (2001) study points to three enabling conditions for 'transformative' participatory governance, namely: a strong central state capacity; a well developed civil society; and an organized political force, such as a party, with strong social movement characteristics.

If this is the case, then questions must be asked of what are the possibilities for moving towards more pro-poor participatory governance in the vast number of societies in which these conditions are absent. Here, other entry points may be necessary which focus on developing the pre-conditions of participatory governance, including awareness building on rights and citizenship; building civil associations and social movements engaged in governance issues; and strengthening institutions of governance, both at the local and central levels. Merrifield's (2002) work raises important challenges for how to promote 'citizenship learning' in places where strong awareness of rights and responsibilities do not previously exist.

Similarly, the work by Fung and Wright (2001) on innovative deliberative mechanisms in the USA, Brazil and India points to three political principles that are fundamental to empowered participatory governance and several design characteristics. The principles include:

- First, each experiment addresses a specific area of practical concern.
- Second, this decision-making relies upon the empowered involvement of ordinary citizens and officials in the field.

- Third, each experiment attempts to solve these problems through processes of reasoned deliberation. (Fung and Wright 2003: 24)

However, they also point to one background enabling condition, that 'there is a rough equality of power, for the purposes of deliberative decision-making, between participants' (ibid., p. 25). Moreover, they go on to point out, robust, democracy-enhancing collaboration is unlikely to emerge and be sustained in the absence of an effective countervailing power (ibid., p. 264) through which citizens can hold these new participatory spaces to account.

What such studies begin to suggest, then, is that while new spaces for participatory governance may offer some possibility for pro-poor change, their transformative potential must be analysed in relationship to the larger power fields which surround and imbue them.

Assessing power relations in participatory spaces

> Power analysis is thus critical to understanding the extent to which new spaces for participatory governance can be used for transformative engagement, or whether they are more likely to be instruments for reinforcing domination and control.

Andrea Cornwall (this volume) reminds us that spaces for participation are not neutral, but are themselves shaped by power relations that both surround and enter them. Inherent in the idea of spaces and places is also the imagery of 'boundary'. Power relations help to shape the boundaries of participatory spaces, what is possible within them, and who may enter, with which identities, discourses and interests. Using the idea of boundary from Foucault and others, Hayward suggests that we might understand power 'as the network of social boundaries that delimit fields of possible action'. Freedom, on the other hand, 'is the capacity to participate effectively in shaping the social limits that define what is possible' (Hayward 1998: 2). In this sense, participation as freedom is not only the right to participate effectively in a given space, but the right to define and to shape that space.

Building on these understandings of power, space and place, I suggest we need to look more closely at three differing continuums of power, if we are to assess the transformative possibility of political space. These involve (i) how spaces are created; (ii) the places and levels of engagement; and (iii) the degree of visibility of power within them. Each of these involves contestation over the boundaries of spaces and places for participation, and the dynamics of power that influence which actors, voices and identities may enter or are excluded from them.

Spaces for participation

In much work on power, the concept is understood as oppositional and in binary terms, regarding the powerful and the powerless; hegemony and resistance; inclusion and exclusion. Other work on power and spaces provides a more nuanced approach. It argues that those who shape a particular space affect who has power within it, but that those who are powerful in one space may in fact be less powerful in another. And, as Cornwall points out, new spaces can be filled by 'old power' and vice versa.

So one dynamic we must explore in examining the spaces for participation is to ask how they were created, and in whose interests and with what terms of engagement. While we are still seeking the appropriate terminology for these categories, our work (Cornwall 2002; Brock et al. 2001; Brock et al. forthcoming) seems to suggest a continuum of spaces, which include:

- *Closed spaces.* Though we want to focus on spaces and places as they open up possibilities for participation, we must realize that still many, many decision-making spaces are closed. That is, decisions are made by a set of actors behind closed doors, without any pretence of broadening the boundaries for inclusion.
- *Invited spaces.* Efforts to widen participation involve the creation of new or 'invited' spaces, i.e. 'those into which people (as users, as citizens, as beneficiaries) are invited to participate by various kinds of authorities, be they government, supranational agencies or non-governmental organisations' (Cornwall 2002: 24). Invited spaces may be regularized, for instance in the case of the constitutionally-created health councils in Brazil, or more transient, through one-off forms of consultation.
- *Claimed/created spaces.* Finally, there are the spaces which are claimed by less powerful actors from or against the power-holders, or created more autonomously by them. Cornwall refers to these spaces as 'organic' spaces which emerge 'out of sets of common concerns or identifications' and 'may come into being as a result of popular mobilisation, such as around identity or issue-based concerns, or may consist of spaces in which like-minded people join together in common pursuits'. (ibid.)

So, as we examine participatory spaces, we must not only examine by whom and how the space was created, but we must also remember that these spaces exist in dynamic relationship to one another, and are constantly opening and closing through struggles for legitimacy and resistance, cooptation and transformation. Closed spaces may seek to restore legitimacy by creating invited spaces; similarly, invited spaces may be created from the other direction, as more autonomous people's movements attempt to use their own fora for engagement with the state. Similarly, power gained in one space, through new skills, capacity and experiences, can be used to enter and affect other spaces. From this perspective, the transformative potential of spaces for participatory governance must always be assessed in relationship to the other spaces which surround them. Creation of new institutional designs of participatory governance, in the absence of other participatory spaces which serve to provide and sustain countervailing power, might simply be captured by the already empowered elite.

Places of participation The concern with how and by whom the spaces for participation are shaped intersects as well with debates on the places, or arenas, where critical social, political and economic power reside. While some of this work (especially within work on gender and power) starts with an analysis of power in more private or 'intimate' spaces, much of the work on public spaces for participation involves the contest between local, national and global arenas as locations of power. There are some who argue that participatory practice must begin locally, in the arenas of everyday life in which people are able to resist power and to construct their own voice. There are others who argue that power is shifting to more globalized actors, and struggles for participation must engage at that level. In between, as well, there are debates on the role of the nation-state, and how it mediates power; on how the possibilities of local spaces often depend on the extent to which power is legitimated nationally, but shared with the locality. On the other hand, work by Mohan and Stokke (2000), for instance, warns us of the dangers of focusing only on the 'local' in a globalizing world.

As we examine the dynamics of spaces and places for participation, we must also keep in mind this second continuum involving the locations and relationships of place, arenas and power. As with the earlier continuum, they show that these levels and arenas of engagement are constantly shifting in relation to the other, that they are dysnamic and interwoven. Local actors may use global fora as arenas for action (e.g. Narmada Dam; Chiapas), just as effectively, or more effectively, as they can appeal to institutions of local governance (Edwards and Gaventa 2001). Conversely, expressions of global civil society or citizenship may simply be vacuous without meaningful links to the local. The challenge is not only how to build participatory governance at differing levels, but how to promote the democratic and accountable *vertical links* across actors and institutions at each level. As Pieterse puts it: 'this involves a double movement, from local reform upward and from global reform downward – each level of governance, from the local to the global, plays a contributing part' (quoted in Mohan and Stokke 2000: 263).

The visibility of power relationships

As we examine the relationships of place and space *vis-à-vis* participation, we must also examine the dynamics of power that shape the inclusiveness of participation within each. Here much of the literature on power is concerned with the degree to which conflict over key issues, and the voices of key actors, are visible in given spaces and places. In earlier work, Gaventa (1980) explored the differences between:

- more pluralist approaches to power, in which contests over interests are assumed to be visible in public spaces, which in turn are presumed to be relatively open
- a second dimension of power, in which the entry of certain interests and actors into public spaces is privileged over others through a prevailing 'mobilization of bias' or rules of the game
- a third dimension of power, in which visible conflict is hidden through internalization of dominating ideologies, values and forms of behaviour

In more recent work building on this model, VeneKlasen and Miller (2002) argue more simply for distinguishing between the visible, hidden and invisible (or internalized) forms of power.

The importance of this for how we analyse the dynamics of participation in differing spaces and places is relatively obvious. Historically, many pluralist studies of power have mainly examined power in its visible manifestations. One looked at who participated, who benefited and who lost in order to see who had power. But as we have seen, power in relationship to place and space also works to put boundaries on participation, and to exclude certain actors or views from entering the arenas for participation in the first place. Or power, in its more insidious forms, may be internalized in terms of one's values, self-esteem and identities, such that voices in visible places are but echoes of what the power-holders who shaped those places want to hear. Such power analysis points again to the importance of establishing the pre-conditions of participatory governance for new institutional mechanisms to lead to change in the status quo. Without prior awareness-building so that citizens possess a sense of their own right to claim rights or express opinions, and without strong capacities for exercising countervailing power against the 'rules of the game' that favour entrenched interests, new mechanisms for participatory governance may be captured by prevailing interests. Or, as Fung and Wright (2003: 263–4) point out, 'where countervailing power is weak or nonexistent, the rules of collaboration are likely to favour entrenched, previously organized or concentrated interests ... Collaboration, under these conditions, is much more likely to become top-down collaborative governance involving experts and powerful interests, even if its impulse originated from bottom-up initiatives.'

Each of these continuums of power, place and space exists in relationship to the others, and affects the complex dynamics of participatory governance in any given context. The local, national and global agenda affect the opening and closure of invited spaces; the visibility of power is shaped by who creates the space; in turn, prior participatory experiences which have helped to overcome forms of invisible and hidden power may strengthen the possibilities for the success of new institutional designs for participation. In any given issue or conflict, there is no single strategy or entry point for participation. Much depends on navigating the intersection of the relationships, which in turn create new boundaries of possibility for action and engagement.

This makes the question of representation – of who speaks for whom across the intersections of spaces and places, and on what basis – a critical one. Representation is found in each continuum, as we look (for instance) at who speaks at the intersection between people's associations and invited spaces; between the local, national and global; or on behalf of the poor and 'invisible'. Effective representation across spaces involves legitimacy, which may be drawn from a number of sources. In new examples of participatory governance, the legitimacy drawn from the principles of representative democracy (i.e. voting, no matter how corrupt) is often pitted against other forms of legitimacy drawn, for instance, from leadership embedded in social movements or neighbourhood associations, while the most positive examples of participatory governance create processes for multiple forms of representation to be legitimate. The politics of intersection is also about identity, and understanding which identities actors use in which spaces to construct their own legitimacy to represent others, or how they perceive the identities and legitimacy of others who speak on their behalf. We need to continue to unpack this question of representation, legitimacy and identity at the intersections of spaces and places, in order to understand more fully the possibilities of deeper forms of participatory governance.

Perhaps some of the most powerful stories of power, and how they constrain participation, are found when these several continuums come together to reinforce one another. For instance, it is the *combination* of the way that fixed spatial locations in turn intersect with histories of closed decision-making spaces (as found in institutions of colonialism or apartheid), which intersect with the capacity to control the visibility of conflict, when power is seen in its most concentrated and hegemonic forms. Given that the history of many of the countries in which participatory governance is being used around the world involves many of these elements, it is no wonder, then, that the dynamics of participation in newly emerging democratic spaces are subject to all sorts of imperfections, manipulations and abuse.

However, intersections of spaces in different ways may also contribute to new possibilities for challenging hegemonic power relations. For instance, the opening of previously closed spaces can contribute to new mobilizations and conscientization, which may have the potential to open those spaces more widely. Power gained in one space may be used to enter new spaces. From the point of view of social actors who are seeking to change power relations, we need also to investigate how this analysis of power and participation opens new entry points and possibilities for transformational change.

Conclusion

The widespread engagement with issues of participation and local governance creates enormous opportunities for redefining and deepening meanings of democracy, for linking civil society and government reforms in new ways, for extending the rights of inclusive citizenship. At the same time, there are critical challenges to ensure that the work promotes pro-poor and social justice outcomes, to develop new models and approaches where enabling conditions are not favourable, to avoid an overly narrow focus on the local, and to guard against co-optation of new mechanisms of participatory governance by entrenched interests of the status quo. An analysis of the power relations which surround and fill new spaces for democratic engagement is critical for an assessment of their transformative potential. Only through such a power analysis can we fulfil the broader agenda of understanding and promoting *both* participatory democracy *and* participatory development, for theorists and practitioners alike.

Note

This chapter builds upon previous papers prepared for the IDS Learning Initiative on Citizen Participation and Local Governance <www.ids.ac.uk/logolink>; the Development Research Centre on Citizenship, Participation and Accountability <www.ids.ac.uk/drc-citizen>. An earlier version was presented at the Conference on 'Participation: From Tyranny to Transformation', Manchester, 27–28 February 2003.

References

Blair, H. (2000) 'Participation and Accountability at the Periphery: Democratic Local Governance at the Periphery', *World Development*, 28 (1): 21–39.

Brock, K., A. Cornwall and J. Gaventa (2001) 'Power, Knowledge and Political

Spaces in the Framing of Poverty Policy', *IDS Working Paper*, 143 (Brighton: Institute of Development Studies).

Brock, K., R. McGee and J. Gaventa (eds) (forthcoming), *Unpacking Policy: Actors, Knowledge and Spaces in Poverty Reduction.*

Clark, M. and J. Stewart (1998) *Community Governance, Community Leadership, and the New Local Government* (London: Joseph Rowntree Foundation).

Coelho, V. S. P., I. A. L. de Andrade and M. C. Montoya (2002) 'Deliberative Fora and the Democratisation of Social Policies in Brazil', *IDS Bulletin*, 33 (2): 65–73.

Commonwealth Foundation (1999) *Citizens and Governance: Civil Society in the New Millennium* (London: Commonwealth Foundation).

Cornwall, A. (2000) 'Bridging the Gap? "Good Governance", Citizenship and Rights', in A. Cornwall, *Beneficiary, Customer, Citizen: Perspectives on Participation for Poverty Reduction,* SIDA Studies, 2, pp. 60–8.

— (2002) 'Making Spaces, Changing Places: Situating Participation in Development', *IDS Working Paper*, 170 (Brighton: Institute of Development Studies).

Cornwall, A. and J. Gaventa (2000). 'From Users and Choosers to Makers and Shapers: Repositioning Participation in Social Policy', *IDS Bulletin* 31 (4): 50–62.

— (2001) 'Bridging the Gap: Citizenship, Participation and Accountability', *PLA Notes*, 40: 32–5.

DFID (2000) *Realising Human Rights for Poor People* (London: DFID).

Edwards, M. and J. Gaventa (2001) *Global Citizen Action* (Boulder, CO: Lynne Rienner).

Ferguson, C. (1999) 'Global Social Policy Principles: Human Rights and Social Justice' (London: DFID).

Fung, A. and E. O. Wright (2001) 'Deepening Democracy: Innovations in Empowered Participatory Governance', *Politics and Society*, 29 (1): 5–41.

— (2003) *Deepening Democracy: Institutional Innovations in Empowered Participatory Governance* (London: Verso).

Gaventa, J. (1980) *Power and Powerlessness: Quiescence and Rebellion in an Appalachian Valley* (Oxford: Clarendon Press).

— (2002) 'Exploring Citizenship, Participation and Accountability', *IDS Bulletin*, 33 (2): 1–11.

Gaventa, J. and C. Valderrama (1999) 'Participation, Citizenship and Local Governance', Background Paper. Conference: Strengthening Participation in Local Governance (Brighton: Institute of Development Studies). <http://www.ids.ac.uk/ids/particip/research/localgov.html>

Goetz, A. M. and J. Gaventa (2001) 'From Consultation to Influence: Bringing Citizen Voice and Client Focus into Service Delivery', *IDS Working Paper*, 138.

Hayward, C. R. (1998) 'De-facing Power', *Polity*, 31 (1): 9–21.

Heller, P. (2001) 'Moving the State: The Politics of Democratic Decentralisation in Kerala, South Africa, and Porto Alegre', *Politics and Society*, 29 (1): 131–63.

Jones, E. and J. Gaventa (2002) 'Concepts of Citizenship – A Review', *IDS Development Bibliography*, 19.

Lister, R. (1997) *Citizenship: Feminist Perspectives* (New York: New York University Press).

— (1998) 'Citizen in Action: Citizenship and Community Development in Northern Ireland Context', *Community Development Journal*, 33 (3): 226–35.

McGee, R. with N. Bazaara, J. Gaventa, R. Nierras, M. Rai, J. Rocamora, N. Saule, E. Williams and S. Zermeno (2003) 'Legal Frameworks for Citizen Participation', *LogoLink Research Report* (Brighton: Institute of Development Studies).

Marshall, T. H. (1950) *Citizenship and Social Class* (Cambridge: Cambridge University Press).

Merrifield, Juliet (2002) 'Learning Citizenship', *IDS Working Paper*, 158.

Mohan, G. and K. Stokke (2000) 'Participatory Development and Empowerment: The Dangers of Localism', *Third World Quarterly*, 21 (2): 247–68.

Narayan, D., R. Chambers, M. K. Shah and P. Petesch (2000) *Voices of the Poor: Crying Out for Change* (Washington, DC: World Bank).

Navarro, Z. (1998) 'Participation, Democratising Practices and the Formation of a Modern Polity – The Case of "Participatory Budgeting" in Porto Alegre, Brazil (1989–1998)', *Development*, 41 (3): 68–71.

Osmani, S. R. (2001) 'Participatory Governance and Poverty Reduction', in A. Grinspun (ed.), *Choices for the Poor: Lessons from National Poverty Strategies* (New York: UNDP).

Skocpol, T. (2003) *Diminished Democracy: From Membership to Management in American Civic Life* (Norman: University of Oklahoma Press).

UNDP (2000) *Human Development Report 2000* (New York: UNDP).

VeneKlasen, L. and V. Miller (2002) *A New Weave of People, Power and Politics: The Action Guide for Advocacy and Citizen Participation* (Oklahoma City: World Neighbors).

Wainwright, H. (2003) *Reclaim the State: Experiments in Popular Democracy* (London: Verso).

World Bank (2001) *World Development Report 2000/2001, Attacking Poverty* (New York: Oxford University Press).

3 | Rules of thumb for participatory change agents

BILL COOKE

This chapter proposes a set of rules for people instigating participatory interventions, particularly participatory development practitioners. These rules are intended for processes involving someone from outside working face-to-face with a group of people. Otherwise, though, they can be applied in any arena, from PRA with poor people through to participatory workshops with policy-making elites.

Part of Uma Kothari's and my argument at the start of *Participation: The New Tyranny*? (Cooke and Kothari 2001) was that participatory development should consider closing itself down. If anything, I hold this view more strongly than I did when the book was published. There are plenty of other ways to engage politically without having to do participatory development. Participatory development appears to continue to thrive none the less. Of course, material interest is one reason for this (see Rule V below), but, I recognize, there are others. Not least, face-to-face participatory processes are apparently very powerful in terms of what they seem to achieve (see the conclusion to Rule I).

The problem is that this apparent power is frequently delusional, concealing the extent to which participatory processes are manipulative (Cooke 2001, 2003b). Simultaneously, important and malign structural forces outside the cognisance and/or influence of participants are ignored and sustained. Dynamic structural factors, the consequence of considered human agency, remain uncontested not just because they are constructed in secret, e.g. by the WTO (Jawara and Kwa 2003), but because participatory processes, prioritizing what happens *within* the participatory group (colloquially termed, in the managerialist participatory tradition, 'the here and now'), foster the assumption that they represent a natural, uncontestable way of things.

The question is whether there is none the less something worth saving about participation. If there is, the challenge is to find modes of non-delusional participatory activity. I am uncertain about whether this is possible, particularly with participatory development. Even attempting to suggest it, in a book like this, by proposing rules which might create an authentically emancipatory version of participation, opens me to charges that I am colluding in the perpetuation of that which I have called to be abandoned. I return to this point in the conclusion.

The title of the chapter is in homage to Shepard's much reproduced *Rules of Thumb for Change Agents* (1975). The phrase *change agent* is likely to irritate, given its apparent managerialist associations, although it originated in a broader tradition (see Lippitt et al. 1958; Cooke 1998). I particularly like it because it foregrounds the otherwise underplayed (in participatory development) agency of the interventionist. The rules are not in any order of priority, and complement one another, although, having said that, following Rule I alone would prevent a lot of harm.

Rule I: Don't work for the World Bank

Instrumentally, credible change agents are principled change agents; and principled change agents know who they won't work for, and why. If not the Bank, then who? According to Schein, inventor of the idea of process consultation: 'any time we help someone we are in effect allying ourselves with the goals and values that they represent. We cannot later abdicate responsibility for the help we have provided if that turns out to have had bad effects on other groups' (Schein 1987a: 127).

What follows is to state the obvious. Greater impact on people's empowerment – in terms of, say, their right to life through healthcare, water and education – is made by decisions taken by the Bank and the IMF on debt repayment than can be made by an infinity of face-to-face participatory events which have no power over debt. And, bluntly, one of the reasons why that debt accumulated was through loans to corrupt and criminal regimes kept in power to sustain a particular world order. Loans were also made by private sector banks to private sector organizations in the Third World. When these creditors defaulted, Third World governments were forced to take the debts on. In an otherwise neo-liberalizing world, private sector debt is nationalized and its repayment extorted from individual, poor, taxpayers (e.g. Chossudovsky 1997).

It is participatory development's institutional *groupthink* (Cooke 2001) that requires the restatement of these basic facts so baldly. Organizations such as the Bretton Woods Project (2003–) produce rigorously researched account of the Bank's dysfunctional behaviour, and Griffiths (2003) produces an insider accounts of its ideological infliction of famine; and the opposition of worldwide anti-globalization movements is widely reported. Yet the participation establishment seems to have no qualms (to put it mildly) and, at least in some cases, has supported the Bank's appropriation of participatory discourse and methods. More basic facts: the World Bank is an organization that sees more neo-liberalism as the remedy for the problems it has visited on the world's poor; and, to the point here, it uses participatory methodologies and practitioners to enforce that agenda (see Brown, this volume). Those participatory practitioners are taking an ideological stance. And, to be fair, there are some practitioners who know this, and will not work for or with the Bank.

Otherwise, though, why do practitioners who might be assumed to be liberal rather than neo-liberal continue to work for the Bank, material interest aside (see Rule V)? Publicly espoused justifications are often along the lines that it is possible to make a difference through a specific Bank project, or more generally that there is the space for alternatives within the Bank, which is not a homogeneous monolith.

A retort to the first of these is that given all the participatory interventions which might be made, why is so much effort dedicated to the Bank's. Moreover, it is breathtaking vanity for participatory practitioners to suggest they can succeed in changing the Bank from within when others better qualified have not been able to do so, from Nobel prize-winning Joseph Stiglitz through to World Development Report author (or not) Ravi Kanbur (Pincus and Winters 2002). Perhaps, rather, participatory practitioners are allowed in through the door precisely because there is no danger of them challenging neo-liberal hegemony, or, worse, because they sustain it.

The point about the Bank not being a monolith works the other way. There is enough in political and organizational theories to show that institutions present different faces to different people the better to incorporate them, to legitimize themselves in society, and to buy critics off (of which more in Rule II). Participatory development also does a more directly neo-liberalizing job for the Bank. A study by the World Development Movement (Marshall and Woodroffe 2001) of country Poverty Reduction Strategy Papers (PRSPs) found that, pro-poor rhetoric aside, the actual changes they proposed, in every country, were neo-liberal prescriptions identical with both previously discredited Structural Adjustment Programmes (SAPs), and with one another. This monolithic homogeneity would be logically surprising if the claims for participation in their production held true, suggesting that participating poor people from countries as diverse as Ghana, Bolivia and Cambodia all chose privatization and user fees, but not redistribution, as the solution to their problems.

Perhaps participatory practitioners are particularly prone to this form of vanity because of what controlling participatory processes does to their self-image. Studies of some of the earliest versions of organized participatory face-to-face groups, known as T(raining)-groups, from the 1950s onwards have shown how they generate a euphoria in both participants and facilitators, so the latter sense they have in their gift some magical power capable of engendering profound personal transformation (Kleiner 1996). Addiction to the sense of well-being that they are apparently able to create can lead practitioners to commit to the cause which permits their participatory practice, oblivious to what that cause is, its consequences, or to the fact that what they are doing is simply a matter of social-psychological technique.

Rule II: Remember: co-optation, co-optation, co-optation

There are other First World critiques (besides those discussed in Rule I) of participatory processes barely acknowledged by participatory development. One prototype contemporary development project was the establishment of the Tennessee Valley Authority (TVA) in the USA under Roosevelt's New Deal. This had contemporary hallmarks – building a dam, electrification, and attempts to ensure the representation and participation of grassroots communities. Selznick's famous 1953 account of the TVA showed how ostensibly autonomous grassroots groups were co-opted, formally and informally, into supporting the programme and goals of the project, and particularly of the project director, and became instruments in policy battles.

At more or less the same time, the Commissioner of the Bureau of (US) Indian Affairs, the New Dealer John Collier, was introducing participatory methods which were, inter alia, to form the basis of action research. The evidence is that Collier's development of these methods was directly inspired by British colonial administration. Participation, for Collier, was a technique for achieving British colonial administrator Lord Lugard's infamous *indirect rule* (Lugard 1965), in which an always limited amount of autonomy was granted with the intent of maintaining the sovereign power of the colonial ruler (Cooke 2003a). Writing in the 1940s Collier used language with present-day resonances, of respecting diverse worldviews, preserving 'community organisation' and so on (Collier 1945: 285); but as his archive makes clear, this was always within the constraints of indirect rule.

Soon after, the T-groups mentioned above first emerged in the United States. These too had co-optative consequences, if not intent. The very first T-group, a workshop conducted in New Britain Connecticut in 1946, also seen in some sources as one of the first action research projects, was an attempt to keep the lid on African American resistance to the apartheid state that the USA then was. Data from that workshop show how participants entered it prioritizing the elimination of racism and structural disadvantages that African American and other ethnic minority communities faced. By its end these were minor concerns; what mattered was having more participatory activities (Lippit 1949; Cooke 2003b).

Both action research and T-groups were synthesized into the management field of Organization Development (Cooke 1998). Many contemporary workplace participatory processes, including those lauded by Chambers (1997), have their roots in OD. The longstanding critique of workplace participation is that it facilitates the co-optation of an otherwise resistant workforce, thinking and behaving autonomously, into a management agenda. The aim is to engender a change of attitude (often cast as 'culture'), sometimes overtly, sometimes covertly, and/or ensure workers take on responsibility for their own management, but with fundamental issues – e.g. organizational purpose and goals, reward structures, resourcing – taken as externally imposed, non-negotiable 'givens' (Cooke forthcoming).

There is another form of co-optation. Burrell's (1997) account of the work of the founder of modern management, F. W. Taylor, argues that often overlooked in accounts of Taylor's scientific management was its function in adapting people who had previously been European peasant labourers into the modern US labour process, more a process of mechanization than socialization, bypassing language and culture. Taylorism was therefore a technology for proletarianizing peasants. Cammack (2002) argues, from a Marxist perspective, that the World Bank's Comprehensive Development Framework initiative has, at the macro-economic level, a similar purpose, of proletarianizing the poor. Cammack in turn contextualizes Harry Taylor's contribution to *Participation: The New Tyranny?* (2001), which argues that participatory development is a way of inducting the poor into the modern labour market. This time, though, would-be workers have to be socialized into the participatory team work practice required by post-modern corporations. In other words, Harry Taylor shows how participatory development becomes a technique of proletarianization.

Sadly, there is yet a third form of co-optation – of radical participation by the orthodoxy (symbolized by even the World Bank [2003b] claiming to host an 'Empowerment Community of Practice') – which is perhaps the most problematic for the purposes of this book. In the work of participatory theorists – Freire (1972) par excellence – for whom participation is about changing consciousness, emancipation rather than just empowerment has been around for some time. However, there is a longstanding analysis in organization studies which identifies a dynamic in which such radical ideas are co-opted, reduced to technique, and applied for non-emancipatory ends. Ironically, the metaphorical term used to describe this process is 'colonization' (Prasad 2003). A specific example is the work of Saul Alinsky (Cooke 1998). Alinsky's model of participatory grassroots organizing, discussed in *Reveille for Radicals* (1948), was part of a programme which included bringing the means of production into common ownership, and critiqued the US labour movement for racist collusion with monopoly capital. But his method (along with that of others) was appropriated, neutralized and transformed by Lippitt et al. (1958), in their standard work which produced a generic model of change interventions and, in passing, brought the term 'change agent' to prominence.

Rule III: Data belong to those from whom they were taken

This rule, too, is a carry-over from workplace participation, as is the word 'data' which is technocratic, and could be broadened to 'information'. Schein (1987b) prescribes not just with whom data collected from a particular group should or should not be shared, with informants' informed permission, but proposes a prior issue to be resolved, namely whether those who instigate and carry out any data collection from a social collective – community or work organization – actually have the right to do so. Not least there is a recognition here that data collection, particularly participatory data collection, is in itself a social intervention that changes things, by, for example, subjecting what was previously private to a public gaze, within/without the collective from which the data were gathered.

One of the most substantial appropriations of data in international development has been the World Bank's Voices of the Poor project. Word-processing at its most literal, the utterings of poor people around the world have been collected, translated, selected and discarded, edited, collated, categorized, copyrighted and given an ISBN (World Bank 2003a). They have become functional sub-components assembled to create a World Bank-brand product, where the claims for participation are, as always, belied by the Bank's imposition of its own interpretation, its meta-narrative, which in turn epitomizes the participatory development establishment's reservation for itself of the last word. That these commodified voices can now be purchased in three volumes, written in English, for a total of $60, suggests that poor people have no psychological or literal ownership of something claimed to be theirs.

This is bad enough; but, as someone trained in a different (non-development) participatory tradition, it is some of the day-to-day, evidently unthinking, abuses of appropriated information that are most shocking. These include:

- The use of photographs of participants – people – in presentations and publications without their consent, informed or otherwise.
- The physical duplication of data about social (dis)ordering, wealth distribution, resource allocation, family relationships, willy-nilly, without reference to those they concern, and from whom they were gathered,

in learning materials (e.g. course handouts), reports and academic articles.

- The use of material gathered in one role, as a participatory change agent, in another, typically as an academic in a journal, again without participants' informed consent, editorial input, right of reply or even their knowledge of publication.
- Public disclosure of information – in conferences, but also in bars and departure lounges favoured by international development agents, not to mention faculty staff rooms – in the absence of those from whom it was collected and to whom it belongs.

This is all behaviour not tolerated by or of First World practitioners working with First World clients. Group therapists are struck off for repeating confidences. Junior management consultants are exemplarily fired for talking about their clients on the train home. Exploitation of privileged information happens; but it is not supposed to. Standard texts on consultancy make clear the requirement for confidentiality on the part of consultants, often in the context of differentiating consultants' from academics' rights and responsibilities for the data that they handle (Kubr 2003; Schein 1987b). The appropriation of information is extraction, as sure as the taking of natural resources or the attempts to patent the genes of commonly held plant stock. But its consequences are also uniquely malign, in that it exposes those from whom it has been extracted to the scrutiny, surveillance and intervention of powerful others.

Rule IV: Work only in languages you understand as well as your first

One of the features which make participatory data so commodifiable is their frequent pictorial form. Pictorial data can be very rich, and have intrinsic worth; however, the argument that they are also valuable because they facilitate work with non-literate communities is disingenuous. Before this, they serve a purpose for the practitioner unable to speak the language of those with whom she or he is working. When working in England, with English speakers, literacy has never been a problem, even though some of the people with whom I have worked will have been illiterate; there is a lot that can go on in a participatory process without the participants having to be able to read and write. It is far more difficult, of course, if I can't understand the language of my participants; I have to invent, or use already invented forms of pictorial representation, so I can continue the processes of co-optation and appropriation.

A case relating to this rule is, again, that of PRSPs. As we have seen, participatory processes are supposed to have ensured 'ownership' of their content – the standard, homogenous package of neo-liberal interventions (Marshall and Woodroffe 2001). Yet, in Cambodia, PRSP documentation was not available in the Khmer language by the time the final draft was put before cabinet (ibid., p. 36). In such situations it is the change agents who are not just illiterate, but inarticulate. Yet somehow this is not seen to preclude their ability or, indeed, assumed right to act. What qualifies people to intervene in such circumstances, where they cannot even talk directly with those they claim to be helping, other than the power they carry with them as the representatives of a development agency? And how are change agents seen by those they claim to help when they can't even speak their language? Would it matter to us if a practitioner able to speak only Khmer was invited by a foreign power to address us? How many times has it happened in the UK Treasury? What does it say about power relationships with the world's poor that this kind of thing is unthinkingly accepted as OK for them?

The other way (besides pictures) that First World consultants get round their incompetence, literally, in their inability to speak the language of those whose lives they intervene in, in the most intimate detail, is to work alongside a 'local consultant', who thus is differentiated from the 'international consultant'. Of course, 'alongside' hardly does justice to the power relationship; without that local consultant the work often could not take place. The local consultant often provides not just day-to-day translation in the literal sense; but a 'meta'-translation in the sense of Jankowicz (1994), that is, providing an overall framework of local meaning within which specific encounters can be interpreted and understood, i.e. telling the international consultant what is really going on. The local consultant may also deal with relatively mundane, but intervention-breaking issues, like working out how to get from place to place. The local consultant is often therefore essential to the participatory intervention. Whereas the local consultant could probably do the work without the international consultant, the international consultant could not do the work without a local consultant. That both are required evidences a mix of racism and colonialism. That 'local consultants don't have the report-writing capacity', is racist, unless the report-writing gene really is ethnically distributed; the real colonialist motive is that 'we' need 'one of us' to be relied on to report what is 'really' going on. This is not, in First World workplace participation terms, an 'authentic' relationship.

Rule V: Always work for local rates, or for free

Of course, one way to achieve a more equal relationship between local and international consultants would be for them to be paid the same. But they rarely are; the local consultant, without whom the intervention often cannot happen, and who is often capable of doing the work alone, gets paid 'local rates' (less); the international consultant, often incapable of doing the work without a local counterpart, gets paid 'international rates' (more).

The unfairness of this will be evident to all involved in an intervention, as will the hypocrisy of change agents who claim to be working to end poverty but whose weekly per-diem expenses, never mind their fees, often amount to more than average annual per capita incomes; likewise, facilitators conducting participatory public sector effectiveness or anti-corruption workshops often earn more in their daily rate than the monthly salary of a permanent secretary.

Moreover, do participatory development practitioners seriously believe that those whom they are working on do not know the cost of the hotels in which they stay? Do they not know the implications, in terms of wealth rankings, of the visible trappings of the participatory intervention: the four-wheel drive, kits of sterile hypodermics, the presence of government and donor representatives? Are the privileges of their existence – education, healthcare, status – really invisible to those with whom they are working? Certainly, it is rarely talked or written about. Again, in the process of group-think, there is collusion in not mentioning the glaringly obvious.

Much of the participatory development discourse is about material well-being. Ignored, however, is its positive effect on the material well-being of its practitioners, and for their employing institutions. This is why this rule will not be followed. It is none the less a serious problem at the heart of participatory development; many of its practitioners have to do it to make a living, and there are organizations, many of them businesses sheltering behind an academic façade, which rely on the income from participatory development consultancies to survive. Quasi-profiteering behaviour distorts and corrupts (in a general rather than criminal sense). It makes it harder, for example, for the practitioner to say no to work; and it encourages the development of client–patron relationships between donors and supposedly independent development institutions and individual practitioners. Again, 'we all know' that this happens; but it is never acknowledged.

Rule VI: Have it done to yourself

In the 1950s, when the Tavistock Institute for Human Relations established itself as the first centre in the UK for participatory social interventions, anyone working for the Tavistock, as a condition of employment, was obliged to undergo a programme of psychoanalysis (Trist and Murray 1990). The intention was that no one should intervene in the social lives of others without having subjected themselves to the most intensive of self-analysis, so that there could be no hidden or unspoken intra-psychic agendas on the part of the practitioner. This is perhaps extreme; and there are, for me, issues to be taken with the various versions of psychoanalysis. However, the theory at least of participatory practice in work organizations (if not, it is accepted, the reality) is thick with the need for a deep personal reflexivity on the part of the practitioner.

One straightforward aspect of this is the expectation that practitioners model, collectively and individually, that which they expect of others. In participatory development that would, for example, mean practitioners making transparent gender relationships or wealth rankings in the communities and institutions in which they live and work. Not only is this indicative of good-will, and an honest thing to do in its own right, demonstrating that we are not asking dispossessed people to share intimate and private information that we ourselves choose to conceal; it is also good practice. The very process of undergoing the procedures we inflict on others affords the practitioner first-person insights into participants' micro-political and affective realities consequent on participatory intervention.

Tacit in this paper's homage to Shepard is a third variety of reflexivity. This is the need for practitioners to incorporate into their self-awareness all the experiences and understandings of what it means to be a practitioner which have already been codified in articles, books and so on. The shared exhilaration of dealing with the 'here and now' distracts from the need to do the harder intellectual work of reading and critical thinking. The material is extensive – and it begins, as I have suggested here, with the pre-war work of Selznick, of Collier, through Alinsky, from Shepard's article, through the work of Schein (1987a), and to its adaptations in, for example, Cooke (1997).

Rule VII: Historicize theory and practice

As with my citation of fads such as T-groups, in my listing of these theorists I have also gone way back into history, into apparently pre-development times. There is a fundamental issue here about learning from experience, about not repeating on Third World people methodologies without acknowledging the potential problems long recognized in the First World.

There is also a broader and equally important concern, that we need to take a historical perspective to be able to put the role and function of participatory development into perspective and context; again, the focus on the here and now that participatory work encourages can discourage us from assessing how it fits into longer-term processes and trends. What should be particularly discomforting in this chapter, for example, is participation's debt to colonization and indirect rule mentioned above, in relation to Collier. Collier's work was able to be written back into histories of participation because histories began to be written by and for his imperial, indirectly ruled, participationed subjects, that is Native Americans during the New Deal (e.g. Biolsi 1991).

Collier was for his times a liberal and even anti-racist figure, and he paid a price for this under McCarthyism. But these histories, written by and for 'the participants', challenge Collier's own account of what actually happened, identify negative as well as positive impacts and, fundamentally, his right to provide the authoritative narrative about that period of engagement between the United States and Native American nations, many of which, as Collier's critics pointed out, had had their relationships and rights *vis-à-vis* the USA formally defined by treaty.

The question all this prompts for contemporary participatory development is the extent, first, to which its practitioners and advocates are able and willing to situate their theorizing and practice. Not only are there the here-and-now disincentives; but the short-termism of the international participatory development industry, with its flying visits to a series of different nations, makes it very difficult to take this historical view. Second, it also discourages even the micro-historical assessment of specific interventions over, say, five or six years, never mind decades. There are, of course, those who work internationally but still have a long-term relationship with those with whom they are working; there are also those who relocate themselves so that they are not working internationally; but they are the exception. Participatory change agents should ask themselves how they would appear in histories of the engagement with development written by or for participants; and must realize that whether or not they are being actually written, they are inevitably placed in a historical context by those with whom they work.

Conclusion

This set of rules is not exhaustive. I make no claim that together they will address all the concerns I have previously raised about the social psychological limits of participation (Cooke 2001). Since there is also no single critical meta-position on participatory development, these rules are not claimed to address all the concerns and critiques of others either.

Further, even though the effect of the rules on redeeming participatory development would be partial, I am none the less pessimistic about their being adopted by its establishment. They have already been described as provocative, and they are intended so to be. I also think that they are, for participatory development, impossibilist. At the same time, they are also perfectly reasonable and practicable.

To explain, the rules are provocative because they deliberately seek to challenge and reveal the entrenched interests and attitudes of the participatory development establishment; and they are impossible because they cannot be achieved within the institutional structures and shared frames of meaning which construct and reproduce the overlapping ideas of development, and of participatory development. To illustrate: many of the First World institutions which manufacture development could not survive financially if they had to follow Rule I and Rule V. It is an intrinsic, defining, feature of development that it provides it own self-legitimizing meta-narrative which gives meaning to the experiences and actions of those it would develop, its subjects and objects. Rule III would make this much harder. Rule VI, if it made wealth and power relationships transparent, would (one hopes) further bring into question the authority and legitimacy of development professionals in their own eyes (again one hopes) and in the communities of First World policy-makers and academics in which they operate and compete.

Yet at the same time I would suspect that to non-participatory development audiences there is nothing particularly challenging about these rules. Debated some of them may be; but that, for example, there are causes which participatory practice should not support would be taken for granted. That much (but by no means all) of what I anticipate being so difficult for participatory development derives from my own background in managerialist organizational participation suggests that it is not intrinsically politically radical. Instead it derives from a technocratic set of ethics, developed from the engagement between practicality and principle. If the rules I propose are therefore seen as unrealistic, this points to the problematic nature of the development reality that the change agents who would avoid them choose to inhabit and sustain. For all the claims of participation as an end as well as means within participatory development, it is very much about technique; and it is the end to which this means is put, the development part of participatory development, that stops it being emancipatory. Indeed, one appropriation yet to be fully critiqued is participatory development's understanding of 'participation', so that, within the development world, 'participation' and 'participatory development' are taken and promoted as meaning the same thing. If participation is worth redeeming it requires a wedge be driven between the two words 'participatory development'; and the former should also be turned against the institutions and ideologies of the latter. But, as Rule VII shows, we have been here before and, according to Rule II, the prognosis is not good.

References

Alinsky, S. (1948) *Reveille for Radicals* (New York: Random House).

Biolsi, T. (1991) ' "Indian Self-government" as a Technique of Domination', *American Indian Quarterly* (Winter): 23–7.

Bretton Woods Project (2003–) Homepage; <http://www.brettonwoodsproject.org> (accessed 2 September 2003).

Burrell, G. (1997) *Pandemonium: Towards a Retro-Organization Theory* (London: Sage).

Cammack, P. (2002) 'The Mother of All Governments: The World Bank's Matrix for Global Governance', in R. Wilkinson and S. Hughes (eds), *Global Governance: Critical Perspectives* (London: Routledge), pp. 36–53.

Chambers, R. (1997) *Whose Reality Counts* (London: IT Publications).

Chossudovsky, M. (1997) *The Globalization of Poverty* (Penang: Third World Network).

Collier, J. (1945) 'United States Indian Administration as a Laboratory of Ethnic Relations', *Social Research*, 12 (May): 265–303.

Cooke, B. (1997) 'From Process Consultation to a Clinical Model of Development Practice', *Public Administration and Development*, 17 (3): 325–40.

— (1998) 'Participation, Process and Management', *Journal of International Development*, 10 (1): 35–54.

— (2001) 'The Social Psychological Limits of Participation?', in B. Cooke and U. Kothari (eds), *Participation: The New Tyranny?* (London: Zed Books).

— (2003a) 'A New Continuity with Colonial Administration: Participation in Development Management', *Third World Quarterly*, 24 (1): 47–61.

— (2003b) 'Managing Organizational Culture and Imperialism', in A. Prasad (ed.), *Postcolonial Theory and Organizational Analysis* (New York: Palgrave).

— (forthcoming) 'The Managing of the (Third) World', *Organization*.

Cooke, B. and U. Kothari (2001) 'The Case for Participation as Tyranny', in B. Cooke and U. Kothari (eds), *Participation: The New Tyranny?* (London: Zed Books).

Freire, P. (1972) *Pedagogy of the Oppressed* (London: Penguin Books).

Griffiths, P. (2003) *The Economist's Tale* (London: Zed Books).

Jankowicz, A. D. (1994) 'The New Journey to Jerusalem: Mission and Mission in the Managerial Crusade to Eastern Europe', *Organization Studies*, 15 (4): 479–508.

Jawara, F. and A. Kwa (2003) *Behind the Scenes at the WTO* (London: Zed Books).

Kleiner, A. (1996) *The Age of Heretics* (London: Nicholas Brealey).

Kubr, M. (2003) *Management Consulting: A Guide to the Profession*, 4th edn (Geneva: ILO).

Lippitt, R. (1949) *Training in Community Relations* (New York: Harper).

Lippitt, R., J. Watson and B. Westley (1958) *The Dynamics of Planned Change* (New York: Harcourt Brace).

Lugard, F. D. (1965) *The Dual Mandate in Tropical Africa*, 5th edn (London: Frank Cass).

Marshall, A. with J. Woodroffe (2001) *Policies to Roll Back the State and Privatise? Poverty Reduction Strategy Papers Investigated* (London: World Development Movement).

Pincus, J. R. and J. A. Winters (2002) 'Reinventing the World Bank', in J. R. Pincus and J. A. Winters (eds), *Reinventing the World Bank* (Ithaca, NY: Cornell University Press).

Prasad, A. (2003) 'The Gaze of the Other', in A. Prasad (ed.), *Postcolonial Theory and Organizational Analysis* (New York: Palgrave).

Schein, E. H. (1987a) *Process Consultation*, Vol. 2 (Reading, MA: Addison Wesley).

— (1987b) *The Clinical Perspective in Fieldwork* (Beverly Hills, CA: Sage).

Selznick, P. (1953) *TVA and the Grass Roots* (Los Angeles: University of California Press).

Shepard, H. A. (1975) 'Rules of Thumb for Change Agents', *Organization Development Practitioner* (November): 1–5.

Taylor, H. (2001) 'Insights into Participation from Critical Management and Labour Process Perspectives', in B. Cooke and U. Kothari (eds), *Participation: The New Tyranny?* (London: Zed Books).

Trist, E. and H. Murray (1990) 'Historical Overview: The Foundation and Development of the Tavistock Institute', in E. Trist and H. Murray (eds), *The Social Engagement of Social Science*, Vol. 1 (Philadelphia: University of Pennsylvania Press).

World Bank (2003a) Publications <http://publications.worldbank.org/ecommerce/catalog/product?item_id=372464> (accessed 2 September 2003).

— (2003b) Community of Practice <http://lnweb18.worldbank.org/ESSD/sdvext.nsf/68ParentDoc/CommunityofPractice?Opendocument> (accessed 10 October 2003).

TWO | Rethinking participation

4 | Relocating participation within a radical politics of development: critical modernism and citizenship

GILES MOHAN AND SAM HICKEY

> [M]uch of the theory construction in development studies has been introduced with no explicit considerations concerning basic ontological, epistemological, and methodological positions ... Further, it is required of a theory that the normative premises and political priorities it embodies are thoroughly exposed. (Martinussen 1997: 345–6)

> [T]hinking about participation (in development) ... has lacked the analytical tools ... and an adequate theoretical framework. (Shepherd 1998: 179)

The absence of a coherent theory of participation that seeks to explain and articulate the role of agency within development processes closely informs the limitations of the participatory movement, and helps explain the ideological malleability that has beset participation in practice. As we and others have argued, the failure to theorize the potential contribution of participation to a transformatory political process has resulted in the depoliticization of participation and its rendering as a technical fix for complex problems of uneven development (Chapter 1, this volume; Cleaver 1999; Rahman 1995). In this chapter we address these concerns by theorizing a radical approach to participation based around citizenship while rooting our normative premise in a critical modernist epistemology. Here, we define 'radical' in broad terms, as being socialist and transformative.

Our focus on citizenship and critical modernism derives from an analysis of both empirical and conceptual developments within and around the field of participation. In Chapter 10 we analyse the empirical evidence concerning those approaches to participatory development and governance that appear to have led to (or have the promise of leading to) a transformative form of development, particularly through the empowerment of marginal groups and people. Underpinning these progressive developments in participatory praxis are a series of commonalities. In each case, participation is aligned with a radical (often socialist) political project of social justice; articulated with a notion of citizenship; and engaged with development as an immanent process of social change rather than in the form of specific interventions. This promotion of participatory citizenship from a broader and radical political project might contribute towards creating the conditions within which participation can be transformative, particularly the process of disentwining modes of economic and political accumulation.

Below, we outline the contemporary theoretical and conceptual approaches to participation with which we are engaging and seek to reformulate. We begin by outlining the claims of the 'critical modernist' approach as a means of capturing the complex and political character of popular agency within development processes, as against the claims of 'alternative' and 'post' readings of development. This then takes us into an examination of the (democratic) values that underpin such a transformatory politics of difference, before we develop a radical notion of citizenship that helps us understand, analyse and plan for deeper empowerment and transformation.

Of theory and analysis: relocating and politicizing participatory thinking

In Chapter 1 we argued that there have been three main responses to the criticisms raised against participation. One is largely practical in seeking to scale-up the 'populist' approach to participation in development to ever-higher levels of policy-making. Here we focus on the other two responses, one theoretical and one conceptual/analytical, which both constitute efforts to overcome the 'atheoretical' tendency within participatory development noted by Shepherd above. The first of these rejects 'participation' in its current form as a 'mainstream' approach to development, and seeks either to relocate participation within a more radical theoretical and political approach, usually 'alternative development', or to reject it from a 'post-development' position. The second response seeks to confront both the critique ranged against participation as being an insufficiently political notion to capture agency, and the broadening of the participation agenda to encompass issues of governance (Gaventa, this volume) by developing a new 'conceptual toolkit'. Although broadly sympathetic with these responses, we argue that neither is sufficient by itself, and that there are flaws within the approaches currently being pursued under this agenda. Our attempt is both to resolve the problems within each and then to unite them into a more thoroughgoing response.

Relocating participation in a radical theoretical home

Theoretical debates over participatory development reflect contemporary debates in development more broadly, with the more radical positions emanating from broadly 'alternative' or 'post' development positions. For example, the 'post-development' approach views 'participation' as inherently linked to the failed project of 'development' (e.g. Rahnema 1992), with its inherent tendency towards imperializing dominance and cultural homogeneity rather than empowerment. Instead, expressions of popular agency should realize themselves in multiple ways, escaping from the 'limping vessel of development [and] striking out for new horizons in smaller craft' (Esteva and Prakash 1992: 51). From within the 1970s school of 'alternative development' (e.g. Fals Borda 1998; Rahman 1995) comes a rejection of the way in which participation has been mainstreamed and thus 'domesticated away from its radical roots' (Cleaver 1999: 608), and an attempt to relocate participatory development within this 'golden age' of radical participation.

For us, the post-development approach seems likely to repeat the localist fallacy that already pervades participatory development and encourage fragmentation rather than the multi-scaled strategies that we argue are necessary for participation to become transformative (see Chapter 10). To advocate the abandonment of modernity in favour of a potentially romanticized view of pristine, bounded islands of alternatives seems very far from the intentions of those social movements on which post-development theorists claim to base their work. Rather, we want to link the agency of belonging to and engaging with multiple political communities to an alternative reading of modernity that does not abandon its positive elements through a catch-all rejection of anything deemed 'western'. Indeed, sanitizing discourses which might potentially do damage to the 'other' and consigning people to a Never-Never land of alternatives to development seem excellent ways of denying them any agency (Kiely 1999).

According to proponents of alternative development, 'participation ... was always radically conceived as a struggle against political and economic exclusion from exercising control over public resources' (Fals Borda 1998: 161). Since its emergence in the 1970s (Nerfin 1977), its task has been defined as being 'to transform the claims of these discarded citizens into rights' (Friedmann 1996: 171). Particularly innovative at the time was the proposition that citizenship participation occurs within multiple and overlapping political communities from the local to the global level (Friedmann 1992), a contribution we draw on in the next section. However, the alternative development approach was less convincing in terms of theory and praxis, particularly its tendency to reify 'actually existing development' as a caricature of eurocentric modernization, to underplay the role of the state, to glorify the local 'community', and failing to specify the requisite socio-political agency and/or institutional support required to realize a project of alternative development (Pieterse 1998; Sanyal 1994). Foreshadowing many of the deficiencies of participatory development, the salience of this critique warns against 'returning' participation to the alternative development approach.

Moreover, both the 'alternative' and 'post' development routes for participation tend to offer a populist reading of popular agency, and align it with strategies that caricature rather than seek to analyse and engage with 'development' as a complex underlying process of social, economic and political change. As such, they fail to meet the epistemological and ontological requirements of a social science theory outlined by Martinussen at the outset of this chapter. Neither is able to account for the ways in which political economy shapes agency within development, a key failing given the critique that both power and politics are absent from participatory development. Below, we link our understanding of agency within development processes to the 'critical modernity' approach, which seeks to chart a path between the voluntaristic tendency of populist thinking and structuralist accounts of political economy, while retaining a sense of the radical and political.

Critical modernism and the left: between political economy and populism

Critical modernism emerged as a response to the failure of the populism, post-modernism or political economy approaches to capture adequately the complex positioning of structure and agency within contemporary development arenas. As an approach, it is primarily distinguishable from the post-modern/post-development rejection of development, in part to stress that most countries of the South have never been 'modern' in the sense understood by post-modernists. In this section we elaborate on critical modernism as a socialist-inspired framework which seeks to balance a normative vision with a dialogic political praxis that is sensitive to different rationalities and modernities.

Critical modernism begins from the premise that rather than reject development *tout court* we need to 'rethink' it (Peet and Hartwick 1999). Theoretically it is rooted in Marxism, feminism and post-structuralism and retains a belief in the central tenets of modernism – democracy, emancipation, development and progress – but begins from a critique of capitalism 'as the social form taken by the modern world, rather than on a critique of modernism as an overgeneralized discursive phenomenon' (ibid., p. 200), the latter being the realm of post-structuralist deconstruction. This faith in modernism is also 'scientific' in that it requires evidence for analysis and action, rather than faith. It is here that affinities with certain populist approaches to participatory knowledge exist, but these are to be rigorous, debated and contested. This avoids romanticizing the plight of the poor and treating all 'local knowledge' as pure and incontrovertible. As Peet and Watts (1996: 38) argue, within critical modernism 'rationality is contended rather than abandoned'.

This assertion rests on the belief that modernity is not a singular entity which unfolds in a linear fashion. Rather, the 'ideas and practices of modernity are themselves appropriated and re-embedded in locally situated practices, thus accelerating the fragmentation and dispersal of modernity into constantly proliferating modernities' (Arce and Long 2000: 1). These 'multiple modernities' (Comaroff and Comaroff 1993) destabilize and provincialize the notion of an ideal European modernity and replace it with one that seeks to understand 'the encounters between multiple and divergent modernities' (Arce and Long 2000: 159) in societies containing a 'multiplicity of rationalities' (ibid., p. 160). Seen thus, development is a 'resolutely dialectical process [which is] a sort of mixing, syncretism and cross-fertilization rather than a crude mimicry or replication' (Watts 2003: 26). This recognition enables an analysis of the contending rationalities of multiple modernities as opposed to abandoning modernity and rationality altogether.

However, this is not an ethically rootless process in which all identities and rationalities are equally valid. We argue below that some differences are more important than others, and for critical modernism, as with Corbridge's post-Marxist notion of a 'radical modernism' (1994), the bottom line is material well-being. The existence of widespread poverty both within and between countries is the starting point for an ethics of development (Corbridge 1998). The pragmatic ethics of critical modernism is to understand these basic needs and to find ways of meeting them, and of responding to the multiple ways in which the poor often speak out in angry, public and radical ways against this condition.

Difference, empowerment and emancipation If development is committed to a politics of social justice, how can it resolve the tension between a universal value of justice and multiple, situated rationalities? Harvey (1993) sees this as a problem for post-modernism which rightly questions the naturalness of different ethical positions but largely ducks the political ramifications of this by positing a politics of anything-goes relativism. Rather than get mired in an impasse over universalism and anti-universalism, we locate our epistemology within a socialist political economy, which seeks social justice through a transformation away from capitalism as currently formulated. As we argue, this is not the same as rejecting modernity, simply the interpretation of modernity as necessarily about capitalist rationality. Furthermore, one practical way of navigating between the universal values of socialism and particular rationalities is through a dialogic process whereby different rationalities are contested; something missing from much instrumental participatory learning.

The first means of addressing this, Harvey continues, is to 'break out of the local', meaning a move beyond a reactionary form of resistance by deconstructing the supposed homogeneity of self-defined communities. Young (1993) takes this on by seeing groups as heterogeneous and relational. She states: 'Groups should be understood not as entirely other, but as overlapping, as constituted in relation to one another and thus as shifting their attributes and needs in accordance with what relations are salient. In my view, this relational conception of difference as contextual helps make more apparent both the necessity and possibility of political togetherness in difference' (Young 1993: 123–4).

This idea of 'togetherness in difference' is based on the interspersion and interaction of different groups. While differences exist, there is also the recognition that relational identities require multiple others so that the identity of one depends upon other/s, which gives groups a mutual stake in one another's existence. At various levels this opens the possibility that alliances exist since only some differences are intractable.

The key to Young's politics of difference is that it 'requires not the melting away of differences, but institutions that promote reproduction of and respect for group differences without oppression' (Young 1990: 47, cited in Harvey 1993: 105). Young (1990) sets out what constitutes oppression so that we have a sense of what a strategy which *avoids oppression* might look like. These sources of oppression are *exploitation* (the transfer of the fruits of the labour of one group to another), *marginalization* (the expulsion of people from useful participation in social life), *powerlessness* (the lack of authority, status of sense of self which permits a person to be listened to with respect), *cultural imperialism* (the stereotyping in behaviours so that the oppressed group's culture is denied value and the dominant culture is imposed), and *violence* (the fear and reality of unprovoked attacks).

While this gives us a framework for resolving differences within a struggle for justice, there is still the problem of which or whose difference claims are valid and which are not. For Harvey this epistemological task of judging validity requires a renewed engagement with political economy, as captured by the critical modernist approach adopted here. Understanding the political economy of the processes shifts the focus in two ways. First, political economy alerts us to similarity as much as difference, thus providing a basis for alliances and connections between different groups. Many of these commonalities are generated by the globalization of capital and hence point to a broadly socialist critique. Second, by understanding the relational formation of group identities we do not ignore claims by groups which we find oppressive, but look at how their presence shapes and is shaped by those groups seeking emancipation.

These observations reveal the type of politics envisaged by critical modernism and link squarely to our arguments below regarding the notion and practice of citizenship as the primary conceptual and strategic means by which transformative forms of participation can be realized. The basis of critical modernism is radical democracy which 'believes in direct popular control over all the resources and institutions used and inhabited by people, from field to forest, factory to family, university to neighbourhood, art gallery to website' (Peet and Hartwick 1999: 206). This approach is 'radical, reproductive, and participatory' in which 'institutions are fundamentally characterized by cooperative effort among equal partners' (ibid., p. 207). The notion of equality does not imply consensus but reflects the values that underpin the democratic interaction. Following a broadly Habermassian line, decisions are arrived at through discussion or 'reasoning' which is pragmatic rather than idealistic. That is, it is the best that reasonable people can achieve under prevailing conditions rather than being the transcendent Reason envisaged in classical Enlightenment thought. In terms of active citizenship, people adhere to decisions and share responsibility precisely because they have participated in the discussion rather than being 'bound' or 'obliged' by law. It is to conceptualizing this form of participatory citizenship that we now turn.

Reconceptualizing participation as citizenship

As noted earlier, an important conceptual response to the backlash against participation has been a series of moves towards capturing the wider sense in which popular agency exists and broadening the participation debate to encompass aspects of governance. This includes a shift from social capital to 'political capital' (e.g. Baumann 2000), and research into the notions of 'political space' (Webster and Engberg-Pedersen 2002) and 'political capabilities' (Whitehead and Gray-Molina 1999; Williams, this volume), as well as a focus on 'citizenship'. While each of these approaches contains the potential to advance debates, we would argue that citizenship offers certain advantages both as a form of analysis and as a guide towards policy and strategic action, although this potential remains unfulfilled.

The notion of 'citizenship participation' recently emerged as a means by which the convergence of people's agency and their participation in specific interventions might be understood (Gaventa 2002).[1] The links between 'citizenship' and 'participatory development' can be conceptualized in terms of the interaction between a series of institutional norms and agency-led practices, whereby 'Citizenship can be defined as that set of practices (juridical, political, economic or cultural) which define a person as a competent member of society, and which as a consequence shape the flow of resources to persons and social groups' (Turner 1993: 2).

Relocating 'participation' within citizenship analysis situates it in a broader range of sociopolitical practices, or expressions of agency, through which people extend their status and rights as members of particular political communities, thereby increasing their control over socioeconomic resources. The question for participatory interventions becomes how they can enhance the 'competency' of participants to project their agency beyond specific interventions into broader arenas, thereby progressively altering the 'immanent' processes of inclusion and exclusion. The notion of citizenship also captures the broadening of the participation agenda, whereby the social and political agendas of 'participation' and 'good governance' have increasingly converged (Gaventa 2002: 1), both as a result of the state moving 'closer to the people' and the infiltration of participatory approaches within bureaucratic institutions. This section goes beyond an exhortation that 'citizenship matters' for participation towards a more thorough analysis of the specific form/s of citizenship that are likely to underpin the transformative potential of participation.

Participation and citizenship The links between participation and citizenship are most clearly expressed within 'civic republican' as opposed to 'liberal' theories of citizenship (Miller 1995). Civic republicanism is founded on 'the collective and participatory engagement of citizens in the determination of the affairs of their community' (Dietz, quoted in Lister 1997: 24). As such, the citizen 'plays an active role in shaping the future of his or her society through political debate and decision-making' (Miller 1995: 443). Civic republican theory thus defines citizenship in terms of membership within a particular political community, whereas liberal conceptions tend to rely on legal definitions concerning the formal status of citizens, and focus on narrow forms of 'political participation' (e.g. voting). This juridical focus tends to mask the fact that the 'sociological realities are those of subjects, clients and consumers, not those of citizens of equal worth and decision-making capacity' (Stewart 1995: 74).

Against this, 'membership in a community can be a broader, more inclusive category' (Silver 1997: 79), wherein 'citizenship' constitutes not only a set of legal obligations and entitlements 'but also the practices through which individuals and groups formulate and claim new rights or struggle to expand and maintain existing rights' (Isin and Wood 1999: 4). This participatory notion of citizenship is particularly 'attractive to women and other marginalised groups' (Lister 1997: 28), as it offers the prospect that citizenship can be claimed 'from below' through their own efforts in organized struggles, rather than waiting for it to be conferred 'from above'. Here, participation becomes not merely a means by which citizenship roles are reproduced and obligations fulfilled, but of extending citizenship to previously marginal groups.

Broadening and gendering citizenship: the informal and the hidden The distinction between 'public' and 'private' spheres is a perennial problem within citizenship analysis. In particular, mainstream republican notions of citizenship have been criticized for extolling a model of citizenship that could only be fulfilled by the publicly active, property-owning, white male. As such it has too often 'excluded many classes of potential citizens, including women, indigenous minorities, slaves, colonial subjects, the working classes' (Werbner and Yuval-Davis 1999: 7). In order to formulate a substantive notion of citizenship that includes those participatory arenas that are relied upon by 'subordinate' social groups, feminist writers in particular have sought to broaden the scope of what can be considered 'public' (Lister 1997: 24–9; Young 1990: 118–20).

In order to retain citizenship as an essentially political notion, this requires making a distinction between 'political citizenship' in a broadly defined public sphere and 'personal politics' within the private arena (Lister 1997: 38), while focusing on the dialectical relationship between people's expressions of agency within each sphere. The growing awareness that women are often the driving force in local civic and political action, in what has been conceptualized as a local and feminine sphere of 'informal politics' (ibid., pp. 145–94), reflects the fact that informal forms of participation are often the preserve of 'subordinate' or 'excluded' social groups who are denied access to more public forms of participation.[2] In some cases, this marginality may 'allow those who have systematically been disprivileged a "central space" of their own in which to organise the expression of their needs' (Fardon 1988: 774; also Jackson 1999), and lead to the development of alternative forms of citizenship.

Citizenship beyond the state: the rise of sub-national citizenship/s

> [T]he political communities which provide the contexts of democratic citizenship ... are able to encompass group as well as individual citizenship and their social sites are potentially widespread, both subnational and transnational, the city and the region as well as the community and the federation. (Stewart 1995: 74)

Civic republican theory has traditionally framed national citizenship as the pre-eminent political identity, against which any 'sub-national' or 'identity-based' forms of political mobilization must be considered to be divisive and potentially destructive of a unified polity (Oommen 1997). Political analysis of 'sub-national' forms of identity-based political activity has arguably progressed furthest within studies of ethnicity in Africa. Here, such activity has become increasingly framed by reference to civic republican notions of citizenship. This is founded on the recognition that in many post-colonial African states 'individuals participate in two substantive publics' – the national and the ethnic – (Ndegwa 1997: 602), neither of which has managed to eclipse the other.[3] It is recognized that certain aspects of citizenship express themselves more fully in sub-national rather than national communes, particularly in terms of high levels of participation, reciprocity and cooperation within a 'moral economy' of socioeconomic exchange (see Henry, this volume).[4] Such modes of sociopolitical action are frequently absent from the national 'civic' public in Africa, where the imposed character of the colonial state, and the anti-colonial struggle against it, left little room for political participation to emerge on the basis of any generalized moral imperative or overarching sense of 'public interest'.

Political analysis of the links between state and ethnic citizenship tends to stress the extent to which ethnicity is inimical to a wider sense of statehood (Ndegwa 1997; Oommen 1997). However, this is problematic, first because it fails to appreciate the extent to which state formation in Africa was founded on a collection of ethnic identities (Mamdani 1996), and second, because ethnicity may not necessarily damage the ideals of social justice and equality contained within notions of citizenship. Indeed, one close observer of the links between ethnicity and citizenship argues that, in Africa, 'ethnicity is universal; it gives the identity that makes social behaviour possible' (Lonsdale 1992: 328), a claim that resonates with Ruth Lister's (1997) formulation of citizenship as agency. Moreover, ethnicity can contain the seeds of civic virtue, which may even be forged symbiotically with reference to a wider sense of 'nationhood'. Lonsdale distinguishes between 'moral ethnicity' and 'political tribalism', as do Doornbos (1991) and Ekeh (1990), who argue that it is possible to found a political morality on the basis that public resources should be shared equally among different ethnic groups (e.g. Srebrnik 2000).

To frame ethnic political action in terms of 'citizenship' is not to valorize all forms of ethnic or 'identity-based' mobilizations in Africa (Ndegwa 1997), some of which have clearly been politically destructive and even linked to genocide.[5] Rather, our approach recognizes that the politics of national citizenship formation for historically excluded groups begins almost by definition with the particularist claims of identity, which are gradually transformed into more universalist democratic gains through the political process (Foweraker and Landman 1997). As such, 'rather than regarding citizenship and identity as antinomic principles' it might be necessary to 'recognize the rise of new identities and claims for group rights as a challenge to the *modern* interpretation of universal citizenship' (Isin and Wood 1999: 4). From here, it is possible to explore the extent to which this 'recognition politics' develops into what Iris Marion Young termed an 'emancipatory politics of difference' (Young 1990: 163).

Realizing a project of radical citizenship and critical modernism

It is clear from the foregoing argument that realizing transformative participation, as located within a project of radical citizenship and critical modernism, requires strategies that are multi-scaled and span political arenas; that employ dialogic political methodologies along the lines of Habermassian deliberative democracy (Cornwall, this volume); and involve political agents engaged with both structural conditions and popular agency, and dedicated to a broader project of social justice and emancipation. Fuller attention to issues of strategy are given elsewhere (see Cornwall and Gaventa, this volume), and it is neither possible nor proper to think here of strategy in the abstract. The nature of strategy is such that it depends upon concrete openings and possibilities found in 'real' places so we cannot specify *a priori* by whom and in what ways such a politics will be realized.

However, a pressing question in terms of realizing the critical modernist project is: what or who will be the key agents and in which institutional arenas? According to Heller's review of participatory governance reforms, neither the state nor the party can be agents of 'sustained transformative projects' (Heller 2001: 152); rather, what is required is an 'ecology of agents' which blends 'the institutional capacities of the state and the associational resources of civil society' (ibid., p. 158). This is not in the sanitized and simplistic sense of state–civic synergies as promoted under the rubric of partnership (Evans 1997), but in the more political sense of party–social movement dynamics and within the context of a shared socialist-inspired project. Alliances as we noted earlier can come from a revivified political economy that finds similarities of experience around which to coalesce and campaign. Hence, coalitions around certain forms of exclusion and subordination emerge. What we get is a form of radical democracy that transcends the local and forges alliances with a range of regional, national and globalized movements. For example, from a critical modernist perspective, social movements such as the Zapatistas are seen as an expression of marginalized people's demands for rights of greater access to a more generous idea of development, rather than a complete overhaul of its basic tenets of material progress and human betterment (see Chapter 10). Such social movements rarely reject *all* notions of progress, but are rather seeking to localize them and challenge their exclusive and disempowering elements. They appear to find a way of 'relating the universal and the particular in the drive to define social justice from the standpoint of the oppressed' (Harvey 1993, quoted in Lister 1997: 89), and, in so doing, articulate a mode of political action capable of imagining and generating transformative development futures not only for their immediate constituency, but also for a broader community of dispossessed and marginalized peoples.

Conclusion

The intention here has been to locate a radical home for the participatory project that secures its autonomy, room for innovation and links to a transformative project. We develop the notion of citizenship as a meso-level concept linking politics, culture and place. Citizenship analysis arguably has a significant contribution to make towards development theory and practice. As befits development theory, it is an inherently multi-disciplinary concept, relating to socioeconomic, political, legal and cultural spheres. Operating at the meso-level of social theorizing, citizenship represents the type of 'conceptual innovation' demanded by this post-impasse discipline (Booth 1994: 12), with its need to find a path between the failed explanandums of meta-narratives and the methodological individualism of the more voluntaristic actor-oriented approaches, and also between the political and the cultural. Furthermore, the notion of citizenship maintains a 'universalist' normative appeal, while maintaining a capacity to be operationalized within particular contexts.

More specifically, citizenship represents a significant conceptual advance within understandings of participatory governance and development for several reasons. First, it offers a means of covering the convergence between participatory development and participatory governance (Gaventa 2002). Second, citizenship links to rights-based approaches since it helps to establish participation as a political right that can be claimed by excluded or marginal peoples, and thus provides a stronger political, legal and moral imperative for focusing on people's agency within development than is currently the case. Moreover, citizenship analysis provides a means of transcending the distinction between imminent and immanent forms of participatory development, situating participation in relation to the politics of inclusion and exclusion that shape popular agency beyond particular interventions. The notion of citizenship thus offers a useful political, social and historical form of analysis within which to situate understandings of participation, as located within the formation of a social contract between citizenry and authority in particular political communities. In sum, citizenship is an inherently political perspective on participation, arguably the chief requirement of contemporary approaches to participation.

Finally, we argue that such forms of citizenship as are conceptualized here must be tied to a radical political project, although one that does not reject modernity since modernity has never been a coherent and teleological process, but one fractured and multiply realized. This ontological reasoning allows for a view of development such that political communities can pursue their different experiences of and desires for modernity. Having said that, we need to be continually aware that the breadth and penetrative influence of capitalist modernity means that it cannot easily be relativized away as one among many modernities, but must be critically engaged with as the pre-eminent force shaping contemporary and future development processes and the role of popular agency therein.

Notes

1 For accounts of the rise of citizenship within social science theory see Heater (1999) and Turner (1999).

2 This resonates with research on women's participation in Africa which argues that the concepts of 'political participation', 'civil society' and 'democracy' need to be expanded to account for the diverse and often informal ways in which women participate as citizens (McEwan 2000; Tripp 1998).

3 This tension has been classically formulated as existing between two different types of political community that compete within the same state, namely the 'civic' (the formal state institutions) and 'primordial' (mainly primary associations based on kinship or ethnic ties) (Ekeh 1975). While this binary divide does not exist in reality, this analytical construct illuminates the dialectical relationship between the two spheres which, for Ekeh, 'foments the unique political issues that have come to characterise African politics' (Ekeh 1975: 93; echoed by Eyoh 1999: 288).

4 According to Hutchful (1995: 64), local-level 'age and kinship groups, secret societies, and gender organizations were the fount of political accountability in traditional African society'.

5 See Mamdani (2001) on how the 1994 genocide in Rwanda reflected a struggle for the rights and status of citizenship between Hutu 'insiders' and Tutsi 'outsiders'.

References

Arce, A. and N. Long (2000) 'Reconfiguring Modernity and Development from an Anthropological Perspective', in A. Arce and N. Long (eds), *Anthropology, Development and Modernities* (London: Routledge), pp. 1–31.

Baumann, P. (2000) 'Sustainable Livelihoods and Political Capital: Arguments and Evidence from Decentralisation and Natural Resource Management in India', *ODI Working Paper*, 136 (London: ODI). <http://www.odi.org.uk>

Booth, D. (1994) 'Rethinking Social Development: An Overview', in D. Booth (ed.), *Rethinking Social Development: Theory, Research and Practice* (Harlow: Longman), pp. 3–41.

Carmen, R. (1996) *Autonomous Development* (London: Zed Books).

Cleaver, F. (1999) 'Paradoxes of Participation: Questioning Participatory Approaches to Development', *Journal of International Development*, 11: 597–612.

Comaroff, J. and J. Comaroff (1993) 'Introduction', in J. Comaroff and J. Comaroff (eds), *Modernity and Its Malcontents: Ritual Power in Postcolonial Africa* (Chicago, IL: University of Chicago Press), pp. xi–xxxvii.

Corbridge, S. (1998) 'Development Ethics: Distance, Difference, Plausibility', *Ethics, Place and Environment*, 1 (1): 35–53.

— (1994) 'Post-Marxism and Post-colonialism: the Needs and Rights of Strangers', in D. Booth (ed.), *Rethinking Social Development: Theory, Research and Practice* (Harlow: Longman), pp. 90–117.

Doornbos, M. (1991) 'Linking the Future to the Past: Ethnicity and Pluralism', *Review of African Political Economy*, 52: 53–65.

Ekeh, P. (1975) 'Colonialism and the Two Publics: A Theoretical Statement', *Comparative Studies in Society and History*, 17 (1): 91–117.

— (1990) 'Social Anthropology and the Two Uses of Tribalism in Africa', *Comparative Studies in Society and History*, 32 (4): 660–700.

Esteva, G. and M. S. Prakash (1992) 'Grassroots Resistance to Sustainable Development: Lessons from the Banks of the Narmada', *The Ecologist*, 22 (2): 45–51.

Evans, P. (1997) 'Introduction: Development Strategies Across the Public–Private Divide', in P. Evans (ed.), *State–Society Synergy: Government and Social Capital in Development*, IAS Research Series, 94 (Berkeley: University of California), pp. 1–10.

Eyoh, D. (1999) 'Community, Citizenship and the Politics of Ethnicity in Post-Colonial Africa', in P. T. Zeleza and E. Kalipeni (eds), *Sacred Spaces and Public Quarrels: African Culture and Economic Landscapes* (New Jersey: Africa World Press), pp. 271–300.

Fals Borda, O. (1998) *People's Participation: Challenges Ahead*. A synthesis of the World Congress of Participatory Convergence, held at Cartagena, Columbia, 1997 (London: Intermediate Technology Publications).

Fardon, R. (1988) 'Centre, Periphery, Boundary: Some Problems with Spatialising Problems', in P. Geschiere and P. Konings (eds), *Proceedings/Contributions, Conference on the Political Economy of Cameroon: Historical Perspectives* (Leiden: African Studies Centre), pp. 757–75

Foweraker, J. and T. Landman (1997) *Citizenship Rights and Social Movements: A Comparative and Statistical Analysis* (New York: Oxford University Press).

Friedmann, J. (1992) *Empowerment: The Politics of Alternative Development* (Oxford: Blackwell).

— (1996) 'Rethinking Poverty: Empowerment and Citizen Rights', *International Social Science Journal*, 148: 161–72.

Gaventa, J. (2002) 'Exploring Citizenship, Participation and Accountability', *IDS Bulletin*, 33 (2): 1–11.

Harvey, D. (1993) 'Class Relations, Social Justice and the Politics of Difference', in J. Squires (ed.), *Principled Positions: Postmodernism and the Rediscovery of Value* (London: Lawrence and Wishart), pp. 85–120.

Heater, D. (1999) *What is Citizenship?* (Cambridge: Polity Press).

Heller P. (2001) 'Moving the State: The Politics of Democratic Decentralization in Kerala, South Africa, and Porto Alegre', *Politics and Society*, 29 (1): 1–28.

Hettne, B. (1995) *Development Theory and the Three Worlds* (Harlow: Longman).

Hutchful, E. (1995) 'The Civil Society Debate in Africa', *International Journal*, 51: 54–77.

Isin, E. F. and P. K. Wood (1999) *Citizenship and Identity* (London: Sage).

Jackson, C. (1999) 'Social Exclusion and Gender: Does One Size Fit All?', *European Journal of Development Research*, 11 (1): 125–46.

Kiely, R. (1999) 'The Last Refuge of the Noble Savage? A Critical Assessment of Post-Development Theory', *European Journal of Development Research*, 11 (1).

Lister, R. (1997) *Citizenship: Feminist Perspectives* (Basingstoke: Macmillan).

Lonsdale, J. (1992) 'The Moral Economy of Mau Mau: Wealth, Power and Civic Virtue in Kikuyu Political Thought', in B. Berman and J. Lonsdale, *Unhappy Valley: Conflict in Kenya and Africa*, Book Two (London: James Currey), pp. 315–504.

McEwan, C. (2000) 'Engendering Citizenship: Gendered Spaces of Democracy in South Africa', *Political Geography*, 19 (5): 627–51.

Mamdani, M. (1996) *Citizen and Subject: Contemporary Africa and the Legacy of Late Colonialism* (Oxford: James Currey).

— (2001) *When Victims Become Killers: Colonialism, Nativism, and the Genocide in Rwanda* (Princeton, NJ: Princeton University Press).

Martinussen J. (1997) *State, Society and Market* (London: Zed Books).

Miller, D. (1995) 'Citizenship and Pluralism', *Political Studies*, 43: 432–50.

Ndegwa, S. (1997) 'Citizenship and Ethnicity: An Examination of Two Transition Movements on Kenyan Politics', *American Political Science Review*, 91 (3): 599–616.

Nerfin, M. (ed.) (1977) *Another Development: Approaches and Strategies* (Uppsala: Dag Hammarskjold Foundation).

Oommen, T. K. (1997) *Citizenship, Nationality and Ethnicity: Reconciling Competing Identities* (London: Polity Press).

Peet, R. and E. Hartwick (1999) *Theories of Development* (New York: Guilford).

Peet, R. and M. Watts (1996) 'Liberation Ecology: Development, Sustainability and Environment in an Age of Market Triumphalism', in R. Peet and M. Watts (eds), *Liberation Ecologies: Environment, Development and Social Movements* (London: Routledge), pp. 1–45.

Pieterse, J. N. (1998) 'My Paradigm or Yours? Alternative Development, Post-development, Reflexive Development', *Development and Change*, 29: 343–73.

Rahman, M. D. A. (1995) 'Participatory Development: Towards Liberation and Co-optation?', in G. Craig and M. Mayo (eds), *Community Empowerment: A Reader in Participation and Development* (London: Zed Books), pp. 24–32.

Rahnema, M. (1992) 'Participation', in W. Sachs (ed.), *The Development Dictionary* (London: Zed Books), pp. 116–31.

Sanyal, B. (1994) 'Ideas and Institutions: Why the Alternative Development Paradigm Withered Away', *Regional Development Dialogue*, 15 (1): 23–35.

Shepherd, A. (1998) *Sustainable Rural Development* (Basingstoke: Macmillan).

Silver, H. (1997) 'Poverty, Exclusion and Citizenship Rights', in C. Gore and J. B. Figueiredo (eds), *Social Exclusion and the Anti-poverty Policy: A Debate* (Geneva: International Institute of Labour Studies/UN Development Programme).

Srebrnik, H. (2000) 'Can an Ethnically-based Civil Society Succeed? The Case of Mauritius', *Journal of Contemporary African Studies*, 18 (1): 7–20.

Stewart, A. (1995) 'Two Conceptions of Citizenship', *British Journal of Sociology*, 46 (1): 63–78.

Tripp, A. M. (1998) 'Expanding "Civil Society": Women and Political Space in Contemporary Uganda', *Comparative and Commonwealth Studies*, 36 (2): 84–107.

Turner, B. S. (1993) 'Contemporary Problems in the Theory of Citizenship', in B. S. Turner (ed.), *Citizenship and Social Theory* (London: Sage), pp. 1–18.

— (1999) *The Sociology of Citizenship* (London: Sage).

Watts, M. (2003) 'Development and Governmentality', *Singapore Journal of Tropical Geography* (April): 1–33.

Webster, N. and L. Engberg-Pedersen (eds) (2002) *In the Name of the Poor: Contesting Political Space for Poverty Reduction* (London: Zed Books).

Werbner, P. and N. Yuval-Davis (1999) 'Women and the New Discourse of Citizenship', in N. Yuval-Davis and P. Werbner (eds), *Women, Citizenship and Difference* (London: Zed Books), pp. 1–38.

Whitehead, L. and G. Gray-Molina (1999) 'The Long Term Politics of Pro-Poor Policies', Background Paper, prepared for World Bank World Development Report 2000/1 <http://www.worldbank.org/poverty/>

Young, I. (1990) 'The Ideal of Community and the Politics of Difference', in L. Nicholson (ed.), *Feminism/Postmodernism* (London: Routledge).

— (1993) 'Together in Difference: Transforming the Logic of Group Political Conflict', in J. Squires (ed.), *Principled Positions: Postmodernism and the Rediscovery of Value* (London: Lawrence and Wishart), pp. 121–50.

5 | Spaces for transformation? reflections on issues of power and difference in participation in development

ANDREA CORNWALL

In many countries around the world conventional models of political participation have come to be complemented by a new architecture of democratic practice. Innovative experiments with participatory methodologies and a plethora of new intermediary institutions, in which publics are invited to join statutory and other stakeholders in deliberation over resource allocation or priority-setting, are creating new opportunities for public involvement in governance (Fung and Wright 2001; Fischer 2000; Heller 2001; Goetz and Gaventa 2001). Levering open arenas once closed off to citizen voice or public scrutiny and drawing on alternative visions of democracy, these moves have helped to widen political space for citizens to play more of a part in making and shaping the decisions that affect their lives (Brock et al. 2001; Webster and Engberg-Pedersen 2002).

In this chapter, I seek to identify entry-points through which better to understand the dynamics of power and difference in these new democratic spaces. I suggest that the concept of space, and of participation as a spatial practice, is a particularly useful frame. Talking in terms of spaces for participation conveys the situated nature of participation, the bounded yet permeable arenas in which participation is invited, and the domains from within which new intermediary institutions and new opportunities for citizen involvement have been fashioned. It also allows us to think about the ways in which particular sites come to be populated, appropriated or designated by particular actors for particular kinds of purposes; its metaphorical qualities allow attention to be paid to issues of discursive closure, to the animation or domestication of sites for engagement, to the absence of opportunity as well as to the dynamism of political agency in forging new possibilities for voice. By illuminating the dynamics of power, voice and agency, thinking spatially can help towards building strategies for more genuinely transformative social action.

Spaces for change?

A lot of attention has been placed, in recent years, on creating anew or lending new life to existing institutions that provide opportunities for dialogue and deliberation between different kinds of stakeholders. These differ from the kinds of structures supported by successive waves of local institution-building (see, for example, Esman and Uphoff 1993), in that they are designed as mechanisms for enabling public engagement in governance, rather than simply as instruments for local development and, as such, primarily implementation-focused. These 'invited spaces' offer one important vehicle through which development intervention can support more transformative participation.[1]

Such 'invited spaces' take a variety of forms. They might be simply constructed opportunities for 'the people', or their representatives, to come together with those who represent public authorities. Or they might involve more complex multi-stakeholder institutions involving representatives from civil society, the private sector, government, donors and lenders. Some of these institutions are transient, ephemeral even, consisting of one-off listening exercises or consultative events, such as a Participatory Rural Appraisal exercise or a Citizens' Jury. Others are more durable, regularized institutions that take the shape of, for example, water users or village development committees, or form part of governance mechanisms at other levels, such as municipal health councils or national advisory bodies.

For analytic purposes, this chapter treats certain 'family resemblances' between these institutions as the basis for categorizing them. One of the most significant is that these institutions tend to be artefacts of external intervention. Distinguished from 'popular spaces', those arenas in which people join together, often with others like them, in collective action, self-help initiatives or everyday sociality, 'invited spaces' bring together, almost by definition, a very heterogeneous set of actors among whom there might be expected to be significant differences in status. While the nature of public representation within these institutions varies enormously, 'invited spaces' assemble people who might relate very differently if they met in other settings, who may be seen (even if they don't see themselves) as representing particular interests, and who generally have rather different stakes in, accountabilities for and responsibilities following from any given outcome.

Gaventa's chapter in this volume contextualizes the emergence of spaces for citizen involvement in governance on a broader political canvas, highlighting a series of entry-points for realizing more active citizenship. In this chapter, my concern is with the challenge of inclusive participation, and my focus is more narrowly on the dynamics of power and difference within 'invited spaces', although, as I suggest, the broader configuration of political institutions within which these spaces are located clearly impinges on what happens within them, making them sites that are constantly *in* transformation as well as potential arenas *of* transformation.

The chapter is structured as follows. I begin with an exploration of the concept of space: one that is necessarily partial.[2] I go on to draw on the work of theorists of space and power to proffer some preliminary entry points for analysing participation as a spatial practice. This necessarily entails a level of generality so the lack of empirical detail in this chapter needs to be contextualized against the case it makes for the kind of situated ethnographic and historical research that is needed if we are to understand better the transformative possibilities of participation. I conclude with reflections on the implications of this kind of analysis for the identification of strategies and tactics for engagement, and for meeting the challenge of meaningful representation and voice of 'hitherto excluded' (Stiefel and Wolfe 1994) social actors in participatory governance.

Of spaces and places

Spatial metaphors abound in contemporary development discourse. There is much talk, these days, about 'opening up', 'widening', and 'extending' opportunities for citizens to participate in decision-making, and of 'deepening' democratic practice. Talk of 'arenas' conveys spaces where voices and ideas jostle for attention while 'political space' is not only something taken up, assumed or filled, but something that can be created, opened, reshaped (Webster and Engberg-Pedersen 2002). Less frequently heard, yet critically important, are other spatial terms that speak about and to issues of representation and power: 'positioned', 'situated'; and 'dislocated', 'displaced'. And there are more.

The terms that have gained currency in the rhetoric of development institutions in recent years also have distinct spatial dimensions. 'Participation' evokes images of people coming together – in lines to vote, or in circles to deliberate. On a more metaphorical level, efforts to engage participation can be thought of as creating spaces where there was previously none, about enlarging spaces where previously there were very limited opportunities for public involvement, and about allowing people to occupy spaces that were previously denied to them.

Looking at uses of the term 'empowerment' is equally revealing. 'Empowerment' is often described in terms of processes that help marginalized or oppressed people to recognize and exercise their agency (cf. Rowlands 1997; Friedmann 1992). In spatial terms, this evokes expansion, yet different kinds of empowerment initiatives position those they work with in rather different ways. Price-Chalita, for example, talks of the '*appropriation of the spatial*' in feminist accounts of empowerment, as 'creating new spaces, occupying existing spaces, or revalorizing negatively-labelled spaces' (Price-Chalita 1994: 239, original emphasis). She cites bell hooks, who evokes marginality 'as much more than a site of deprivation. It is also the site of radical possibility, a space of resistance' (hooks 1990, cited in Price-Chalita 1994). Contemporary mainstream development appropriations of the term 'empowerment' retain some of the developmental goals associated with self-actualization. But the primary emphasis of institutions like the World Bank seems to be on *relocating* the poor within the prevailing order: bringing them in, finding them a place, lending them opportunities, *inviting them to participate* (cf. Narayan et al. 2000).

The contrast here between spaces that are chosen, fashioned and claimed by those at the margins – those 'sites of radical possibility' – and spaces into which those who are considered marginal are invited, resonates with some of the paradoxes of participation in development. Yet the boundaries between such spaces are unstable: those who participate in any given space are also, necessarily, participants in others; moving between domains of association, people carry with them experiences and expectations that influence how they make use of their agency when they are invited to participate, or when they create their own spaces (cf. Lefebvre 1991). And the scope that 'invited' or 'popular' spaces offer for political agency is, in turn, influenced by a host of contextual factors. Analysed through the lens of the concept of space, the political ambiguities of participation become all the more evident. Taking a closer look at the kinds of spaces that have been created in recent years for the participation of ordinary people in the affairs of governance, more ambiguities arise.

Making spaces

In any given place, there are many different domains for participation. Officialized spaces, such as public consultations, exist alongside unofficial spaces and the spaces of everyday life. These spaces are not separable; what happens in one impinges on what happens in others, as relations of power within and across them are constantly reconfigured. Understanding their production, the actors, policies and interests giving rise to them, and the configuration of other spaces surrounding them is critical to making sense of their democratic potential.

Whether through engaging with older institutionalized spaces in new ways or creating new institutions, efforts to involve the public more directly in processes of governance are underpinned by the view that to do so makes for better citizens, better decisions and better government (Mansbridge 1999; Bohmann and Rehg 1997; Gaventa 2002). The production of spaces for participation might be theorized within the civic republican tradition of citizenship theory as a means by which citizens can realize more active participation in the polity.[3] For Habermas, the creation of public spaces outside the domain of the state is held to be an essential pre-condition for citizen engagement that does not simply serve to legitimate the existing political system. Habermas's 'public sphere' is less a designated space in itself than a more generalized and diffuse web of institutions that provide opportunities for people to interact with others, test out their views and share their experiences, and gain a sense of themselves as belonging to a broader political community. Habermas (1984) develops from his conception of the public sphere his theory of communicative action, placing an emphasis on the possibilities of attaining consensus through the exercise of rationality in public deliberation.

Habermassian assumptions underpin many forms of participation in development, from the naïve populism of applications of PRA in which 'the poor' are assembled to represent their 'realities' and negotiate 'action plans' to the proliferation of sectoral co-management and consultative committees. An explicit aim of the space-making activities of development organizations – whether the creation of temporally bounded opportunities for consultation or more durable intermediary institutions in which civil society representatives are invited to participate – is to provide opportunities for poor and marginalized people to contribute to development activities intended to benefit them, whether as beneficiaries, consumers or citizens. Amid what would appear to be a general awareness that such spaces are permeated with relations of power, and that representatives from civil society might need some form of capacity-building in order to make use of the opportunity to take part, much is vested in these spaces and their ability to deliver agreed-on priorities and policy choices.

A body of critique has arisen around the core assumption in Habermas's work that an 'ideal speech situation' can exist in which procedures ensure equality of voice of all of those present, and in which rational deliberation produces genuine consensus (see, for example, contributors to Benhabib 1996; Fraser 1992). There are echoes here with critiques of participatory development that highlight entrenched biases that result in persistent exclusion (Chambers 1974; Cohen and Uphoff 1980; Guijt and Kaul Shah 1998; Mosse 1995). One of the most incisive of these critiques is put forward by Margaret Kohn (2000), who suggests that far from providing an arena in which all voices can be equally raised and heard, deliberative spaces are discursively constituted in ways that permit only *particular* voices and versions to enter into debate. What remains salient from work on deliberative democracy is the extent to which official spaces, that bring together civil society representatives with the state and other non-state stakeholders (such as the private sector), can potentially help citizens to engage meaningfully in shaping public policy, or whether the forms of exclusion that operate within and around them are so potent that they are simply pseudo-democratic instruments through which authorities legitimize already-taken policy decisions.

Situating participation

Foucault argues that 'space is fundamental in any exercise of power' (1984: 252); making available, claiming and taking up spaces need to be seen, then, as acts of power. But these acts are not always about the exercise of power over others, whether directly or indirectly (cf. Foucault 1979, 1984). Viewing participation as a spatial practice helps draw attention to the productive possibilities of power as well as its negative effects. Lefebvre contends: 'Space is a social product ... it is not simply "there", a neutral container waiting to be filled, but is a dynamic, humanly constructed means of control and hence of domination, of power' (Lefebvre 1991: 24). Social relations, Lefebvre contends, exist only in and through space; they have no reality outside the sites in which they are lived, experienced and practised. And every space has its own history, and is threaded through with the traces of other histories, in other spaces, its own 'generative past' (ibid., p. 110). Like Lefebvre, de Certeau draws attention to practices that animate any given domain: 'space is a practiced place' (1984: 117), he argues; it is those practices that come to constitute particular spaces that infuse them with power.

Spaces come to be defined by those who are invited into them, as well as by those doing the inviting. People move between domains of association in everyday life in which the ways they come to be seen by others, and see themselves, may be strikingly different, with implications for the extent to which they are able to influence and indeed act as agents in particular spaces. Someone who is voluble and assertive in one setting may be silenced in another; someone looked up to with respect in one sphere may find themselves patronized and even derided in another. The mutual impingement of relations of power and difference within and across different arenas conditions possibilities for agency and voice. For no matter how equitable the intentions that inform the creation of an arena for participation might be, existing relationships cannot be simply left at its boundary; rather, the traces of these relationships, and of previous experiences in other spaces, continue to exert an influence on what is said, and what is sayable, within any given space.

Foucault's (1991) work on 'governmentality' is especially useful in situating some of these contradictory effects. The art and activity of government, Foucault argues, need to be seen as consisting of attempts to constitute governable subjects. As such it is about defining the very boundaries of action – 'the conduct of conduct' – rather than simply acting directly on people.

Foucault's work alerts us to the constantly shifting ground upon which struggles for control are waged, and to the ways in which discourses – ways of thinking and doing, as well as of speaking – shape the very boundaries of agency. He highlights the ways in which power permeates and courses through spaces, sparking a multiplicity of points of resistance as well as producing and embedding particular institutional forms, patterns and practices.

Spaces in which citizens are invited to participate, as well as those they create for themselves, are never neutral. Infused with existing relations of power, interactions within them may come to reproduce rather than challenge hierarchies and inequalities. Yet the 'strategic reversibility' (Foucault 1991: 5) of power relations means that such governmental practices and 'regimes of truth' in themselves are always sites of resistance; they produce possibilities for subversion, appropriation and reconstitution. For 'government' is no monolith and the project of 'governmentality' is an ever partial, contingent and contested enterprise: a constantly moving dance of domination and resistance. Foucault argues:

> There is not, on the one side, a discourse of power and opposite it, another discourse that runs counter to it. Discourses are tactical elements or blocks operating the field of force relations; there can exist different and even contradictory discourses within the same strategy; they can, on the contrary, circulate without changing their form from one strategy to another, opposing strategy. (Foucault 1979: 101–2)

Discourses of participation might be viewed, following Foucault, less as a singular, coherent, set of ideas or prescriptions, but as a configuration of strategies and practices on constantly shifting ground. They may be at one time oppositional and at another conducive to the interventions of particular kinds of agents, whether states or supra-national institutions. Spaces produced by hegemonic authorities can be filled with those with alternative visions, whose involvement transforms their possibilities. Spaces created with one purpose in mind may be used by those who engage in them for something quite different. Efforts to control outcomes can only be partial, and the impotence of initiating agencies to direct or close down emergent processes is part of their inherent dynamism. Factoring in the agency of those who are invited to take up, or come to inhabit, spaces suggests that nothing can be prejudged.

Contestation and resistance

Sites for citizen engagement in governance span a 'public sphere' that is far more extensive, and diffuse, than the conventional divide between 'civil society' and 'the state' would permit. Many of the interventions that characterize the current landscape of development seek to hybridize and transform existing institutions, lending them new life and new purpose, as well as to create new ones. In contemporary development contexts, in which the boundaries of the nation-state have become ever more permeable, the practice of 'governmentality' in the interventions extended and supported by foreign governments and supranational agencies reconfigures the domain of the 'public' (cf. Tandon 2002), and with it sites for contestation and compromise.

If Lefebvre and Foucault alert us to the importance of spatial practices and to the relations of power that produce and permeate social spaces, Scott's (1986, 1990, 1998) work helps to highlight the dynamism of power relations. Scott's analytic tools depend on a series of dichotomies that situate forms of resistance in an artificially autonomous domain, as if they were not themselves constituted by power (Mitchell 1990). However, his explicit concern with the spatiality of power and resistance offers useful analytic tools for making sense of the shaping of spaces, and for exploring the potential of differently located spaces. Scott's early work on everyday forms of resistance details instances in which what people *appear* to be doing masks subtle tactics that subvert the strategies of the powerful (Scott 1986). Exploring the extent to which such 'weapons of the weak' are deployed in spaces for participation may be instructive: agendas can be shaped as much through pretending not to understand, remaining silent, staging an argument, talking all at once, as by articulating positions openly.

In other spaces, beyond the gaze of those in authority, Scott (1990) argues, resistance is voiced in 'hidden transcripts': backstage commentaries through which speakers define countervailing realities in their own terms. In some respects, it is these 'hidden transcripts' that traditions like Participatory Action Research seek to work with: enabling the construction of alternative versions of the world, to fashion networks of solidarity and build people's confidence in their own knowledge and capabilities, and with it a sense of entitlement (cf. Freire 1972). But, Scott's analysis would suggest, to do so relies on creating spaces that are at a remove from spaces inhabited by those in authority, even if – as Lefebvre argues – such spaces are never completely insulated from the effects of power. One of the ironies of the efforts of development agencies to foster autonomous spaces for popular organization and self-reliance is that their very presence and agency as instigator may come to affect, rather fundamentally, what these spaces might come to represent to those who participate in them. The very act of soliciting the 'voices of the poor' can all too easily end up as an act of ventriloquism as 'public transcripts' are traded in open view.

A further insight from Scott's (1998) more recent work is the extent to which analysing spatial practices of participation as part of a broader project of 'state simplifications' that render populations 'legible' – whether through institutions like Participatory Poverty Assessments or user groups – work to *constitute* a particular kind of measurable citizen who can be rendered amenable to intervention. However, what emerges from these spaces may tell, and indeed be *made* to tell, very different kinds of stories.[4] Dominant discourses may be refracted through artefacts such as these to substantiate and legitimize the interventions or policy prescriptions of the powerful, or construct such an all-encompassing mediating frame that it is barely possible to imagine, let alone articulate, alternative versions.

Exactly the same technologies of space-making may be used by a social movement or consultants hired to inform the lending priorities of a supra-national bank; Scott's work alerts us to the need to position those who instigate processes of space-making, and those who define its contours. Yet, to return to Foucault's notion of 'strategic reversibility' of discourse, there are always chinks of possibility through which alternative counter-narratives can be woven, and around which 'discourse coalitions' (Hajer 1995) can be built. The 'weapons of the weak' can be used to buy time and lever space; 'hidden transcripts' articulated and strengthened in more closed, familiar spaces can serve as the basis around which to build new story-lines with which to contest policy space; and while Scott's notion of 'non-state' spaces is problematic as it represents simply a residual category to 'state spaces' when the two may be more densely interlinked than his analysis suggests, possibilities for agency and alliances exist within any configuration of actors and institutions.

Spatial practices, agency and voice

Thinking of spaces less as concrete locales than as sites that are constitutive as well as expressive of power relations focuses attention on questions of agency: on strategies and tactics (de Certeau 1984) and on 'spatial practices'; and on the lived experience of particular spaces, and how they come to 'condition(s) the subject's presence, action and discourse, his [*sic*] competence and performance' (Lefebvre 1991: 57). A gamut of cultural, social, historical and political contextual factors are all tangled together in shaping the boundaries of what is possible in any given encounter. For all the rules of open and free exchange, and ideals of listening and mutual understanding, 'invited spaces' are always already permeated with the power effects of difference (Fraser 1992; Benhabib 1996).

At a very basic level, discourses of participation make available particular subject positions for participants to take up, bounding the possibilities for agency as well as for inclusion. Being constructed, for example, as 'beneficiaries', 'clients' or 'citizens' influences what people are perceived to be able to contribute or entitled to know or decide, as well as the perceived obligations of those who seek to involve them. Participants can make use of these constructions, positioning themselves in such a way as to imbue their interventions with moral authority, turning the tables and contesting the frame; transforming tokenism into opportunities for leverage. But the ways in which participants are constructed by others – and perceive themselves to be constructed – within any given space for participation means that they are never neutrally positioned players. Their location as speakers fundamentally affects the nature and effects of their participation: it influences what they say, and how and whether they are heard. This might appear self-evident, but it poses some fairly fundamental challenges to the ideals underpinning participatory and deliberative processes (cf. Fraser 1992; Benhabib 1996; Kohn 2000), challenges that Habermas (1997) himself has acknowledged in more recent writings.

While procedures to increase the presence of more marginal actors in spaces for participation are necessary conditions for their formal involvement, they may not be sufficient to enable such actors to participate substantively (Knight and Johnson 1997; Kohn 2000; Pozzoni 2002). Drawing on the work of Bahktin (1983), Kohn (2000) argues that speech acts within any given deliberative context are also acts of power: using a particular 'speech genre' to make themselves understood, speakers reproduce embedded relations of power, signalling at once their own social position and their attitude towards the listener. And some speakers are better equipped than others to make themselves heard in particular social spaces. Others may find themselves labelled by their accent, or the words they use, as soon as they open their mouths. Couple this with entrenched prejudices that colour the way words might be heard, and questions of voice become all the more complex.

Having a voice clearly depends on more than getting a seat at the table. In participatory arenas in which 'experts' are present, even the most well-equipped middle-class layperson may end up feeling cowed. More so those who have spent their lives being on the receiving end of prejudice, and may, as Freire (1972) argued, have so internalized discourses of discrimination that they are barely able to imagine themselves as actors, let alone agents. Exercising voice in such a setting requires more than having the nerve and the skills to speak. Resisting discursive closure, reframing what counts as knowledge and articulating alternatives, especially in the face of apparently incommensurable knowledge systems, requires more than simply seeking to allow everyone to speak and asserting the need to listen.

Making a difference: towards more transformative participation

Making real the promise of transformative participation calls for processes that strengthen the possibilities of active citizen engagement *both* with those institutions into which the powerful extend invitations to participate, and those through which citizens make and shape their own conditions of engagement and find and use their own voice (Cornwall 2000; Gaventa, this volume). And it rests on strategies to enhance citizens' political capabilities in the public policy domain, from the ability to make sense of complex budgetary or expenditure information, to having the language with which to argue with technical specialists: on equipping ordinary people with the 'weapons of the powerful'. But these strategies don't come in toolkits or one-size-fits-all boxes. They are contextual and contingent, conditional on a host of complexities, from the nature of existing governance arrangements, the history of engagement with power, and the particularities of identities, locations and forms of activism in any given context.

What is clear is that more attention needs to be paid to issues of difference, and the challenge of inclusion (Mansbridge 1999; Benhabib 1996; Kohn 2000). The social and power relationships that exist within the range of domains of association across which people move in the course of their everyday lives intimately affect their ability to enter and exercise voice in arenas for participation. Any newly-created space quickly comes to be filled with expectations, relationships, institutions and meanings that have been brought from elsewhere, and which impinge upon how that space comes to be experienced. Unless we do more to understand these processes of impingement, and the power relations that imbue these spaces, the best-intentioned participatory endeavour can simply reproduce the status quo. Yet at the same time, it is important to acknowledge that while spaces made available by the powerful may be discursively bounded to permit only limited citizen influence, colonizing interaction and stifling dissent, the contingency of participatory processes and the unexpected effects that they can have lends even the most instrumental of interventions the potential for transformation.

What, then, can be done to foster more transformatory practice? Different strands of the literature on participation offer different solutions: perhaps one starting point is to do more to bring them together. The first element lies in the kind of innovations in institutional design suggested by those working with deliberative democracy (see Bohman and Rehg 1997; Fung and Wright 2001). These range from changing the rules of representation and the ways decisions are made, to styling new institutions, from intensive, large-scale deliberative events at which cross-sections of the public are presented with evidence and convened around a series of policy questions to participatory advisory panels that meet regularly. Archon Fung, reviewing a range of mechanisms for public involvement and deliberation, argues that 'design characteristics ... should be deliberate choices rather than taken-for-granted habits' (2003: 28) that pervade much of the decision-making that is done through conventional institutions. Yet this literature has less to say about dealing with difference, either in positionality and status, or in knowledges. Deliberation privileges particular kinds of strategies (e.g. calling upon expert 'witnesses'), which frame what is know-able as well as say-able.

Strategies are needed that allow participants to engage with reframing debates, where necessary, to allow them to articulate their own perspectives and experiences. For this, we might turn to participatory research methodologies as a second element. Various schools of participatory research – from Participatory Action Research to Participatory Rural Appraisal – explicitly seek to enable marginalized actors to articulate what they know, contesting the hegemony of 'experts' to build countervailing knowledge that recognizes people's lived experience and constructions of their own realities. While some conflate these rich traditions into a singular critique, others miss the radical potential of even the most mainstreamed of participatory methodologies, PRA (see Pratt 2001). Emma Jones and SPEECH (2001) describe, for example, how the use of PRA in a rural South Indian village helped introduce new 'rules of the game' that began to transform the ways in which women were able to assert themselves in various spaces. Participatory methods can transform the business-as-usual patterns of domination of meetings and help create space for alternative world-views to emerge and be articulated (cf. Chambers 1997). Unleashing people's creativity, and drawing on pictures, drama, song and other forms of expression, methodologies that are so derided by the proponents of the *Tyranny* critique, can prove surprisingly valuable in giving people who are so often ignored a chance to have their say.

Institutions like committees might involve only 'the usual suspects'. PRA exercises might result in people simply parroting the discourses of the developers and their preferred solutions. Used alone, or in combination, neither may provide sufficient scope for contesting, and reshaping, the boundaries of the possible (Hayward 1998). The third required element comes from another strand of participation, this time from the experience of popular mobilization. Here the example of the feminist movement might serve as a particularly useful one, as it so successfully enabled women to reframe and define for themselves their own scope for agency rather than take their place within established discursive spaces. What this third element adds is an awareness that transformative participation is not just about interventions in and through 'invited spaces' to transform the way that they work, strengthening their inclusiveness and representativity. In order to make the most of channels for citizen influence, strategies like popular education, assertiveness training, building argumentation skills, informing people about their rights and about the policies that they are being consulted about, or mobilizing to put on pressure from 'outside' may be required.

As Fraser (1992), Price-Chalita (1994) and Kohn (2000) suggest, analysing feminist experiences, effective participation within the 'public sphere' may indeed come to depend on access to other spaces, 'sites of radical possibility' from which marginalized actors are able to define themselves and only then to act. In these sites, marginalized groups can learn the skills for effective engagement, acquire the information they need, and build the political agency through which to make a difference (Webster and Engberg-Pedersen 2002). Developing alternative narratives, or 'story lines' (Hajer 1995) within these spaces and extending alliances from these sites through new or existing networks, can help build the basis for new 'discourse coalitions' that contest existing framings and open up new policy spaces (Hajer 1995; Grindle and Thomas 1981; Schönwälder 1997). Tempting as it might seem for donors to seek to fund and direct the production of these spaces, doing so may domesticate their 'radical possibility' and possibly neutralize them in the same way as 'gender' did for feminism in development.

While some combination of these three elements might help make a difference to inclusion and voice, to realize the potential of 'invited spaces' to contribute towards transformative participation, far more needs to be known about when, and under what conditions, they work to produce the effects that are assumed of them. There is much that activist researchers can do to generate new ethnographies of participation that help locate spaces for participation in the places in which they occur, framing their possibilities with reference to actual political, social, cultural and historical particularities rather than idealized models of democratic practice. But there are also ways of learning and sharing that build on some of the strategies for change identified here. Bringing activists and bureaucrats together to share their stories of change, for example, could help spark reflection, inspiration and a renewed energy to transform inequities. More experimentation with new procedures and processes may help in getting a more practical, context-specific, understanding of pre-conditions for more inclusive and deliberative participation. Exchanges of information and the development of new tactics among social movements and those working to prise open spaces within institutions of governance, would build solidarity as well as creating new knowledge and channels for communication. Given the sorry state of mainstream efforts to promote participation in development, all this and more is needed to bring about the kinds of changes in power relations that genuinely transformative participation demands.

Notes

I would like to thank John Gaventa, Karen Brock, Emma Jones and my colleagues in the Citizenship, Participation and Accountability Development Research Centre, especially Vera Schattan Coelho, Ranjita Mohanty, Bettina von Lieres, John Williams and Carlos Cortez, for stimulating discussions on many of the themes addressed in this paper, from which my thinking has benefited enormously. Thanks too to John Gaventa, Rosie McGee and Peter Houtzager for helpful comments on an earlier version of the arguments presented here, which were published as an IDS working paper under the title of 'Making Spaces, Changing Places: Situating Participation in Development' (Cornwall 2002).

1 Building on earlier distinctions between 'invited participation', instigated through institutional mechanisms or technologies of participation, and more autonomous, organic forms of participation (Cornwall 2000; Cornwall and Gaventa 2001), recent work in the IDS Participation Group has come to distinguish between 'invited' spaces and 'popular' or 'autonomous' spaces (Brock et al. 2001; Cornwall 2002).

2 There is a huge literature in geography on questions of space. Massey (1994) and Harvey (2000) are two obvious reference points.

3 There is a vast, and often confusing, literature on different strands of citizenship thinking; on questions of political community, identity and belonging, and citizenship as practice see Lister (1998), Dryzek (2000) and Mouffe (1992). See also Chapter 4 by Mohan and Hickey in this volume.

4 The *Voices of the Poor* study for the World Bank (Narayan et al. 2000) is a fascinating case in point, providing a rich tapestry of decontextualized voices that could be used to support any number of potential lines of argument.

References

Bakhtin, M. (1983) *The Dialogic Imagination*, ed. M. Holquist (Austin: University of Texas Press).

Benhabib, S. (1996) 'Toward a Deliberative Model of Democratic Legitimacy', in S. Benhabib (ed.), *Democracy and Difference: Contesting the Boundaries of the Political* (Princeton, NJ: Princeton University Press).

Bohman, J. and W. Rehg (1997) *Deliberative Democracy: Essays on Reason and Politics* (Cambridge, MA: MIT Press).

Brock, K., A. Cornwall and J. Gaventa (2001) 'Power, Knowledge and Political Spaces in the Framing of Poverty Policy', *IDS Working Paper*, 143 (Brighton: Institute of Development Studies).

Chambers, R. (1974) *Managing Rural Development: Ideas and Experience from East Asia* (Uppsala: Scandinavian Institute of African Studies).

— (1997) *Whose Reality Counts? Putting the First Last* (London: Intermediate Technology Publications).

Cohen, J. and N. Uphoff (1980) 'Participation's Place in Rural Development: Seeking Clarity Through Specificity', *World Development*, 8: 213–35.

Cornwall, A. (2000) *Beneficiary, Consumer, Citizen: Perspectives on Participation for Poverty Reduction* (Stockholm: Sida).

— (2002) 'Making Spaces, Changing Places: Situating Participation in Development', *IDS Working Paper*, 170 (Brighton: Institute of Development Studies).

Cornwall, A. and J. Gaventa (2001) 'From Users and Choosers to Makers and Shapers: Repositioning Participation in Social Policy', *IDS Working Paper* (Brighton: Institute of Development Studies).

de Certeau, M. (1984) *The Practice of Everyday Life*, trans. S. F. Rendall (Berkeley: University of California Press).

Dryzek, J. (2000) *Deliberative Democracy and Beyond. Liberals, Critics and Contestations* (Oxford: Oxford University Press).

Esman, M. and N. Uphoff (1993) *Local Organisations: Intermediaries in Rural Development* (Ithaca, NY: Cornell University Press).

Fischer, F. (2000) *Citizens, Experts and the Environment: The Politics of Local Knowledge* (Durham, NC, and London: Duke University Press).

Foucault, M. (1979) *The History of Sexuality, Part I* (London: Penguin Books).

— (1984) 'Space, Knowledge and Power', in P. Rabinow (ed.), *The Foucault Reader* (New York: Pantheon Books), pp. 239–56.

— (1991) 'Governmentality', in G. Burchell, C. Gordon and P. Miller (eds), *The Foucault Effect: Studies in Governmentality* (Chicago, IL: University of Chicago Press).

Fraser, N. (1992) 'Rethinking the Public Sphere: A Contribution to the Critique of Actually Existing Democracy', in C. Colhoun (ed.), *Habermas and the Public Sphere* (Cambridge, MA: MIT Press).

Freire, P. (1972) *Pedagogy of the Oppressed* (London: Penguin Books).

Friedmann, J. (1992) *Empowerment: The Politics of Alternative Development* (London: Blackwell).

Fung, A. (2003) 'Recipes for Public Spheres: Eight Institutional Design Choices and their Consequences', *Journal of Political Philosophy*, 11 (3): 338–67.

Fung, A. and E. O. Wright (2001) 'Deepening Democracy: Innovations in Empowered Participatory Governance', *Politics and Society*, 29 (1): 5–41.

Gaventa, J. (2002) 'Introduction: Exploring Citizenship, Participation and Accountability', *IDS Bulletin*, 33 (2): 1–11.

Goetz, A.-M. and J. Gaventa (2001) 'Bringing Citizen Voice and Client Focus into Service Delivery', *IDS Working Paper*, 138 (Brighton: Institute of Development Studies).

Grindle, M. and J. Thomas (1981) *Public Choices and Policy Change* (Baltimore, MD: Johns Hopkins University Press).

Guijit, I. and M. Kaul Shah (eds) (1988) *The Myth of Community: Gender and Participatory Development* (London: IT Books).

Habermas, J. (1984) *The Theory of Communicative Action, Vol. I: Reason and the Rationalization of Society* (Boston, MA: Beacon Press).

— (1997) *Between Facts and Norms: Contributions to a Discourse Theory of Law and Democracy*, trans. W. Rehg (Cambridge, MA: MIT Press).

Hajer, M. (1995) *The Politics of Environmental Discourse: Ecological Modernization and the Policy Process* (Oxford: Clarendon Press).

Harvey, D. (2000) *Spaces of Hope* (Berkeley: University of California Press).

Hayward, C. R. (1988) 'De-facing Power', *Polity*, 31 (1).

Heller, P. (2001) 'Moving the State: The Politics of Democratic Decentralization in Kerala, South Africa, and Porto Alegre', *Politics and Society*, 29 (1): 1–28.

Jones, E. and SPEECH (2001) '"Of Other Spaces": Situating Participatory Practices: A Case Study from South India', *IDS Working Paper*, 137 (Brighton: Institute of Development Studies).

Knight, J. and J. Johnson (1997), 'What Sort of Equality Does Deliberative Democracy Require?', in J. Bohman and W. Rehg (eds), *Deliberative Democracy: Essays on Reason and Politics* (Cambridge, MA: MIT Press).

Kohn, M. (2000) 'Language, Power and Persuasion: Toward a Critique of Deliberative Democracy', *Constellations*, 7 (3): 408–29.

Lefebvre, Henri [1974] (1991) *The Production of Space* (London: Verso).

Lister, R. (1998) 'Citizen in Action: Citizenship and Community Development in a Northern Ireland Context', *Community Development Journal*, 33 (3): 226–35.

Long, N. and J. van der Ploeg (1989) 'Demythologizing Planned Intervention: An Actor Perspective', *Sociologica Ruralis*, XXIX (3–4): 227–49.

Mahmud, S. (2002) 'Making Rights Real in Bangladesh Through Collective Citizen Action', *IDS Bulletin*, 33 (2): 31–9.

Mansbridge, J. (1999) 'On the Idea that Participation Makes Better Citizens', in S. Elkin and K. Soltan (eds), *Citizen Competence and Democratic Institutions* (University Park: Pennsylvania State University Press).

Massey, D. (1994) *Space, Place, Gender* (Minneapolis: University of Minnesota Press).

Mitchell, T. (1990) 'Everyday Metaphors of Power', *Theory and Society*, 19 (5): 545–77.

Mosse, D. (1995) 'Authority, Gender And Knowledge: Theoretical Reflections on the Practice of Participatory Rural Appraisal', *KRIBP Working Paper*, 2 (Swansea: Centre for Development Studies).

Mouffe, C. (ed.) (1992) *Dimensions of Radical Democracy: Pluralism, Citizenship, Community* (London: Verso).

Narayan, D., R. Chambers and M. K. Shah (2000), *Crying Out for Change* (Washington, DC: World Bank).

Pozzoni, B. (2002) 'Citizen Participation and Deliberation in Brazil: The Case of the Municipal Health Council of São Paulo'. Unpublished M Phil Dissertation, University of Sussex, IDS.

Pratt, G. (2001) 'Practitioners' Critical Reflections on PRA and Participation in Nepal', *IDS Working Paper*, 122 (Brighton: Institute of Development Studies).

Price-Chalita, P. (1994) 'Spatial Metaphor and the Politics of Empowerment: Mapping a Place for Feminism and Postmodernism in Geography', *Antipode*, 26 (3): 236–54.

Rowlands, J. (1997) *Questioning Empowerment: Working with Women in Honduras* (Oxford: Oxfam).

Schönwälder, G. (1997) 'New Democratic Spaces at the Grassroots? Popular Participation in Latin American Local Governments', *Development and Change*, 28: 753–70.

Scott, J. C. (1986) *Weapons of the Weak: Everyday Forms of Peasant Resistance* (New Haven, CT: Yale University Press).

— (1990) *Domination and the Arts of Resistance: Hidden Transcripts* (New Haven, CT: Yale University Press).

— (1998) *Seeing Like a State: How Certain Schemes to Improve the Human Condition Have Failed* (New Haven, CT: Yale University Press).

Stiefel, M. and M. Wolfe (1994) *A Voice for the Excluded: Popular Participation in Development, Utopia or Necessity?* (London: Zed Books).

Tandon, R. (2002) 'Linking Citizenship, Participation and Accountability: A Perspective from PRIA', *IDS Bulletin*, 33: 59–64.

Webster, N. and L. Engberg-Pedersen (eds) (2002), *In the Name of the Poor: Contesting Political Space for Poverty Reduction* (London: Zed Books).

6 | Towards a repoliticization of participatory development: political capabilities and spaces of empowerment

GLYN WILLIAMS

Mainstreaming participation, depoliticizing development

> [I]s the new participatory myth acting more like a Trojan horse which may end up by substituting a subtle kind of teleguided and masterly organized participation for the old types of intransitive or culturally defined participation, proper to vernacular societies? (Rahnema 1997: 167)

Writing at the beginning of the 'PRA boom', Majid Rahnema saw participation's rapid growth as an indication that it had already been politically 'tamed', and was serving important economic, institutional and legitimating functions for a mainstream vision of development. Side-stepping his uncritical celebration of 'vernacular societies', Rahnema raises important questions for those finding themselves inside or outside the 'Trojan horse' today. Does the recent explosion of 'participatory' practices and discourse represent a radical paradigm shift, or the active *de*-politicization, of international development? Certainly, within its officially recognized forms, participatory development appears to be wholly compatible with a liberalization agenda, able to marshal poor people's voices in support for the World Bank's policy prescriptions.[1] As a result, criticisms of participatory development have been fleshed out carefully over the last ten years, not just in the rhetoric of self-proclaimed anti-developmentalists, but also through careful reflection on field experiences by practitioners and academics alike. In this chapter, I highlight this depoliticization critique before offering an agenda for the repoliticization of participatory development.

The first criticism is that participation stresses personal reform over political struggle, whereby a 'revelatory' moment occurs in which 'communities' uncover their previously hidden knowledge and 'uppers' cast off their professional biases (Chambers 1994). There is little on how such instances of revelation are built into longer-term projects or alliances for change, or indeed the various forms of resistance they might face.

A second reservation is that participatory development privileges 'the community' as the site where empowerment is assumed to occur. All too often, 'communities' are treated as fixed and unproblematic and idealized in terms of their content (Mohan 2001). By homogenizing communities, and uncritically boosting 'the local' as the site for action, participatory development both draws a veil over repressive structures (of gender, class, caste and ethnicity) operating at the micro-scale, and deflects attention away from wider power relationships that frame the construction of local development problems (cf. Fine 1999; Mohan and Stokke 2000).

The third criticism, that participation has become the 'new tyranny' of development, deserves slightly longer elaboration. Participation's claims to openness and transparency, combined with its massive institutional reach, have led critics fundamentally to question the 'empowerment' it is intended to achieve. The argument is that participation actively 'depoliticizes' development; incorporating marginalized individuals in development projects that they are unable to question (Kothari 2001); producing 'grassroots' knowledge ignorant of its own partiality (Mosse 2001); and foreclosing discussion of alternative visions of development (Henkel and Stirrat 2001). Alongside this portrayal of grassroots agency, participatory development also denies development experts' role in shaping processes of participation (Cooke, this volume). By obscuring the agency and motivations of development workers, important questions about the nature of management and leadership are bypassed, and key aspects of the development process are thus removed from public scrutiny.

These concerns echo those raised by James Ferguson in his study of the development business in Lesotho (Ferguson 1994). In this reading, participation merely adds to the 'anti-politics machine': it is a Foucauldian exercise of power that rewrites the subjectivity of the Third World's poor, disciplining them through a series of participatory procedures, performances and encounters.[2] At the same time, the discourse of participation legitimates that power: through their incorporation, swathes of intended 'development beneficiaries' are deemed to have shifted from objects to empowered subjects – or even authors – of their own development. In this way, any blame for project 'failure' is displaced from macro-level concerns, and re-localized on to 'the people', leaving the anti-politics machine free to grind onwards.

There are, however, important limitations to this 'depoliticization' critique. First, in some versions of this argument there is an almost conspiratorial air of intentionality, as implied in Rahnema's phrase: 'teleguided and masterly organized'. Participatory development may have become an international and powerful discourse, but it is not an intentional project capable of being controlled by a narrow set of 'interest groups', be they local southern elites or policy-makers in Washington.

The second point is that some of these critiques suffer almost as much as celebratory accounts of participatory development do from a reductionist view of power. Participatory development projects may well re-script people's subjectivities in terms of others' choosing and incorporate them within a development process far less benign than its promoters might suggest. But while participation may appear to be all-pervasive, this account of its operation is in danger of ignoring the fact that any configuration of power/knowledge opens up its own particular spaces and moments for resistance.

Seeing these possibilities for resistance we should not forget the lessons learned from Scott's 'weapons of the weak' (Scott 1985). To take the 'incorporation' of participatory events at face value is to ignore people's ability for feigned compliance and tactical (and self-interested) engagement. Furthermore, there is the ever-present possibility that while participatory development projects can seem all-consuming to practitioners and academics evaluating them, they may play a relatively small part in their intended beneficiaries' lives (Kumar and Corbridge 2002; Williams et al. 2003a). Limited engagement or even exit thus provide means of passive resistance to the 'tyranny of participation'.

In a more positive sense, we need to remember that within Foucault's own writing, systems of power/knowledge are practically grounded and evolving, thus providing space within themselves for alternative discourses and knowledges to emerge. By examining the particular ways in which the discourse and practices of participatory development play out in concrete situations, we can look for opportunities for their *re*-politicization. If, as the contributors to *Participation: The New Tyranny?* suggest, participation appears both all-pervasive and fraught with contradictions, it surely also provides the conditions for these contradictions to be exploited by a range of different actors. Two important questions thus emerge. The first is methodological: how should we evaluate participatory practices as a form of development? The second is more practical: if participation has gained institutional power within development practice, what can this power be made to *do*? Answers to this second question are always inherently political: they are about seeking ways in which the contradictions and opportunities of participation can be exploited to forward particular programmes, values and interests.

In the rest of this chapter I sketch out preliminary answers to both questions. My response to the methodological question is that a more realistic evaluation of participatory development should focus on participation's wider political impact. I then turn to how participation should be used, and take up Mohan and Stokke's (2000) call to 'develop a new political imaginary', highlighting where the potential for a radicalized or repoliticized participatory development might lie.

Re-evaluating participation: institutional analysis and political capabilities

In approaching the first question, two methodological shifts are required in evaluating participatory development. The first is to move beyond individual instances of participation to look at the institutional impact of participatory techniques and values. Both proponents and critics alike have perhaps focused too much on the minutiae of participatory methods and events, and too little on their wider context. To some extent, the literature on participation has already begun this analysis through its own internal critique. Blackburn and Holland's collection, *Who Changes?* (1998), reviews initiatives to embed participation more deeply within development practice, and the institutional difficulties that such attempts face. Throughout their collection changes in practice of development professionals themselves are seen as central to better participation. Recommendations to enhance a participatory ethos include institutional change and a set of micro-tactics for reform-minded individuals to push participation within their own institutions (IDS Workshop 1998a, 1998b). In combination, these individual and institutional changes are intended to spread the 'benign virus' (Blackburn 1998: 167) of participation; we are therefore presented with a series of *managerial* strategies that will deepen participation's impact. However, a discussion of *political* changes needed for participation is largely absent here.

It is this absence that suggests a second shift in methodology, towards a more explicitly political analysis of participation. In their work on assessing anti-poverty policies, Whitehead and Gray-Molina outline key issues such an evaluation could draw upon. They examine the degree to which development initiatives improve the *political capabilities* of the poor, defined as 'the institutional and organizational resources as well as collective ideas available for effective political action' (Whitehead and Gray-Molina 1999: 6). In their view: 'an analysis of political capabilities requires a closer examination of the rules of political engagement as actually played, including the transformation or manipulation of rules over time. Critically, political capabilities involve the ability to create new rules, transform social preferences, as well as secure new resources as they become available' (ibid., p. 7). In this reading, political capabilities provide the set of navigational skills needed to move through political space, and the tools to reshape these spaces where this is possible. A key distinction here would be a focus on uncovering the knowledge and performances required to (re-)negotiate political space rather than trying to quantify levels of political capital in the abstract. Understanding the processes by which cultural capital (in Bourdieu's sense) is deployed to political ends would therefore be far more important than attempts to produce political

'institutional mappings' equivalent to those of the World Bank's Social Capital Assessment Tool (Krishna and Shrader 1999).

Moore and Putzel (1999) have used Whitehead and Gray-Molina's definition of political capabilities in arguing for the rehabilitation of political analysis within aid and development work more generally.[3] For Moore and Putzel, important criteria for the success of development projects are the degree to which they contribute to the mobilization and sustained political action of the poor. They argue that the structural constraints poor people face (of political exclusion, fractured identities and physical isolation) mean that their political mobilization is largely *re*-active. Despite increased globalization and the privatization of development, developmental activities of the state remain key sites for struggle as it is here that there is a chance that forms of recognized authority can be called to account. For Moore and Putzel, an important part of poor people's political empowerment is thus the degree to which states create and shape opportunities for the poor to engage in government-focused struggles for rights and resources.

These opportunities may not be present everywhere. Whitehead and Gray-Molina (1999: 5) suggest, on the basis of their fieldwork in Bolivia, that their arguments are relevant to a sub-section of developing countries where there are 'reasonably stable boundaries, and relatively coherent systems of public policy-making and implementation'. This is because the long-term construction of political capabilities explicitly requires constituencies of the poor (national or sub-national) involved in interaction with a responsive (or 'democratic' in a loose sense) state. Whether political capabilities are relevant within *extreme* cases of authoritarianism or state failure is therefore open to empirical question. However, James Fox's work on Mexico does at least suggest that these capabilities can survive periods of repression (Fox 1996).

Although participation is not central to these authors' work, their wider arguments suggest that political analysis should be given more prominence in the evaluation of participatory development. Some important questions that such an analysis would address include the following:

- *To what extent do participatory development programmes contribute to processes of political learning among the poor?* Equally important here are knowledge of formal political rights and increased awareness of the *de facto* local rules of the game, which can sharpen understanding of appropriate strategies and allies.[4]
- *To what degree do participatory programmes reshape political networks?* It is often the reshaping of linkages *beyond* the local that will be a key determinant of success/failure for poor participants. The ways in which

the existing roles of brokers and patrons are challenged or reinforced is of importance here – and these political intermediaries should not be assumed to be always and everywhere a negative force.[5]

- *How do participatory programmes impact upon existing patterns of political representation, including changes to the language of political claims and competition?* Challenging repressive or exclusionary political norms is crucial to the longer-term success of participatory practice – and here an analysis of local cultures of leadership and governance may be important in understanding both the potentials and limits to this change.[6]

These questions can redirect analysis of participatory projects towards explicit recognition of the political aspects of development, but are also important guides for a self-critical participatory practice. With regard to both, whether or not they are able to produce more 'positive' and effective development in the sense used here, they can at least guide a fuller and more honest evaluation of the outcomes (intended or otherwise) of participation on the ground (cf. Williams et al. 2003b). At stake here is not merely the effectiveness of participatory processes in accumulating local stocks of social capital, but their contribution to the political empowerment of sections of the poor. As Moore and Putzel argue: 'It is useful to think of empowerment in terms of increasing the political capabilities of the poor ... It is the political capabilities of the poor that will determine whether they can employ social capital ... constructively or create social capital where it is lacking' (Moore and Putzel 1999: 13).

This produces very different reading of the politics of participation from that in Blackburn and Holland's collection: the central question is not 'how do we strategize to embed participation within development institutions and agendas?', but 'what longer-term political value do participatory processes have for the poor?'

In particular, taking poor people's changing ability to engage *with the state* as the analytical end-point focuses attention on the particular sites where decisions are made, influence is held and authority is located. This itself may provide a fruitful contrast with analyses of participation that describe its disciplinary effects as being systemic, and the agency behind them simultaneously both all-powerful and diffuse. As Andrea Cornwall (2002) has indicated, a more careful reading of Foucault would question the particular qualities of different spaces of participation, both within and against/outside the state. Linking this understanding of political space with an assessment of political capabilities can in turn suggest a range of ways in which participation can be used to call state power to account.

In further developing such an approach, the literature on comparative politics is useful. Ethnographic understandings of state power that develop context-specific answers to the three questions posed above are crucial here. Understanding formal political rights and the *de facto* rules of the game; the constitution of local political society; and discourses of political claims and cultures of leadership are all vital in assessing how participation is being, and could be, used.[7]

Learning from participation: 'success' and 'failure' in South Asia

Reading recent South Asian case studies, one can find numerous instances of the *de*-politicizing effects of participatory development. Mosse's assessments of the Western Indian Rainfed Farming Project show that participatory consultation exercises were both a strategic game whereby villagers tried to second-guess the resources to be won, and simultaneously important events in legitimizing the programme for audiences of powerful outsiders (Mosse 1994, 2001). In their account of the programme's counterpart in Eastern India, Kumar and Corbridge note that trying to ensure the participation of the very poorest within the project was always an unrealistic target: 'the Project has been less successful in targeting the poor, than richer families have been in targeting the Project' (Kumar and Corbridge 2002: 14). Furthermore, the project's longer-term effects of 'thinning of the social networks of the poorest and most vulnerable' (ibid., p. 18) have undermined the political capabilities of the poor.

If read simply in comparison to their intended outcomes, the failure of these programmes on the ground – through routinization, the capture and co-option of schemes, the reproduction of the power of village elites – is both familiar and unsurprising. In part, the idealism of a naïve understanding of participatory development writes 'failure' into such projects from the outset. In so far as the poor are supposed to become 'empowered' by dint of their engagement in participatory events alone, this view of participation does not merely raise the standard for developmental 'success', it sets it impossibly high. Most participatory development projects simply do not command *enough* power to transform radically the structural inequalities that reproduce poverty. To this extent, judgements of projects that see their problems merely as 'failures' *within the act of participation itself* are tilting at windmills. To blame development professionals for not truly taking on board participatory values, or locally powerful figures for acting in self-interested ways, may protect the purity of a mythic participatory ideal but it fails to elucidate participation's potential and limitations in changing development practice. Instead, and as Mosse, Kumar and Corbridge note, the 'failures' of these projects are to be found elsewhere: they were shaped by donor and Forest Department agendas to provide relatively efficient service-delivery rather than any more radical programme of emancipation.

Where more positive examples of the power of participatory development projects exist, some form of transformative political agenda often explicitly underpins their effectiveness. Starting with an example from 'inside' the state, the People's Campaign for Decentralized Planning in Kerala (launched 1996) shows how a more radical version of participatory development can capture the popular imagination. Although the resources made available for local planning are qualitatively different from other experiments in decentralization, the mechanisms (including PRA) and institutions (the *panchayats* or village councils) used to engage the public are widespread in India. In explaining why participatory planning works here rather than elsewhere, Heller (2001) notes the central importance of synergies between political institutions and social mobilization. Specifically, elements of the ruling Communist Party saw decentralization as a means to extend their electoral support beyond its working-class core, and used earlier experience in linking with the mass-based Kerala Popular Science Movement to galvanize mass participation. The wider lesson is that state-sponsored participatory development is effective, because it is associated with a genuine attempt to reshape state power.

In contrast, the Rajasthan-based MKSS shows the potential for participatory mobilization outside and explicitly *against* the state. The MKSS campaigns for the right-to-information on a range of government activities important to the poor, including welfare and development programmes. The movement has used photocopies of official documents to confront corrupt practices. In its *jan sunwais* (public hearings), the MKSS aims at collective, local verification of official accounts to pick up misdeeds that would be invisible through higher-level audit processes. In parallel, the MKSS has organized large-scale protests to put pressure on the state legislature to provide a legal basis for freedom of access to government information. As Jenkins and Goetz (1999) note, the MKSS uses information as a radical resource; rather than using participatory techniques to generate and offer up a 'grassroots viewpoint' to the state, the MKSS's success is explicitly based around participation challenging the official record. Chambers's ideals of 'sharing' are seen as naïvely consensual by comparison: if knowledge is indeed power, then those (ab)using it are unlikely to give it up lightly.

In both of these 'successful' examples, and in others such as mobilizations around the Maharastra Employment Guarantee Scheme (Joshi and Moore 2000), a number of common points emerge. First, they share a clear political direction and aim to produce fuller and more active citizenship.

'Moving' the state towards a decentralized mode, or opening it up to effective public scrutiny, are examples of *progressive* agendas that could build poor people's political capabilities in the longer run.[8] Second, they reshape political networks by building alliances not limited to the poor themselves and extending beyond the grassroots: cross-class and cross-institutional linkages (with different branches of government, NGOs and/or parties) are part of their success.[9] Third, the poor took these programmes and movements seriously because they at least offered the hope of significant change. Although Moore and Putzel note that poor people's political capital is limited, these examples suggest that they will gamble it on genuine opportunities for constructive engagement when these arise. Finally, in these examples, grassroots participation was not reified, either as the only mode of operation, or as an end in itself. Rather, it was one among several tactics for achieving the empowerment of the poor. In the final section, I expand on this idea of tactical engagement to locate the points at which the growing power of participatory development practice can be harnessed towards progressive political goals.

Towards the repoliticization of participation

An overtly political analysis is not simply useful for evaluating existing projects and programmes; it can also highlight participation's contribution within a more emancipatory practice. Here I expand on participation's potential to develop 'a new political imaginary' of empowerment by thinking through the ways in which it currently works, and can be made to work, within developmental processes and discourses. In doing so, attention must also be given to the spatial and temporal aspects of empowerment that participation is to achieve. It is through this reappraisal that the scope for participation's repoliticization may be explored, and the differences between participatory and other forms of development can be made explicit.

Looking first at the forms of development process demanded by a participatory agenda, the dangers of institutionalized participation are that it can place excessive demands on the time of all concerned. Governmental and NGO resources can be poured into participatory activities that have little influence on key managerial decisions, and build only cynicism among their lay participants. By contrast, when the dynamics of local political society are more supportive, 'official' moments can open up spaces of empowerment at the grassroots; be used to extract public promises from politicians, bureaucrats and managers; and/or make explicit wider political conflicts and agendas. More generally, participatory development's claims to transparency and openness may provide a key pressure-point at which to deploy and build the political capabilities of the poor and their allies. Intelligent pursuit of these claims could allow both greater public scrutiny of development managers' actions, and opportunities for political learning.

With regard to increased public scrutiny, participation's avowed ethic of self-critical reflection turns the spotlight on development institutions' behaviour, values and actions to a greater extent than before. This could provide political leverage to uncover and challenge decisions that would otherwise remain hidden: for example, pressurizing officials to account for their use of discretionary power can be an important way of curbing their excesses. Furthermore, attempts made to contain participation within certain arenas can be opened to question. At the intra-project level, grass-roots participants are usually not empowered to criticize or evaluate key decisions concerning project objectives, staffing or finance; at a wider level, participation is generally ghettoized within social development, and absent from other spheres of government activity. A repoliticized practice could explicitly challenge these boundaries, tactically pressing for the extension of participatory 'rules of engagement' into other arenas.

With imaginative use, the practical mechanisms of participation's 'new public management' culture (Desai and Imrie 1998) can also be turned into important resources in building political capabilities. Within Kerala and other examples of mass participation in local government, 'success' is not only found in the individual projects that are completed, or the instances of corruption that are challenged, but also through the wider institutional learning that occurs. 'Moving' the state, or the development agency, to the grassroots can increase the density of contacts between power-holders and the population at large, making the former more visible. Social activism would use this increased visibility to ensure that the everyday and mundane spaces of participation become opportunities to build public understanding of how power works.

In terms of the discourse promoted by participatory practice, the picture is again ambivalent. In part because of the focus on participatory processes rather than theoretically informed understandings of power, participation remains a highly malleable discourse in political terms. One possibility is that it could be used to spread debate on the nature of political rights (see Waddington and Mohan, this volume). If modernist top-down development caused a disjuncture between 'elite' and 'vernacular' ideas of development (Kaviraj 1991), participation could at least hold the possibility of building a common language community between the architects and recipients of development programmes. Here it may well be participation's claims to 'listen' and 'represent' – however problematical – that provide a foothold to place elements of alternative developmental visions on the political agenda. Again, using the claims of participation's idealized self-image as an entry-point to challenge its actual practice may be a useful strategy in forwarding a more radical vision of empowerment. In doing so, explicit and open debate of political values will be required to avoid returning to a romanticized vision of 'local' cultures and to build support for anti-oppressive agendas.

Although a transformative participation can have no pre-defined or 'teleguided' goals, some features of a new political imaginary of empowerment can be traced. In spatial terms, this imaginary would require a developmental practice that aimed towards achieving relative levels of empowerment within networks, rather than producing bounded, localized spaces of liberation. As noted above, political analysis guides us towards the range of state and non-state actors engaged in participatory development projects. More radically, thinking in terms of political networks recognizes how the degree to which these actors appear to be at the 'centre' or 'periphery' of any particular struggle over developmental resources is both dynamic and highly context-specific. Majid Rahnema's metaphor of participation as a 'Trojan horse' is thus somewhat inappropriate: instead of the clandestine penetration of 'authentic' local spaces, we have at least a degree of two-way traffic that refashions and reproduces the spaces of political action.[10]

Finally, a change in temporal focus is also needed if an empowering political practice is to be created. Here it is vital that 'empowerment' is not treated as a change in status created at a particular moment in time. Rather, empowerment should be seen as a relative (and reversible) process built from within longer-term political projects. Development programmes have their own trajectories, and political institutions have their own life-cycles; participation, and its potential for empowerment, should not be seen outside these. In practice, even where participatory projects are successful, we will witness periods in which their effects are routinizing rather than revolutionary. Similarly, for the poor, everyday participation in democratic forums may appear to do little more than reconfirm the status quo, and provide public acts of legitimation for power brokers.[11]

The challenge for a repoliticized participatory practice is to recognize and develop the political capabilities that may be present within such periods of apparent quiescence. Cornwall provides a typology of spaces of participation, but movement between these categories is always possible. 'Movements and moments' of participation can bed down into 'regularised relations' whereby 'citizens become part of the machinery of governance' (Cornwall 2002: 18), but the latter can also be vital pre-conditions for the emergence of active mass campaigns. As a result, progressive visions of development have to be tactically agile in their use of participation, carefully combining mass mobilization, the institutionalization of gains, and learning to navigate the reshaped spaces of participation. All are important, and it would be both simplistic and wrong to label any one mechanism as more 'radical' or 'authentic' without careful contextualization.

Conclusions

In this chapter, I have attempted to move beyond both the naïve boosting of participatory development and the potentially disabling 'tyranny' critique by thinking through issues of methodology and practice. With regard to the former, I have argued that there is a marked absence of constructive political analysis within current evaluations of participatory development. This silence has in turn perpetuated participation's political malleability, and its ready co-option within processes where underlying neo-liberal worldviews are not called into question. The alternative presented here is to highlight questions of politics by examining the effects of participation on political capabilities: how, if at all, do specific instances of participation contribute to processes of political learning, reshape networks of power, and change patterns of political representation? As an alternative basis for evaluation, this focus on political capabilities moves debate on because it takes questions of power seriously. Power over participatory encounters is not simply a result of individual choices and values, but neither is it systemic, totalizing and irresistible in the sense expressed by some of participation's detractors. A careful reading of Foucault draws attention to the particularities of participatory development: both the discourses and practices through which it has spread, but also the space for movement and contestation it creates.

As such, the questions raised in this chapter are not only of use to a detached academic analysis: they can also inform a radicalized development practice. Actually existing participation, for all its shortcomings, provides a range of opportunities through which the power of development can be actively called to account. In exploiting these opportunities a radicalized practice should not only be sure of its underlying values, it must also be imaginative in its forms of engagement, using to the full those elements of participatory processes and discourses that support its political agenda. In doing so, careful attention needs to be given to the contexts of individual instances of engagement. Equally importantly, the spatial and temporal dimensions of empowerment envisaged within repoliticized participatory development need to transcend the search for isolated moments of liberation or professional 'reversals'. Nor should it champion a post-developmental retreat to 'the local' to escape participation's totalizing power. Rather, it should encompass longer-term political projects and reshaped political networks that embed within themselves a discourse of rights and a fuller sense of citizenship.

Notes

1 *Voices of the Poor* gave the Bank's *World Development Report 2000/1* 'ethnographic interest', but in contrast to the intentions of PRA these voices do little to interrupt the dominant 'expert' voices.

2 Ferguson's central concern was the spread of 'governmentality' in Foucault's sense, but given NGOs' prevalence within the subsequent expansion of PRA, it may be more appropriate to focus on participation's impact *beyond* the state. This 'NGO governmentality', expressed through particular forms of 'professionalism' and procedures of reporting and accounting, acts to discipline smaller NGOs across the South, shaping their activities, and limiting the range of officially recognized projects, actors and activities within the NGO sector (Mawdsley et al. 2001).

3 Whitehead and Gray-Molina argue that, far too often, 'politics' is invoked as a reason for policy failure: it becomes an external, negative and residual category within a narrow technocratic assessment of poverty alleviation measures.

4 This is not to suggest that the poor are ignorant of the former, and certainly not of the latter. Their experience and knowledge – as with that of outside analysts – will, however, be both situated and partial. The importance of such a process of political learning would be to discuss collaboratively both how power works and *how things could be different*.

5 It is here that wholly negative views of politics most severely misread local realities. The motives behind lower-level bureaucrats' reinterpretations of development policy, or local politicians' management of the spaces of participation, are often more complex than discourses of rent-seeking would suggest (Srivastava et al. 2002; Véron et al. 2003). Instead, these brokers and patrons are key mediators of the power of participatory development.

6 This analysis would seek to understand why particular elements of political culture are valued, and imagines how things could be different.

7 Ethnographies of state power often develop separately within different global regions. In the South Asian context, important recent collections include those of Chatterjee (1997); Fuller and Bénéï (2001); Kohli (2001); and Wyatt and Zavos (2003).

8 The adjective needs stressing if we want to avoid the fact that political capabilities have a 'dark side': for accounts of how extremely capable agents are able to generate political capital from mobilization around religious or caste hatred see, *inter alia*, Brass (1997); Jeffrey (2002); Williams (2001).

9 Moore and Putzel note that a much undervalued resource within current understandings of anti-poverty programmes is the ability of political leaders to broaden the ranks of such allies considerably.

10 If populist anti-developmental critiques tend to celebrate 'the local', there is perhaps a contrasting trend for political scientists to privilege the national scale and the 'commanding heights' of the state. A networked view of power would recognize that a multiplicity of spaces of empowerment can be created, and that contesting or redrawing the existing spatial hierarchies of the state can be an important part of their production.

11 It is important not to discount the strategic value of routinized power for

many among the poor, when for them the *reliability* of power-holders can be a key concern. The poor know only too well the limitations to their own participation and power: for them secure access to known power brokers (who, ideally, could be held accountable to a benign higher authority) is perhaps a much more attractive scenario than Chambers's 'flux' (Chambers 1997).

References

Blackburn, J. (1998) 'Conclusion', in J. Blackburn and J. Holland (eds), *Who Changes? Institutionalizing Participation in Development* (London: IT Publications), pp. 167–78.

Blackburn, J. and J. Holland (eds), *Who Changes? Institutionalizing Participation in Development* (London: IT Publications).

Brass, P. (1997) *Theft of an Idol: Text and Context in the Representation of Collective Violence* (Princeton, NJ: Princeton University Press).

Chambers, R. (1994) 'The Origins and Practice of Participatory Rural Appraisal', *World Development*, 22 (7): 953–69.

— (1997) *Whose Reality Counts?: Putting the First Last* (London: IT Publications).

Chatterjee, P. (1997) *State and Politics in India* (Oxford: Oxford University Press).

Cornwall, A. (2002) 'Making Spaces, Changing Places: Situating Participation in Development', *IDS Working Paper*, 170 (Brighton: Institute of Development Studies).

Desai, V. and R. Imrie (1998) 'The New Managerialism in Local Government: North–South Dimensions', *Third World Quarterly*, 19 (4): 635–50.

Ferguson, J. (1994) *The Anti-politics Machine: 'Development', Depoliticization, and Bureaucratic Power in Lesotho* (Cambridge: Cambridge University Press).

Fine, B. (1999) 'The Developmental State is Dead – Long Live Social Capital?', *Development and Change*, 30: 1–19.

Fox, J. (1996) 'How Does Civil Society Thicken? The Political Construction of Social Capital in Rural Mexico', *World Development*, 24 (6): 1089–103.

Fuller, C. J. and V. Bénéï (eds) (2001) *The Everyday State and Society in Modern India* (London: Hurst and Company).

Heller, P. (2001) 'Moving the State: The Politics of Democratic Decentralisation in Kerala, South Africa, and Porto Alegre', *Politics and Society*, 29 (1): 131–63.

Henkel, H. and R. Stirrat (2001) 'Participation as Spiritual Duty; Empowerment as Secular Subjection', in B. Cooke and U. Kothari (eds), *Participation: The New Tyranny?* (London: Zed Books), pp. 168–84.

IDS Workshop (1998a) 'Reflections and Recommendations on Scaling-up and Organizational Change', in J. Blackburn and J. Holland (eds), *Who Changes? Institutionalizing Participation in Development* (London: IT Publications), pp. 135–44.

— (1998b) 'Towards a Learning Organization – Making Development Agencies More Participatory from the Inside', in J. Blackburn and J. Holland (eds), *Who Changes? Institutionalizing Participation in Development* (London: IT Publications), pp. 145–52.

Jeffrey, C. (2002) ' "A Fist is Stronger than Five Fingers": Caste and Dominance in Rural North India', in R. Bradnock and G. Williams (eds), *South Asia in a Globalising World: A Reconstructed Regional Geography* (Harlow: Pearson).

Jenkins, R. and A.-M. Goetz (1999) 'Accounts and Accountability: Theoretical Implications of the Right-to-information Movement in India', *Third World Quarterly*, 20 (3): 603–22.

Joshi, A. and M. Moore (2000) 'Enabling Environments: Do Anti-Poverty Programmes Mobilise the Poor?', *Journal of Development Studies*, 37 (1): 25–56.

Kaviraj, S. (1991) 'On State, Society and Discourse in India', in J. Manor (ed.), *Rethinking Third World Politics* (New Delhi: Sage), pp. 225–50.

Kohli, A. (ed.) (2001) *The Success of India's Democracy* (Cambridge: Cambridge University Press).

Kothari, U. (2001) 'Power, Knowledge and Social Control in Participatory Development', in B. Cooke and U. Kothari (eds), *Participation: The New Tyranny?* (London: Zed Books), pp. 139–52.

Krishna, A. and E. Shrader (1999) 'Social Capital Assessment Tool', Paper presented at the Conference on Social Capital and Poverty Reduction, World Bank, Washington, DC, 22–24 June.

Kumar, S. and S. Corbridge (2002) 'Programmed to Fail? Development Projects and the Politics of Participation', *Journal of Development Studies*, 39 (2): 73–103.

Mawdsley, E., J. Townsend, G. Porter and P. Oakley (2001) *Knowledge, Power and Development Agendas: NGOs North and South* (Oxford: INTRAC).

Mohan, G. (2001) 'Beyond Participation: Strategies for Deeper Empowerment', in B. Cooke and U. Kothari (eds), *Participation: The New Tyranny?* (Zed Books, London), pp. 153–67.

Mohan, G. and K. Stokke (2000) 'Participatory Development and Empowerment: The Dangers of Localism', *Third World Quarterly*, 21 (2): 247–68.

Moore, M. and J. Putzel (1999) 'Thinking Strategically about Politics and Poverty', *IDS Working Paper*, 101 (Brighton: Institute of Development Studies).

Mosse, D. (1994) 'Authority, Gender and Knowledge: Theoretical Reflections on the Practice of PRA', *Development and Change*, 25: 497–526.

— (2001) '"People's Knowledge", Participation and Patronage: Operations and Representations in Rural Development', in B. Cooke and U. Kothari (eds), *Participation: The New Tyranny?* (London: Zed Books), pp. 16–35.

Rahnema, M. (1997) 'Participation', in W. Sachs (ed.), *The Development Dictionary: A Guide to Knowledge as Power* (Hyderabad: Orient Longman; originally published by Zed Books, 1992).

Scott, J. (1985) *Weapons of the Weak. Everyday Forms of Peasant Resistance* (New Haven, CT: Yale University Press).

Srivastava, M., S. Corbridge, R. Véron and G. Williams (2002) 'Making Sense of the Local State: the Employment Assurance Scheme in Eastern India', *Contemporary South Asia*, 11 (3): 159–78.

Véron, R., S. Corbridge, G. Williams and M. Srivastava (2003) 'The Everyday State and Political Society in Eastern India: Structuring Access to the

Employment Assurance Scheme', *Journal of Development Studies*, 39 (5): 1–28.

Whitehead, L. and G. Gray-Molina (1999) 'The Long-term Politics of Pro-poor Policies'. <http://www.worldbank.org/poverty/wdrpoverty/dfid/whitehea.pdf>

Williams, G. (2001) 'Understanding "Political Stability": Party Action and Political Discourse in West Bengal', *Third World Quarterly*, 22 (4): 603–22.

Williams, G., R. Véron, M. Srivastava and S. Corbridge (2003a) 'Participation, Poverty and Power: Poor People's Engagement with India's Employment Assurance Scheme', *Development and Change*, 34 (1): 163–92.

Williams, G., M. Srivastava, R. Véron and S. Corbridge (2003b) 'Enhancing Pro-Poor Governance in Eastern India: The Role of Action Research in Institutional Reform', *Progress in Development Studies*, 3 (2): 159–78.

World Bank (2000) *World Development Report 2000/2001: Attacking Poverty* (New York: Oxford University Press).

Wyatt, A. and J. Zavos (eds) (2003) *Decentring the Indian Nation* (London: Frank Cass).

THREE | Participation as popular agency: reconnecting with underlying processes of development

7 | Participation, resistance and problems with the 'local' in Peru: towards a new political contract?

SUSAN VINCENT

Participatory development requires, not surprisingly, that people take the time and energy to engage in establishing the basis for, planning, carrying out and/or evaluating some activity or activities that will bring about a change in their own lives. The participation of those at whom an intervention is aimed is meant to ensure that the change will be more appropriate to their needs. It is also assumed to have the effect of empowering them so that they can continue to direct future changes and put pressure on outside forces to support these changes (e.g. Chambers 1997). The location of participatory work is thus focused on the local level and depends upon local interest and capacity to engage in action for change.[1] However, despite the rhetoric that conceptualizes the participatory process as empowering for the 'locals',[2] many observers of participatory practice argue that the process has tended to be coercive instead (Cooke and Kothari 2001a), in part because practitioners resist giving up their authority to direct change (e.g. Pottier 1997).

However, I am interested here in the reasons for resistance on the part of the locals. Following a Foucauldian analysis, some critics argue that the resistance calls attention to the exercise of power. In the case of participatory development, these critics argue that the methods engage the locals in the process of becoming subjects of modernization (Henkel and Stirrat 2001; Kothari 2001). But why would people resist, rather than collude? After all, in many cases the locals have been active participants in the state, in capitalism and in modernity. There is a danger in romanticizing actions read as resistance (Brown 1996), imputing to them a heroic rejection of the state, development, capitalism or modernity. Often, what is read as grand resistance might simply be cynicism about the possibility of achieving their own goals, or a feeling that other activities are more pressing. And if there is, indeed, resistance, what exactly is being resisted?[3] Discovering the reasons for their lack of enthusiasm – what Harrison (2002) calls the 'problem with the locals' – is crucially important to understanding the shortcomings of participatory, or any other type of, development.

This chapter examines a case study in order to uncover some of the reasons why locals may be hesitant about participatory methods. To do this, I argue that we must go beyond the local to explore both historical process and the broad range of contemporary context. The case of the Peruvian community of Matachico demonstrates that local-level planning and implementation have a long history. Interest in engaging in this process has diminished, however, and the reasons can tell us much about the prospects for success of local-level participatory development. The local itself poses a problem, given the high degree of mobility of the people, and the extent to which they are embedded in regional, national and international processes. The global nature of this environment makes it hard to understand how local action, even with a geographically bounded community, could really change the conditions of existence. The case study shows how understandings of the political roles of individuals, communities and governments has changed over the last century, leading to a political contract in which locals are supplicants while outsiders are patrons. The multiple levels of this contract imply that a focus on the local, however complexly conceptualized and empowering, cannot fully solve local problems. These problems have at least part of their origin and means of reproduction elsewhere, and I propose here that the search for a solution must begin with the form of political relationship or contract between the multiple levels of action. This is not to ignore the need for subjects of development to be engaged in planning for the future: one of the great contributions of participatory and alternative models is their requirement that at least some decision-making must be decentralized to the margins. Rather, it is to insist that transformation needs to take place 'upwards' before those at the 'bottom' can have any reason to believe that they can have an effect on the wider origins of their concerns.

Development and participatory practice

The term 'development' has a plethora of meanings. Cowen and Shenton (1995; 1996) point out that the original English meaning of the term referred to an autonomous process of immanent change. They trace the history of the newer meaning of development as a directable process through the ideas of the Enlightenment and the institution of the modern state. This directable process was integrally linked to the immanent one, intended to address problems caused by its cyclical fits and starts (see also Long 2001). This mitigation process has been directed by 'trustees,' in Cowen's and Shenton's terminology, such as the state, multilateral agencies and non-governmental organizations. It is this process of the entrenchment of intentional trustee-led development that leads to a trustee–subject political contract that I trace in Matachico.

It is interesting to note that Cowen and Shenton's historical survey reveals a recurring cycle of communities being formed by processes of development, and then when these same processes engender problems, the community is reasserted as a solution to the destruction (e.g. Cowen and Shenton 1996: 435). Mohan and Stokke (2000) review some of the current formulations of the reassertion of community, or the local. While they note important differences among the approaches, they point to common tendencies to construct the local as a homogeneous and distinct entity and to ignore the role of global economic and political forces. Participatory development methods represent one of the branches they examine. Among their criticisms is the way in which participatory methods maintain the centrality of external agents, in this case, the participatory development facilitator who is constructed in the literature as contradictorily uniquely appreciating the value of local knowledge while denying the value of outsider knowledge (see also contributors to Cooke and Kothari 2001b; Harrison 2002; Pottier 1997).

Let us examine further this paradox of rejection of the external while retaining outsider power. Participatory methods attempt to deny the trusteeship of the state, or other large-scale external agents; through their focus on local-level activities, the people themselves are to articulate and pursue their own development strategies. However, trusteeship is reinstated through the role of the participatory facilitators.[4] Participatory development implies, as I have noted above, that people must actively do something, but it also implies that they engage in a process already established by others. The underlying implication of participatory development is that people will be joining a game the rules of which have already been decided, thus forging a political contract in which they are subjects of trustees.

Even critiques of participatory development that aim to improve practice tend to retain this external trusteeship role. For example, calls to acknowledge the political heterogeneity of the local community lead to fortifying the role of the facilitator. Thus, Guijt and Shah (1998) counsel methods that address local inequalities according to criteria such as gender, race and class (see also Chambers 1997). That is, outsiders retain for themselves the right to guide the process (Pieterse 1998: 348): outsiders decide who participates and how and (although they may not be the same outsiders) what gets funded and what does not. It is not surprising, then, that participatory development has sometimes turned out to be tyrannical in practice. The case study that follows demonstrates how outsiders and outside processes have come to overshadow the will of the people of Matachico to control their lives.

'Been there, done that': a history of participatory development and translocal livelihood in Matachico, Peru

The case study I present here involves a peasant community in the Peruvian central highlands.[5] Peasant communities in Peru have been sites of a tremendous amount of self-directed change in the past – good examples of autonomous participatory development (Long and Roberts 1978: 4). We need to understand why this is no longer the case (at least in places such as Matachico, although other communities may continue)[6] in historical and wider political terms in order to understand why trying to implement a new process of local participatory development is of little interest to the people in Matachico. This analysis illustrates how the political contract that guides people's negotiations with the state and with non-governmental development organizations (NGOs) has changed over time from greater local autonomy to a supplicant–trustee-donor relationship.

The term 'local' usually implies a geographic definition: Matachico is located in the central highlands of Peru along the Mantaro River. It lies along the central highway, about 280km from Lima at an altitude of 3,500–4,200m. As well as being a community in the sense that it revolves around a group of people who live in the same place,[7] it is a peasant community, a *comunidad campesina*, a legal designation accorded in 1936, entailing a community political structure, inalienable rights to land, the need to organize communal work projects, and so on. I will use the term '*comunidad*' when referring to the political institution and the term 'community' when referring to the general grouping of people. The two terms are not interchangeable since not everyone who lives within the political boundaries of the *comunidad* is a member of it. The translocality of the people associated with Matachico adds a further complicating factor (see also Paerregaard 1997). I trace here the history of the *comunidad*/community of Matachico to demonstrate the complex mixture of forces, local and external, which are incorporated within it.

The very construction of Matachico as a *comunidad* is a product of Peruvian state-building combined with how the *comunidad* has self-consciously worked to plan its own development. The Peruvian government created a legal definition of a *comunidad indígena* (indigenous community), the precursor to the *comunidad campesina*, in the 1919 constitution. That the government created this legal entity was in part in response to lobbying from civil society groups that held a pro-indigenist perspective. However, the state institution of the *comunidad* was also tied to developing statehood: it had the effect of bringing the peasants under the control of the government and into the national capitalist economy (Mallon 1983: 232).

The *comunidad* came into being not only because of the patronage of well-meaning activists and the strategizing of an expanding state, however; communities actively organized to seek this designation. Long and Roberts (1978: 4) note that the communities most involved in national markets were the ones who applied for *comunidad indígena* status. Thus, this was part of their own (or at least of powerful *comunidad* members') planning for their development (e.g. Grondin 1978; Winder 1978).[8]

Matachico applied for *comunidad indígena* status in 1935 as part of a locally formulated development strategy. The people had already bought the land in the 1920s, in at least some cases with money earned by men in the region's foreign-dominated mineral and related rail transport sectors. Thus, the process of establishing local political and economic autonomy was closely linked to migration to work in the expanding capitalist sector. The goals they tried to achieve by becoming a *comunidad indígena* included attempts to get control of more land and using the *comunidad* structure to organize local projects, for which state or other sources of funding have been sought, such as getting national acceptance of the school, building a bridge across the Mantaro River, and erecting communal buildings. I return to the *comunidad*'s role in development during the 1980s and 1990s presently.

Once they purchased the land, *mateños* did not give up their jobs outside the community. There was a gradual increase in the expectation that young men would work in either the mining or railway sector over the period from the early part of the century to the 1970s, although some also continued to farm. The extent of farming, along with the balance of subsistence and market production, was partly dependent on traditional production patterns, but was also affected by state agricultural and industrial policy. For example, in the 1970s the government of General Velasco implemented agrarian reform and fostered collective agricultural production. However, alongside this apparent support for agriculture was a policy to promote industry through cheap food prices. The result was food imports and stagnation in national agricultural production (Hunefeldt 1997) as well as increased migration in search of income. State institutionalization of the *comunidad campesina*, however ineffective economically, did extend the state's trustee role in the rural areas and provided a mechanism for other external agents to become trustees as well.

Thus, the *comunidad* came to be the target of development funds, a different role from the earlier one of autonomous self-generated development. All of the major projects that took place in Matachico in the 1980s were coordinated through this local political structure. There was a high degree of interest among residents in being members of the *comunidad*, particularly when a project was in operation. A major foreign NGO-run project that took place at the end of the decade provides an example. This project incorporated some limited participation: although largely designed by the NGO, there was some consultation with the *comunidad*, more specifically with certain influential members, about some aspects of it. People participated in training sessions and attendance at *comunidad* assemblies was high at this time. This project was of the integrated rural development type: it dealt with a variety of issues centring on improvements in agricultural techniques and income generation for both the *comunidad* and for individuals. It was an ambitious project, but a decade later there is little trace of it.

The increase in political violence[9] and the economic crisis at the end of the 1980s led to project resources being scavenged. The foreign NGO directors left Peru before the project was completed and it was left in the hands of a Peruvian NGO. *Mateños* complain that they have not had access to the accounts and this has allowed for speculation that not all of the money and resources left by the foreign agency were transmitted to Matachico. None of the income-generating workshops was functioning after the early 1990s and most of the resources intended to improve agriculture are missing, broken or not in use. The disintegration of this project has left people sceptical about the potential for addressing local needs on a *comunidad* basis in any sustained way.

A further experience has left *mateños* unwilling to commit their energy to defining and pursuing their own goals. This is the best recent example of an attempt at locally generated development, and *mateños* feel that it failed. This project involved all residents – the community rather than only the *comunidad* – although the *comunidad* administration participated in its organization and in supplying resources. In this avoidance of the local political structure, it is similar to the projects of the Fujimori era, into which it extends, as we will see below. A core group of villagers and migrants had wanted electricity for some time. When the foreign organizers of the 1980s development project left Peru, they left two pickup trucks to the *comunidad*. These were sold in order to buy a generator to provide electricity to the community. There is some feeling that the generator cost the equivalent of only one of the trucks and many wonder what was done with the proceeds of the other. In any case, the community took the initiative to begin the process of electrification and was able to have electricity for a few hours in the evenings. Later, in the early 1990s, a foreign-sponsored electrification project run by a Peruvian NGO connected them and several neighbouring communities to the regional grid. However, Matachico feels that it did not receive the same benefit as the other communities that had made no effort to electrify before the wider project came, as they were not compensated for their prior investment. Again, they feel there was a lack of transparency in the accounting that left them with unconfirmed suspicions that they had not got their share of the benefits. They are thus wary of engaging in any other self-organized project, especially those related to infrastructure, since other communities might get the same services for less commitment and expense. They have learned that it is better to wait and receive than to exercise their own initiative.

The politics of the 1990s reinforced this tendency. When Alberto Fujimori won the presidency in 1990, he bowed to international pressure and instituted structural adjustment and neo-liberal policies. Ironically, at a time when the trend towards 'smaller government' might have displaced it from its dominant trustee role, the poverty alleviation programme of the Fujimori government led to an emphatically centralized paternalism. Under structural adjustment, ongoing state support programmes were cut and replaced by assistance to those deemed to have suffered by the changes (Beaumont et al. 1996: 19–20). Fujimori concentrated this assistance in the Ministry of the Presidency and used it to reward those who supported his party or to encourage this support. The assistance avoided existing local political entities, such as the *comunidad*, tending to focus on individuals. Women were of particular interest to the regime (Blondet 2002).

Thus, 1990s Matachico had numerous small projects that bypassed the *comunidad*. These projects were planned elsewhere and the people vied to be included in them for the benefits (usually food handouts) they offered. In sharp contrast to the initiative displayed by the community to get electricity, when a church-run NGO which was said to give generous amounts of food wanted to undertake a project in Matachico in 2000, women clamoured to be included, although no one knew what the project's purpose was, nor did they know which church was involved: their focus was on the handout.

The *comunidad*, which had been a vehicle for local strategizing for decades, was in tatters, undermined by the new development regime. Attendance at planning sessions in 1998 to establish local development priorities was very low, as was membership in the *comunidad* and attendance at *comunidad* assemblies. The multiplicity of household income that has existed for most of the last century has become even more pronounced in the last decade and those projects that do appear always involve the contribution of labour. Households do not necessarily have this extra labour to commit to planning projects without a guarantee of success. It is much easier to ask for a pre-designed project, especially those that seem reasonably certain to take place. My interviews with people about development priorities show that they more often mention projects that they think might happen than needs which they mention in other contexts. Palerma's personal dream, for example, was to further her education so that she could get a professional job, something that would almost certainly mean leaving Matachico. However, when asked about her priorities for development, she enthusiastically supported a water and sewerage project that seemed likely to take place if the community asked for it. People lack confidence that local efforts can bring about needed change and have learned instead to rely on outside trustee-patrons.

This does not mean, however, that they trust these outsiders, whether they be NGOs or the government. The former do not open their accounting to recipient communities and, holding the resources, can also make the key decisions about how a project will be carried out. There is also a current of resentment about the state takeover of their electrical system. As I described above, Matachico got electricity through a combination of local initiative and the support of a foreign NGO, with no assistance from the state. The people contributed their labour and consider the physical infrastructure to belong to them. They resent government appropriation of the value of their labour. Now with the state trying to privatize the electric companies,[10] the community will be further removed from owning the product of their labour. While the state can now receive compensation for its work and investment, the community will not. All of these concerns and experiences cause people to be less than enthusiastic about committing further work and energy to projects, even when they very much want the results.

This case study has tried to demonstrate the importance of space and time dimensions in analysing how people conceptualize the potential for investing energy in planning their future. The problems faced in local areas have their origins in diverse places. The lack of resources in Matachico is one problem, but national policies such as those relating to agriculture, and international pressures, such as for structural adjustment programmes, also create conditions with which the people of Matachico must contend. Further, in dealing with local problems and trying to achieve various goals, the people of Matachico have become translocal and active in multifarious activities. This fragmentation of their lives means that Matachico is only one of their spheres of action. Concentrating on the local, as participatory development does, will address only some of the issues people face. The historical focus of this study reveals that endogenous development has been around for a very long time in Matachico.[11] Most importantly, it also indicates that *mateños* have learned that their own efforts are inadequate. A new political relationship with outsiders has arisen in which they are supplicants and expect to be helped not by themselves, but by trustee-donors.

Ways forward: towards a new political contract?

So, what is to be done? Participatory development's emphasis on the local is inappropriate in this context, and its assumption that local empowerment is to be the engine of change improbable. The local is not only politically heterogeneous, as some participatory practitioners acknowledge, it is also hybrid and translocal. Locals demonstrate their lack of faith in participatory methods when they resist participating, or participate only under duress. Do we give up trusteeship and development as a directable process, as Cowen and Shenton might suggest?[12] Certainly, there is evidence that progress cannot advance in a linear fashion without problems, and that not all communities want the same progress, while some may want no directed change at all. However, doing nothing is not an option in the current global context. Cowen and Shenton invoke Marx's bourgeois sorcerer who can 'no longer ... control the powers of the subterranean world that he has called up by his spells' (1995: 43). Given that the Pandora's box of capitalist and, in conjunction, development powers has been opened, there remains the task of trying to minimize the damage. In that vein, then, I conclude with a tentative outline of how 'development' might be managed in a global context.

What we should not do is abandon the notion that people should engage in the planning of their own lives. Perhaps surprisingly, there is still evidence of endogenous development in Matachico. A group of young men, brought together to play football, noticed the deteriorating condition of the footbridge that links Matachico to the highway and raised money and contributed their labour to fix it. Inspired by this, they have since turned to other projects. The *comunidad* itself continues to function, and the community recently coordinated a potable water project with a foreign NGO, albeit hesitatingly and with a lack of enthusiasm. We – those engaged in development practice and critique – should learn from the reasons for their reluctance and suspicion, and do justice to their desire to create their own lives, by turning our gaze upwards. The way for people to address their own needs is to establish a situation in which they do not have to intuit what an external agency might be prepared to offer.[13] For this to be possible, the political contract among citizens, peoples, states and other sociopolitical institutions must be transformed. Participatory development needs to focus more clearly on interactions among groups and institutions, and it is here in the realm of interrelational governance that further restructuring is necessary.

I borrow the concept of a political contract from de Waal (1996, 2000), who writes about famine prevention and democracy. Addressing the debate as to why drought and food shortages occur in all societies, but that famines occur only in some, de Waal critiques Sen's argument that famines are absent in democracies. Rather, de Waal argues that the institutional trappings of democracy are of less relevance here than the character of the political contract between the state and citizenry. In India, for example, famine has been absent since independence largely because protection from famine formed a key element of the anti-colonial struggle and the subsequent political settlement between successive nationalist regimes and the populace, rather than the scrutiny of parliament and a free press.

The challenge, then, is to create a political contract in which citizens' rights, including that to protection from famine, are respected by governments. Replacing the linear and trustee-led notion of development, the concept of a political contract emphasizes the content of relationships among different social groups and institutions. In this way, the problems caused and addressed by intentional development can be mitigated more effectively. In order to achieve this, problems of accountability must be resolved. As the case study illustrates, *mateños* frequently complained about the lack of accountability of agencies working in the community. Importantly, de Waal (1996: 201) argues that where strong social contracts have emerged in Africa, international development agencies have been notably absent. As originally understood by Rousseau, the very basis of contractualism is citizenship rather than clientelistic and patronage-based forms of political relationship that generally prevail within international development.

The issue of accountability is inextricably linked to that of trusteeship. While international agencies may be counterproductive in forcing governments to attend to citizens' needs and rights, there will still be occasions when groups of people are unable or unwilling to pressure governments on their own behalf. Here, de Waal (2000: 1), who focuses four of his eight proposals concerning the establishment of political contracts on accountability, sees a role for civil society actors, such as rights lobby organizations, journalists and academics, as the conscience of government, pressuring it to respond to the needs of more marginal groups. For example, the case study indicates that communities such as Matachico are unlikely to engage in the political negotiations necessary for change until there is some assurance that they will be heard. They would prefer that someone else undertake the time-consuming task of consultation until results are proven, reflecting their accommodation to external trusteeship. However, establishing how the various actors are constituted and involved will not be easy. I have suggested that people, communities, states and institutions might be involved, but what would count as a people's group or community anyway? Anthropological critiques of definitions of 'indigenous' give an idea of the complexity of developing ways to identify groups

(Hodgson 2002). How would the multidimensionality of people's lives be accommodated in their representation? Further, any form of second-party representation must be temporary, leading to a more direct relationship between the groups and the state instead of institutionalizing civil society actors as trustees of the marginal. In this way, an autocratic state would be replaced by one responsive to its citizens' needs, and the clientelistic forms of relationship that generally prevail within international development can be avoided. The content of the relationship between state and citizens would become more direct and symmetrical.

In some ways, this returns us to the wider arguments about increasing citizens' 'voice' and state 'responsiveness' (see chapters by Gaventa and Mitlin, this volume).[14] Decentralization reforms are underway in Peru, to address the problems associated with the centralization of Fujimori's regime, although it is not yet clear that this will be successful. However, the notion of a political contract provides a focus on the 'missing-middle' of these debates, concerning the specific terms and character of the relationships that bind state and citizens together in particular political communities. By locating these relations within historical political processes – particularly concerning the attempts of states to secure hegemony and local efforts to maintain autonomy and ownership of their own development – the debates focus on issues of political agency and political rule, and are embedded within an analysis of underlying processes of politics instead of the prevailing focus on technocratic issues of reform.

Anyone engaged in practices or critiques of processes of intentional development will know that there is no magic bullet. A new political contract will not resolve all problems regarding trustee–subject relations, but should provide mechanisms to manage conflicts more effectively than in the past.[15] Working towards peaceful and equitable global coexistence means radically changing the practices of the powerful, and it is only in this way that the weak will have the opportunity not only to participate, but to set the rules of their own game.

Notes

1 See Mohan and Stokke (2000) and Peters (1996) for critiques of the localism in participatory development.

2 I use this term ironically in the chapter, given the translocality of the people in the case study.

3 Schuurman (cited in Mohan and Stokke 2000) comments that many social movements are the product of an 'aborted modernity project'. That is, the movement is a reaction to failure, not to the intended goals of the project.

4 Notably, Chambers's works on participatory methods (e.g. 1997) are directed at practitioners, not at communities.

5 Anthropological fieldwork in Matachico was carried out over seasons ranging from one to seven months in length in 1984, 1987, 1988, 1995, 1998, 1999, 2000 and 2002. I am grateful to McGill University, the Ontario Graduate Scholarship Program, SSHRC, the Women's Studies Research Center of the University of Saskatchewan, for funding this work.

6 Paerregaard (2002), for example, describes how Usibamba strategizes as a community.

7 This geographic location is only one of the ways in which the people I refer to as '*mateños*' (those from Matachico) might identify themselves. They may also see themselves as transport workers in Lima, members of a mining union, musicians or a multitude of other identities.

8 It is also important to note that local initiatives were fraught with problems, led to dissension and helped some and not others, although there is no space here to pursue this theme.

9 The period of violence which began in 1980 had its roots in the extreme poverty and political marginalization of peasants in regions of the Andean highlands. See Stern (1998) for a good discussion of causes and effects.

10 Peru was convulsed in 2002 by protests against the privatization of electricity in the south of the country in the department of Arequipa. There was significant sympathy in other regions.

11 It must be galling for people in communities such as these to entertain development practitioners exhorting them to participate in their own development as the cure for all their problems when they have been trying, with very little support either from the state or other agencies, to do just this for so long.

12 Cowen and Shenton (1996) refrain from giving any specific suggestions for change. Indeed, since they renounce trusteeship, to suggest change might be hypocritical.

13 Spivak (1995) outlines the difficulty of achieving this situation.

14 Similarly, Ferguson and Gupta (2002) call attention to the vertical encompassing nature of the state that they argue needs to be addressed.

15 Note that there has been a recent rise in political unrest in Peru amid complaints that the government of Alejandro Toledo has not fulfilled its promises of economic prosperity and stability.

References

Beaumont, M., J. Gamero and M. Piazza (1996) *Politica Social y ONGs* (Lima: DESCO).

Behar, R. (1995) 'Introduction: Out of Exile', in R. Behar and D. Gordon (eds), *Women Writing Culture* (Berkeley: University of California Press), pp. 1–29.

Blondet, C. (2002) *El Encanto del Dictador: Mujeres y Política en la Década de Fujimori* (Lima: IEP).

Brown, M. (1996) 'On Resisting Resistance', *American Anthropologist*, 98 (4): 729–35.

Chambers, R. (1997) *Whose Reality Counts? Putting the First Last* (London: IT Publications).

Cooke, B. and U. Kothari (2001a) 'The Case for Participation as Tyranny', in B. Cooke and U. Kothari (eds), *Participation: The New Tyranny?* (London: Zed Books), pp. 1–15.

— (eds) (2001b) *Participation: The New Tyranny?* (London: Zed Books).

Cowen, M. and R. Shenton (1995) 'The Invention of Development', in J. Crush (ed.), *Power of Development* (London: Routledge), pp. 27–43.

— (1996) *Doctrines of Development* (London: Routledge).

de Waal, A. (1996) 'Social Contract and Deterring Famine: First Thoughts', *Disasters*, 20 (3): 194–205.

— (2000) 'Democratic Political Process and the Fight Against Famine', *IDS Working Paper*, 107 (Brighton: Institute of Development Studies).

Escobar, A. (1997) 'Anthropology and Development', *International Social Science Journal*, 49 (4): 497–515.

Esteva, G. (1992) 'Development', in W. Sachs (ed.), *The Development Dictionary: A Guide to Knowledge as Power* (London: Zed Books), pp. 6–25.

Ferguson, J. and A. Gupta (2002) 'Spatializing States: Toward an Ethnography of Neoliberal Governmentality', *American Anthropologist*, 29 (4): 981–1002.

Grondin, M. (1978) 'Peasant Cooperation and Dependency: The Case of the Electricity Enterprises of Muquiyauyo', in N. Long and B. Roberts (eds), *Peasant Cooperation and Capitalist Expansion in Central Peru* (Austin: University of Texas Press), pp. 99–127.

Guijt, I. and M. K. Shah (1998) 'Waking up to Power, Conflict and Process', in I. Guijt and M. K. Shah (eds), *The Myth of Community: Gender Issues in Participatory Development* (London: IT Publications), pp. 1–23.

Harrison, E. (2002) ' "The Problem with the Locals": Partnership and Participation in Ethiopia', *Development and Change*, 33 (4): 587–610.

Henkel, H. and R. Stirrat (2001) 'Participation as Spiritual Duty; Empowerment as Secular Subjection', in B. Cooke and U. Kothari (eds), *Participation: The New Tyranny?* (London: Zed Books), pp. 168–84.

Hodgson, D. I. (2002) 'Introduction: Comparative Perspective on the Indigenous Rights Movement in Africa and the Americas', *American Anthropologist*, 104 (4): 1037–49.

Hunefeldt, C. (1997) 'The Rural Landscape and Changing Political Awareness: Enterprises, Agrarian Producers, and Peasant Communities, 1969–1994', in M. Cameron and P. Mauceri (eds), *The Peruvian Labyrinth: Polity, Society, Economy* (University Park: University of Pennsylvania Press), pp. 107–33.

Kothari, U. (2001) 'Power, Knowledge and Social Control in Participatory Development', in B. Cooke and U. Kothari (eds), *Participation: The New Tyranny?* (London: Zed Books), pp. 139–52.

Long, N. (2001) *Development Sociology: Actor Perspectives* (London: Routledge).

Long, N. and B. Roberts (1978) 'Introduction', in N. Long and B. Roberts (eds), *Peasant Cooperation and Capitalist Expansion in Central Peru* (Austin: University of Texas Press), pp. 3–43.

Mallon, F. (1983) *The Defense of Community in Peru's Central Highlands: Peasant*

Struggle and Capitalist Transition, 1860–1940 (Princeton, NJ: Princeton University Press).

Mohan, G. and K. Stokke (2000) 'Participatory Development and Empowerment: The Dangers of Localism', *Third World Quarterly*, 21 (2): 247–68.

Paerregaard, K. (1997) *Linking Separate Worlds: Urban Migrants and Rural Lives in Peru* (Oxford: Berg).

— (2002) 'The Vicissitudes of Politics and the Resilience of the Peasantry: The Contestation and Reconfiguration of Political Space in the Peruvian Andes', in N. Webster and L. Engberg-Pedersen (eds), *In the Name of the Poor: Contesting Political Space for Poverty Reduction* (London: Zed Books).

Peters, P. (1996) ' "Who's Local Here?" The Politics of Participation in Development', *Cultural Survival Quarterly*, 20 (3): 22–5.

Pieterse, J. N. (1998) 'My Paradigm or Yours? Alternative Development, Post-Development, Reflexive Development', *Development and Change*, 29: 343–73.

Pottier, J. (1997) 'Towards an Ethnography of Participatory Appraisal and Research', in R. D. Grillo and R. L. Stirrat (eds), *Discourses of Development: Anthropological Perspectives* (Oxford: Berg), pp. 203–27.

Spivak, G. (1995) 'Can the Subaltern Speak?', in B. Ashcroft, G. Griffiths and H. Tiffin (eds), *The Post-Colonial Studies Reader* (London: Routledge), pp. 24–8.

Stern, S. (ed.) (1998) *Shining and Other Paths: War and Society in Peru, 1980–1995* (Durham, NC: Duke University Press).

Strathern, M. (2000) 'The Tyranny of Transparency', *British Educational Research Journal*, 26 (3): 309–21.

Winder, D. (1978) 'The Impact of the *Comunidad* on Local Development in the Mantaro Valley', in N. Long and B. Roberts (eds), *Peasant Cooperation and Capitalist Expansion in Central Peru* (Austin: University of Texas Press), pp. 209–40.

8 | The 'transformative' unfolding of 'tyrannical' participation: the *corvée* tradition and ongoing local politics in Western Nepal

KATSUHIKO MASAKI

One dominant trend among academics concerned with 'participatory' development has been to stand on the side of disadvantaged groups and to explore correctives to counter the forces of marginalization at work. Pervasive among researchers has been the zero-sum, sovereign notion that attributes power to those who exercise control over others, thus polarizing domination and resistance. As a consequence, existing studies on 'participation' tend to stress the need to initiate a distinct set of activities to correct power 'imbalances' for the empowerment of those 'barred' from participating competitively in 'participatory' activities. Otherwise, it is often assumed, dominant players are liable to pre-empt the processes to present their agendas as 'local' realities, thereby allowing ongoing social relations to be reproduced and reinforced under what is intended as an 'emancipatory' process.

There are studies, drawing on the Foucauldian notion of power, that supposedly refute the validity of the zero-sum, sovereign view of power. According to Foucault (e.g. 1980, 1982), 'disciplinary power' not only pressurizes individuals to conform to prevailing norms, to subjugate them to constrained positions, but also provides a common frame of reference that serves as a medium for the renegotiations of the interpretations of social standards. However, existing literature on 'disciplinary' mechanisms under 'people's participation' tends to focus narrowly on oppressive aspects of power, at the expense of its productive features (e.g. Mosse 2001). Lurking behind such studies on 'disciplinary' forces is also the zero-sum, sovereign view of power. Such dyadic interpersonal relations as are presumed in the conventional notion offer fertile soil for the perpetuation of 'disciplinary power'.

The conventional perception of power, which juxtaposes domination and emancipation, is convenient for analysts with moral and political commitments, since it provides grounds for arguing for the need to launch counter-measures. But in view of the assertion by Foucault that taken-for-granted norms are ceaselessly being remoulded, is it true that marginal actors exercise little leverage over the unfolding of 'participatory' activities?

If prevailing standards are transient and fluid, is this not because power falls into the hands of both 'dominant' as well as 'less powerful' players, thus interweaving domination with resistance in ongoing power contestation? If both social control and emancipation are immanent in daily social interactions, does not this also mean that the 'tyrannical' attributes inherent in 'people's participation' coexist with 'transformative' forces, as pointed out by Cleaver (1999)? If the two are not diametrically polarized, how should we explore alternative approaches to 'people's participation' that are more conducive to the emancipation of the oppressed?

With these questions in view, this chapter intends to explore a nuanced understanding of the unfolding of 'participation', drawing on research carried out in the Bardiya district of Western Nepal in 2000–01, to examine how 'people's participation' intersects with ongoing local politics. This chapter starts by providing a historical background of Bardiya and elucidating the local *corvée* tradition, a system that demands labour contributions from a subordinate group for flood control projects, and which has provided a fertile soil for local elites to 'tyrannize' development projects in the name of 'people's participation'. This is followed by an overview of the ongoing politics of one village, referred to here by the invented name of Majuwa. As described below, power dynamics in the case study village can be best explained by the 'structuration' perspective (Giddens 1984), according to which social structure not only constrains but also facilitates marginal groups in their daily renegotiations of power. This chapter then examines how 'people's participation' unfolds, with a focus on the cases of flood control projects undertaken in Majuwa. Although the projects were conducted under 'tyrannical' circumstances, in which the *corvée* tradition was appropriated in the name of 'people's participation', the oppressed managed to ameliorate some aspects of the modality of *corvée* by capitalizing on the 'duality of structure' (Giddens 1984). The chapter concludes by drawing some lessons for those seeking alternative, 'non-tyrannical' forms of 'participation' that can lead to the attainment of 'empowerment' for subordinate groups.

Setting the context: Majuwa and the *corvée* tradition

Majuwa is situated in Bardiya, which is the third Tarai district from the western border with India. The Tarai, which is an extension of India's Gangetic plains, stretches along the southern frontier adjoining India. Bardiya was thinly populated, mostly by an ethnic group called Tharus, until it was annexed to Nepal in 1861. The ruler then granted large tracts of land in Bardiya as rewards to his loyal courtiers and generals, who were high-caste Pahadis of hill origin. As a result of the colonization, a majority of Tharus became tenants or labourers for new landlords. Moreover, Pahadi immigrants exacted from Tharus unpaid labour and services for the construction and maintenance of village infrastructure, such as irrigation canals and roads. Local Tharus consequently had to suffer from the double burden of high rents, and *corvée* obligations called *begaari*.

In the Majuwa village, local leaders, most of whom are high-caste Pahadis, continue to rely on the unpaid labour of Tharus to implement various public works. In the case study area, as of November 2000, there were a total of 138 households. Thirty-eight households were those of Pahadis,[1] while the remaining majority of the village population were Tharus. With the renewed emphasis on 'decentralization and participation' in the 1990s, the government has been channelling a larger portion of its budget to villages in Bardiya, including this case study area. Because of the growing availability of governmental funding for local public works, Tharus in Majuwa have come to be compelled to undertake a wider range of *begaari*. As a result, the age-old tradition of *begaari* lingers on in the locality, and its fundamental practice remains largely unchanged; that is, those who actually work in the field, namely tenants and labourers, are responsible for maintaining irrigation canals and other village infrastructure. Pahadis, most of whom use Tharus for tilling their land, have therefore in many cases long been exempted from the *begaari* requirements.

Ongoing local politics in Majuwa

The transition to the multi-party system in 1990 has opened up political opportunities to contest power for Tharus in Majuwa who increasingly express in public their discontent with the *corvée* tradition that has long served as the backbone of the Pahadi dominance. At the same time, it is often difficult to make sense of how a particular village activity unfolds solely from the viewpoint of such binary rivalries as between Pahadis and Tharus. This is because village politics has come to evolve, especially during the 1990s, at complex intersections of power struggles, that manifest themselves along the lines not only of ethnic, but also of party, class, gender and other differences. Owing to the 1990 political transition that resulted in the relaxation of political restrictions, such as those hindering freedom of speech and association, other marginal groups, such as the landless and women, came to enjoy a wider latitude when raising their grievances. Moreover, the intermingling of different facets of power struggles has opened up more space for the 'oppressed' to ally with more dominant players. In this respect, party politics, which came into the open in the 1990s, often play a crucial part, by refracting other social tensions in such a manner as to intensify them.

For example, Tharus at times openly refuse their *corvée* obligations with the help of Pahadi politicians from the opposition camp who, despite their presumed interest in maintaining the *begaari* tradition, often incite Tharus, in pursuit of party politics, to stand in the way of elected representatives. The landless, a majority of whom are Tharus, increasingly demand that they should be allowed to register the plots they occupy or else be provided with alternative land, with recourse to political parties competing with one another to allocate unused public land to dispense patronage. Some women's activities are partly instigated by male party activists who are required to involve themselves in the promotion of emerging female programmes as part of their strategies to strengthen their support bases, while weakening those of their rival parties.

This growing intricacy and dynamics of village politics draws attention to two crucial implications for the analysis of power. First, in making sense of local power dynamics, it is helpful to move away from the conventional notion in which power is perceived to be absent except when exercised by dominant actors over others. Instead, it is more useful to adopt the 'structuration' view put forth by Giddens (1984) to regard power as immanent in daily social interactions, in which structure not only constrains but also facilitates renegotiations of social relations. This is because the 'structural' disadvantages facing marginal groups are often turned into 'structural properties', which enable them to challenge the existing social order in alliance with dominant actors. Such 'duality of structure' is furthered by the increasingly complex nature of local power dynamics that has come to revolve around various facets of tensions along the lines of party, ethnicity, class and gender.

Another important implication is that the interests of various actors are becoming less neatly defined and static and more multi-faceted and fragmented. Male Pahadi leaders increasingly face the dilemma of allowing various marginal groups to challenge ongoing asymmetrical social relations. Given the provisional and multifarious nature of individuals' identities, it is imperative to avoid making assuptions about the interests of social actors from their presumed structural locations in society, and instead to make careful empirical investigations while avoiding the mainstream zero-sum, sovereign conception of power which tends to accord various actors essential, objective interests.

Local patterns of participation in flood control projects

With these subtle and intricate workings of village power struggles in mind, this section examines the unfolding of 'people's participation' with a focus on the cases of flood control projects that were undertaken in the

Majuwa village in the 1990s. Majuwa is of quadrangular shape, two sides of which are bordered by a river. After an exceptionally severe flood in 1951, the river started shifting its course to cause part of the riverbank to be washed away. As a result, a portion of the forest and some of the surrounding farmland have been lost. With a view to containing the erosion of the bank, seven riverbank protection works, called spurs, were constructed in 1993, 1994 and 1996. The 1993 and 1996 projects were undertaken, drawing on the local *corvée* tradition, in line with the government's 'participatory' policy.

In Nepal, since the late 1980s, 'people's participation' has penetrated into the mainstream discourse of development, given the growing realization that top-down, supply-driven approaches did not accelerate development. However, the conventional perception of development, which contrasts the centre and the periphery along the polarized scale of progress and backwardness, continues to set the overall tone of development in Nepal (Pigg 1993; Shrestha 1997). As a result, 'participation' tends to be reduced to an instrument to solicit people's acceptance of, and their labour and financial contributions to, pre-determined projects, rather than serving to open avenues for grassroots activism. This was also the case with the 1993 and 1996 projects, under which the government's involvement was largely confined to delineating the design specifications, and to handing the materials and financial resources to the user groups, with little regard to the actual unfolding of 'people's participation'.

As a result, the 'participatory' process under the 1993 and 1996 projects was ostensibly doomed to be 'tyrannical' in the sense that it entailed the 'illegitimate and/or unjust exercise of power' (Cooke and Kothari 2001: 4) by local elites. Pahadis in Majuwa generally justify *begaari* by projecting themselves as benevolent benefactors who help Tharus to improve their living standards. According to them, since landlords first arrived from the hills back in the nineteenth century, to propagate irrigation in place of rain-fed agriculture, Pahadi migrants have always led Tharus in development, of which the *corvée* practice has been an integral part. This narrative serves as what Foucault terms 'disciplinary power', to constrict the perceptions of Tharus in such a manner as to incline them to become resigned to *begaari*. To uphold the *corvée* standard further, Pahadis have appropriated the prevailing 'participatory' rhetoric, which is a convenient tool to mask the inequalities embedded in *begaari*. The term *jana sahabhagita*, or 'people's participation', which is often used by local politicians as a euphemism, has served to project an impression of their commitment to public welfare.

How were the 'tyrannical' circumstances translated into action under the 1993 and 1996 projects, in view of Foucault's assertion that social norms embodied in 'disciplinary power' are constantly reshaped in myriad ways at the micro-level? 'Disciplinary power' not only constrains individuals' thoughts and actions, but also provides a common frame of reference that serves as a medium through which different actors can renegotiate their interpretations of reality. As pointed out by Foucault, therefore, where and when 'disciplinary power' is in operation, a 'whole field of responses, reactions, results, and possible inventions may open up' (Foucault 1982: 220). The starting point of power analysis should therefore be to focus on 'antagonisms of strategies' (ibid., p. 211), namely how different social actors in particular situations are subjugated to and resist 'disciplinary power'. In view of this productive nature of power, the ensuing section looks into how different actors in the case study village are subjugated to, and bargain over, the pervasive local standard that flood control structures should be built with the mobilization of *begaari* labour.

Renegotiations of the *begaari* norm

Owing to ever-intensifying power contestation in Majuwa, external interventions came to represent an additional arena in which various actors assert or resist existing social relations. Even in such 'tyrannical' circumstances as described in the preceding paragraphs, therefore, Tharu peasants in Majuwa were far from being reconciled to the fate of being the underlings of Pahadis under the river control undertakings. On the contrary, the 1993 and 1996 projects became entangled in ongoing power struggles, and constituted a domain for Tharus to challenge various inequalities embodied in the *begaari* practice. Tharus increasingly raised their grievances that they found it difficult to subsist without remuneration for days on end, given their hand-to-mouth way of life. In their attempt to revitalize the *corvée* tradition, therefore, Pahadi village leaders were facing the dilemma of having to work to reduce the inequality between landlords and their tenants or labourers, which manifested itself in the *corvée* practice.

As a result, the modality of *begaari* was ceaselessly renegotiated during the 1993 and 1996 projects, and was in a state of flux, with the terms incrementally changing in favour of Tharus who not only bargained directly with village leaders, but also covertly relied upon the 'duality of structure', as illustrated in the following two paragraphs. The projects required two types of labour contributions, namely transporting boulders using bullock carts, and building flood control structures at the construction site. For the latter task, Pahadis, who had traditionally been exempted from *begaari*, came to be obliged to provide unpaid labour, although they were not required to contribute on an equal footing. With regard to the transportation of boulders, Tharus successfully bargained for remuneration, albeit at a reduced rate of the market wage. Moreover, the conventional mode of village public works – to superimpose a Pahadi-led user committee on the traditional communal labour system of Tharus – was done away with under the 1996 undertaking, for which a Tharu leader was appointed as the chair of the user committee. In Majuwa, the user committee modality had long served as symbolic capital for Pahadis to display their dominance in decision-making. However, at the time of the 1996 project, it was imperative to rely upon Tharu leaders to solicit *begaari* from other Tharus, given their growing discontent with having been dictated to historically by Pahadis.

The incremental 'transformation' of asymmetrical power dynamics was facilitated by the 'duality of structure' within local politics. Tharus implicitly knew that they could not abruptly uproot the historical Pahadi dominance, and that they had to participate in the project as the underlings of Pahadis. At the same time, their ongoing social interactions, in which asymmetrical relations with Pahadis were constantly being renegotiated, accorded Tharus a practical understanding of the possibilities for challenging the existing social order. While conforming to the general terms of *corvée* obligations, Tharus continually engaged in what Scott (1990) terms 'infra-politics' to work unobtrusively to manipulate the *begaari* rules through undeclared, covert resistance. Children were often sent to the site in order to minimize labour contributions, because supervisors could not be as strict with them as they would be with adolescents or adults. Tharus also tested the limits to which they could expand their discretion, for instance, by breaking for lunch in groups of twos and threes, but many of them at the same time. Pahadi leaders could only let them have their own way. In these ways, the 'structural' constraint was turned into 'structural properties', by means of which Tharus tried out subtle ways of shirking their tasks, while observing the overall *begaari* rules in a seemingly submissive manner. These low-profile moves not only in themselves constituted down-to-earth strategies to minimize appropriations, but also served as building blocks for much more overt changes in the *corvée* practice, as mentioned in the preceding paragraph.

Such 'duality of structure' was also promoted by the increasingly complex nature of village politics, in which different facets of power struggles came to be interwoven, especially in the 1990s. This was because individuals' subjectivity was becoming less neatly defined and more incoherent at the dynamic intersections of party, ethnic, class and gender struggles. As a consequence, Pahadis were increasingly compelled to assist Tharus to challenge existing social relations, though this contradicted their presumed interests in defending them. In pursuit of party politics, Pahadis from the opposition camp, with a view to standing in the way of the elected representatives, incited Tharu peasants to resist providing labour for the flood control projects, contrary to the Pahadis' ostensible interests which were to defend *begaari* founded on their historical supremacy. The elected leaders in the case study village were increasingly expected to arrange land grants for Tharu peasants, though this would inspire the latter further to challenge the *corvée* tradition, thriving on the skewed distribution of land. This dilemma has arisen from the countrywide context in which political parties have competed with one another in distributing unused government land to the landless, with a view to strengthening their respective support bases.

Despite the advent of the multi-party system in 1990, historical Pahadi–Tharu rivalries have not manifested themselves along party lines. This is because the main political parties are dominated by Pahadis who, building on their caste and kinship affiliations identical to those of many party leaders, deal with their party organizations at the district level and above. At the same time, the multi-party system has opened up opportunities for marginal Tharus to ally with other dominant individuals, partly because it serves to compel Pahadi leaders to cater to the plight of Tharus for votes. Moreover, since political parties have been diversifying the profiles of their candidates, and given the preference of Tharus to have leaders from similar social and economic backgrounds, a growing number of Tharus have come to assume elected posts within local government. In this way, owing to the 'duality of structure', Tharus' disadvantaged position has been turned into 'structural properties' for them to weaken Pahadi dominance. It can therefore be concluded that, in this village, electoral politics has served to restrain the 'tyranny of participation'.

Non-linear progression of 'participatory' processes

As Pahadis and Tharus came to participate in *begaari* on a more and more equal footing, and as the *corvée* requirements facing Tharus were also relaxed incrementally, the historically asymmetrical relations between the two groups were gradually ameliorated. This led to the further erosion of the tenability of the *begaari* standard because its basic premise was increasingly called into question, that is the assertion that Pahadis should guide Tharus into advancement. Instead, local Pahadi leaders were ironically compelled to defend their historical dominance, by relaxing the *corvée* obligations for Tharus.

However, renegotiations during the projects did not constitute a monotonous, unilateral transition towards the amelioration of the historical Pahadi domination. On the contrary, the adjustment to inequitable practices of *begaari* also backfired on some Tharu peasants in the form of renewed oppression by Pahadis, not only in the context of the flood control projects, but also in other spheres of daily social interactions. Positive changes in the project rules cover just some aspects of a complex web of social relations that subjugate Tharus to disadvantaged positions.[2]

Nor can the evolution of 'people's participation' under the 1993 and 1996 projects be relegated to a binary process of Pahadis' attempts to perpetuate, and Tharus' resistance to challenge, the *begaari* norm. Instead, the 'participatory' process did not always progress in such a 'logical' manner, but entailed some 'unexpected' turnarounds, given the mutable and often contradictory nature of people's subjectivity.

It is therefore imperative to avoid reducing village interactions to such binary dynamics of assimilation to, and resentment at, the *corvée* tradition. Pahadis were far from being a coherent whole interested in perpetuating *begaari*, nor were Tharus monolithic in their resentment of the *corvée* tradition. Because the discontent of Tharu peasants had grown to an unprecedented level during the 1993 project, Pahadi leaders did not even propose to implement the 1994 undertaking through *begaari*. At the same time, Tharus also felt ambivalent about leaving the construction of flood control structures to a private builder, while at the same time feeling relieved from the *begaari* burden. This was because Tharus also shared a narrative, often drawn upon by local politicians in upholding the *corvée* tradition, that contractors put profits before quality.

The *begaari* modality was thus reinstated under the ensuing 1996 project. The flood control structures built by the builder in 1994 had soon started showing signs that they might collapse in due course, as the ends were under water, thus adding fuel to the pervasive image that a contractor is liable to cut corners to maximize profits. In view of the dismal performance of the 1994 project, Tharus, whose livelihoods were also at stake, felt the need to protect their village as much as they resented the *corvée* practice.

Because villagers' identities are not given and fixed, but are fluid and fragmented, it is imperative to avoid deducing a likely course of a 'participatory' process abstractly from actors' reified representations in society. Individuals' subjectivity was constantly readjusted and modified through day-to-day social interactions, in which ongoing social relations were ceaselessly renegotiated. Instead of analysing the 'tyrannical' elements inherent in 'people's participation', 'in terms of the dyadic relationships between "goodies" and "baddies"', to borrow the phrase by Stirrat (1996: 76), it is therefore imperative to examine how a 'participatory' process unfolds by making empirical inquiries into situation-specific practices of different actors.

Towards 'transformation'? Participation in the 2001 flood control project

The cases of the 1993 and 1996 flood control projects offer a warning against polarizing 'tyranny' and 'transformation', since oppression and resistance are so interwoven that it is implausible to juxtapose them. As illustrated in the preceding sections, 'transformative' changes are immanent in daily power struggles, rather than standing in opposition to 'tyranny'. This point was also ascertained from another flood control project that a donor agency launched in Majuwa in 2001, to construct additional flood control structures.

The major objective of the donor-supported project, entitled the 'Participatory Disaster Management Programme' was to 'enhance the capacity of local communities in disaster management'. According to one official in charge of this project, Majuwa was chosen as one of the target areas, given its 'commendable' records of 'community mobilization' for the past flood control projects. The donor did not heed divergent meanings that different village actors attached to the tradition of 'people's participation', since it regarded the 'community' as a cohesive, homogeneous entity, in line with the underlying approach prevailing among donor agencies.

Village elected representatives were entrusted by the donor to organize the 'community' for the project, who then attempted to put the *corvée* tradition into action, but in vain. At the time, another road construction project was about to be launched with villagers' *begaari* contributions. Moreover, at the onset of monsoon, the busy season for farmers was fast approaching. This provided Tharu peasants with grounds to refuse openly to offer *begaari*, thereby preventing the project from being started. As the donor and village leaders came under increasing pressure to initiate the construction of flood control works, it was decided by village elected representatives to assign the *begaari* obligation to landowners, instead of passing it to their tenants, as had usually been done in the past. Landlords, a majority of whom were Pahadis, had to pay a market-rate wage to their Tharu tenants, if the former were to depute the latter to provide labour.

In this way, just as under the flood control projects in the 1990s, the modification to the project plan evolved out of the day-to-day struggles of Tharus to renegotiate the *begaari* practice. At the same time, in comparison with the adjustments made under the previous projects, this new change struck me as a major departure from the past, when *begaari* had always been the responsibility of tenants, not their landlords. However, this was not the case from the viewpoint of Tharu peasants, a discrepancy that warns against analysts imposing their own cognitive interests on the non-theoretical flow of social interactions.

Through my fieldwork, I had built up rapport with various Tharu peasants who divulged stories of the historical plight of Tharus and their daily struggles. I was expecting that those informants would describe the news as a major breakthrough in their resistance to the existing social order. On the contrary, none of them took this modification as a special step forwards; for them it was another incident in their continual struggles to redress social injustice. In the past the mode of *begaari* had ceaselessly been renegotiated and modified. The alteration of the donor project plan evolved out of a series of minor adjustments that had continually been made to the *begaari* tradition. Through years of assiduous resistance, Tharu peasants had even managed to obtain remuneration, albeit at rare intervals, as exemplified by the above-mentioned case of the transportation of boulders under the flood control projects in the mid-1990s. In this sense, the 'new rule' of *begaari* was just an extension of the few exceptional cases that had occasionally occurred, despite the historically predominant pattern of non-payment for *begaari*.

As pointed out by Giddens, social interactions entail 'an interweaving of short-term purposes and long-term projects' (1995: 35), in contrast to the synchronic view prevailing among analysts to associate time with changes, thus underplaying recursive social practices across time. In the case of the donor-supported project, the longstanding struggles against *begaari* across generations constituted 'storage capacity' (ibid.) that Tharus drew upon to demand the 'new rule' under the 2001 project. This leads us to conclude, by drawing on the two terms coined by Cowen and Shenton (1996), that it is crucial to pay attention to how 'imminent' participatory development interventions engage with more 'immanent' processes of day-to-day struggles.

To make sense of the seemingly 'restrained' reaction of Tharu peasants, described in the second last paragraph, it is also relevant to cite Bourdieu, who cautions that social scientists risk projecting regularities and logic on to non-theoretical and informal flows of social interactions (Bourdieu 1990: 80–97). Bourdieu picks up a calendar as a metaphor of scientific construction. A calendar 'substitutes a linear, homogenous, continuous time for practical time which is made up of islands of incommensurable duration, each with its own rhythm, a time that races or drags, depending on what one is doing' (ibid., p. 84). Analysts should bear in mind that, by virtue of attributing formal properties to the uncertainty surrounding 'people's participation', 'scientific' analyses are liable to divert attention away from the transient nature of the actual participatory processes on the ground. As demonstrated by this donor-supported project, as well as the previous flood control undertakings in the mid-1990s, even under 'tyrannical' circumstances, 'participatory' interventions continue to be reshaped and remade by ongoing power struggles in local contexts. It is thereby imperative to heed the micro-level practices of local actors over time, which cause power relations to be ceaselessly renegotiated and modified.

Conclusions: rethinking 'tyranny' and 'transformation'

The flood control projects described in the preceding sections were implemented under 'tyrannical' circumstances, in that the pervasive 'participatory' rhetoric was appropriated by Pahadis to uphold the *corvée* tradition, or *begaari*, which fell heavily on Tharus. At the same time, the *begaari* standard was ceaselessly renegotiated and the modality of *corvée* was incrementally adjusted in favour of Tharus. Under the case projects, the *begaari* standard not only exerted pressure on villagers to conform to the norm, but also served as a medium for local actors to assert or challenge existing social relations. This chapter attests to the assertion of Foucault that 'disciplinary power' not only subjugates individuals to constrained positions, but also helps them to contest ceaselessly the interpretations of pervasive norms.

The continual remoulding of the *corvée* standard can be grasped within the context of ongoing village politics in which Tharus turn 'structural constraints' into 'structural properties', in response to the limitations and opportunities arising in their daily social interactions. This 'duality of structure' was facilitated by the increasing complexity of village politics in which people's identities became increasingly fluid, multi-faceted and incoherent. Pahadis, who were faced with the daily dilemma of retaining their dominance, constantly readjusted their stance on the existing social order. This often enabled Tharus to ally with Pahadis in their ongoing power struggles to ameliorate the historically asymmetrical relations between the two groups.

Given such subtle and intricate workings of power, this chapter shows that the potential for a 'transformative' evolution of 'participatory' activities is inherent in the daily flow of social interactions, in contrast to the pervasive assumption that a separate process of counter-measures should be launched. Instead, the modification to the *begaari* mode evolved out of the daily struggles of Tharu peasants constantly to seek opportunities for renegotiating ongoing power dynamics, a finding that underlines the importance of understanding popular agency as an immanent social force as distinct from participation in imminent interventions.

If external interventions are to make better contributions to the cause of marginal groups, it is imperative to start out by considering how the daily flow of social interactions can potentially play a part in ameliorating potential biases in 'participatory' processes. It would only then be feasible to devise strategies that build upon opportunities arising from daily social interactions, as well as make up for limitations of local struggles to overcome entrenched inequalities.

In the case of the flood control projects, external agents could have incited Tharus to take to overt protests against the *begaari* tradition, with a view to blocking the implementation of the projects. It would have been a grave mistake to launch such a campaign, however, since Tharus and Pahadis would become simplistically juxtaposed as 'goodies' and 'baddies'. The case projects show that Pahadis did not necessarily seek to defend the *corvée* practice, but often faced the dilemma of having to relax *begaari* to maintain the tradition. Had outside 'supporters' intervened in the projects with disregard to the fluid, multi-faceted and often fragmented nature of individuals' identities, their initiatives would have unnecessarily alienated Pahadis by depriving them of opportunities for self-imposed adjustments.

For comprehending such transient, incoherent social practices, thus capitalizing on the intermingling of 'tyrannical' and 'transformative' potentials in daily lives, it is crucial for external agents to conduct ethnographic investigations. Past guidelines on 'participatory' interventions, on the other hand, are overly concerned with a formal, pre-determined process of designing, executing and evaluating action programmes. Without more informal, contingent and spontaneous encounters, it is not feasible to gain a nuanced understanding of how local actors constantly rework their stances in view of ongoing renegotiations of power. A less formulaic approach is therefore a key to preventing external agents from preconceiving what constitutes 'tyrannical' situations. The importance of evading the projection of analysts' presumptions on to subtle and intricate social interactions is also exemplified by the case study of the donor-supported project, taken up in the preceding section.

To exercise reflexive vigilance against the potential risk of imposing regularities on to non-theoretical flows of social interactions, it is crucial to move beyond the 'tyranny/transformation' antinomy. As explained at the outset of this chapter, the polarized scale of 'tyranny' and 'transformation' is largely unresolved even among those studies that supposedly follow Foucault. This is attributable to a commitment shared by many researchers to take the side of 'marginal' groups, and so to overemphasize the oppressive nature of power, drawing upon the conventional view of power. To arrive at an alternative concept that elucidates the 'tyranny/transformation' nexus, it is useful to bring together the Foucauldian notion and Giddens's 'structuration' theory, capitalizing upon their common orientation to regard both domination and resistance to be immanent in day-to-day lives. By combining the two facets of power, it is possible to gain an overarching picture of societal dynamics, without which external agents would remain liable to force their unfounded presumptions with disregard to the uncertain and contingent nature of how 'participatory' interventions engage with the everyday struggles of subordinate groups on the ground.

Notes

This chapter is partly drawn from my PhD dissertation (entitled 'The Politics of the Policy Process: "Participatory" River Control in Nepal'), awarded by the University of Sussex in the UK in 2003. The input of my supervisor, Dr Jude Howell, is gratefully acknowledged. Thanks also go to Garett Pratt at the IDS for useful comments and ideas.

1 Twenty-five of all the Pahadi households were of high caste, while the rest of Pahadis were either *Matwalis* (alcohol drinkers) or of untouchable caste. The latter two groups of Pahadis hardly figure in the historical power contestation over *begaari*. This is because they earn their livelihoods from a combination of livestock rearing, backyard farming and working as day labourers in nearby towns. Since none of them works as a tenant or *kamaiya*, nor uses irrigation canals as a cultivator, they are rarely obliged to participate in public works. In this chapter, the term Pahadis denotes the twenty-five high-caste households.

2 For further details, see my PhD dissertation.

References

Bourdieu, P. (1990) *The Logic of Practice* (London: Polity Press).

Cleaver, F. (1999) 'Paradoxes of Participation: Questioning Participatory Approaches to Development', *Journal of International Development*, 11: 597–612.

Cooke, B. and U. Kothari (2001) 'The Case for Participation as Tyranny', in B. Cooke and U. Kothari (eds), *Participation: The New Tyranny?* (London: Zed Books), pp. 1–15.

Cowen, M. and R. Shenton (1996) *Doctrines of Development* (London: Routledge).

Foucault, M. (1980) 'Two Lectures', in C. Gordon (ed.), *Power/Knowledge: Selected Interviews and Other Writings 1972–1977 by Michel Foucault* (New York: Harvester Wheatsheaf).

— (1982) 'Afterword: The Subject and Power', in H. L. Dreyfus and P. Rabinow (eds), *Michel Foucault: Beyond Structuralism and Hermeneutics* (Brighton: Harvester Press).

Giddens, A. (1984) *A Constitution of Society: Outline of the Theory of Structuration* (Cambridge: Polity Press).

— (1995) *A Contemporary Critique of Historical Materialism*, 2nd edn (London: Macmillan).

Mosse, D. (2001) '"People's Knowledge", Participation and Patronage: Operations and Representation in Rural Development', in B. Cooke and U. Kothari (eds), *Participation: The New Tyranny?* (London: Zed Books), pp. 16–35.

Pigg, S. L. (1993) 'Unintended Consequences: The Ideological Impact of Development in Nepal', *South Asia Bulletin*, 13 (1 and 2): 45–58.

Scott, J. C. (1990) *Domination and the Arts of Resistance: Hidden Transcripts* (New Haven, CT and London: Yale University Press).

Shrestha, N. R. (1997) *In the Name of Development: A Reflection of Nepal* (Kathmandu: Educational Enterprises).

Stirrat, R. L. (1996) 'The New Orthodoxy and Old Truth: Participation, Empowerment and Other Buzz Words', in S. Bastian and N. Bastian (eds), *Assessing Participation: A Debate from South Asia* (Delhi: Konark).

9 | Morality, citizenship and participatory development in an indigenous development association: the case of GPSDO and the Sebat Bet Gurage of Ethiopia

LEROI HENRY

> People in the cities feel obligated to support their locality. It is a natural phenomenon that starts from the family. If you talk about the well-being of society, you start from your home then go to your neighbour. The obligations start with supporting your family, your clan, your house [territorially defined grouping of related clans], then the other Gurages, then the rest of Ethiopia. (Development association activist)

Rather than reducing our understanding of participatory development to debates over the pros and cons of participatory techniques, researchers must ground their understanding of participatory development in the social organization, cultures and identities of indigenous agents of development. Critiques of participatory development have attacked its practice-driven nature and weak theoretical underpinning, particularly an inadequate conceptualization of community and power (Cooke and Kothari 2001). This chapter explores the relationships between an indigenous development association and the communities it serves and focuses on how the process of community participation in development is socially constructed. I illustrate how participation in development projects is an element of citizenship, defined as participation in the social, political, economic and cultural affairs of political communities. As such the social rights and obligations that constitute citizenship are embedded in developmental practices. I apply approaches used in African Studies, particularly the study of ethnicity (highlighted in Chapter 4 of this volume) to assist in understanding the role of citizenship in the construction of community participation in development. I explore what it means to be a good Gurage citizen and argue that the dominant understandings of Gurage citizenship are related to fulfilling the obligations around participating in communal affairs, including development projects. Furthermore, this approach differs from other approaches to citizenship in development studies by focusing on non-state forms of citizenship and analyses the obligations that activate citizenship in addition to the rights enjoyed by citizens.

The processes of development that I outline may appear instrumental and non-empowering and indeed for some may not constitute participatory development. However, this form of participation must be understood in the context of the rights and, particularly, the obligations embedded in dominant notions of Gurage civic virtue. When analysed in these terms, this form of participation increases the legitimacy of development interventions in three ways. First, it increases the effectiveness of projects by reducing overheads and securing leadership. Second, financial sacrifices ensure that communities are vested with ownership of projects, which increases sustainability. Third, resource mobilization legitimizes the position of the rural people as recipients of assistance from the urban population by demonstrating their commitment to the project and Gurage notions of citizenship. As such, participation in development is also central to the construction of Gurage identities.

I begin by outlining the limitations in current thinking about the relationship between citizenship and participatory development. From there I propose an approach to citizenship based on an analysis of the moral elements of ethnicity. I then introduce a case study of the Gurage People's Self-help and Development Organization (GPSDO) and the Gurages before discussing their dominant discourses relating to rights and obligations reflecting mutual interdependence and rural dependence in Gurage notions of citizenship. I highlight the process of development and leadership focusing on examples of initiation, consultation, resource mobilization and implementation. I then outline how a range of sanctions underpins the process of participation in development and explore the meanings attributed to participation in development and particularly the obligations on the elite. I conclude by discussing the implications of this approach to citizenship as civic virtue.

Citizenship and participation

Current approaches to citizenship and development are influenced by, among others, the work of Lister (1997, 1998). In rejecting formal and legalistic approaches she conceptualizes citizenship as relationships that form the basis of membership of political communities (Lister 1997). Contemporary development discourses use citizenship as a means of understanding the relationships between individuals and/or groups and political authorities. This is an overtly political process of transforming the objects of development from passive consumers to active citizens with rights to participate in institutions that affect their life on the basis of equality (Cornwall and Gaventa 2000). In this way they can assert accountability on the basis of citizenship – holding rights to be protected from, and which are protected by, the state.

However, these approaches are of limited use when analysing participation in indigenous development associations. First, this conception of citizenship is based almost exclusively on rights while overlooking obligations. To conceptualize the relationships between participation and citizenship one must investigate collective action as practices that activate citizenship status which includes obligations to act as citizens (Lister 1997). Understanding citizenship as entailing rights and obligations allows us to conceptualize citizenship as a process rather than a static framework (Turner 2001). However, international development research tends to focus on the rights of groups and individuals but overlooks the responsibilities inherent in membership of political communities. As I outline below, this has important implications for the study of participatory development which often involves the sacrifice of resources as a precursor to gaining benefits.

Second and relatedly, while acknowledging the existence of a plurality of citizenships there is a tendency to confine analysis to relationships with the state. This literature accepts the importance of identities in the construction of citizenship. For example, Gaventa suggests that how people understand themselves as citizens has an impact on their perceptions of rights and responsibilities. In turn, this notion of relationships between citizenship and identity allows us to conceptualize citizenship beyond the nation-state (Gaventa 2002). However, when discussing the relationships between citizenship and diversity the focus is on the legitimacy of group demands of the state rather than using citizenship to conceptualize social practices and other relationships within non-state political communities.

I focus on an ethnically based NGO and how citizenship has been structured as a web of rights and obligations that relate to participation in the affairs of the group, including development activities. Hence, I examine a form of ethnic citizenship, specifically the moral elements of membership of an ethnic group. Non-state forms of citizenship in Africa, particularly ethnicity, tend to be regarded in negative terms. For example, Mamdani (1996) contrasts the rights-based privileges of citizenship inherited from colonizers enjoyed in towns and the 'tribal traditions' exercised by subjects in rural areas. While politically mobilized ethnic sentiment can have negative outcomes, these approaches focus on a very narrow conception of ethnicity and overlook the potentially progressive and transformative aspects of ethnic identities.

In this chapter I use the concept of civic virtue (Lonsdale 1992) as an analytical tool to explore the relationship between citizenship and development by focusing on the moral component of membership of groups. Civic virtue refers to an idealized form of citizenship consisting of a moral framework of rights and obligations and conceptions of justice and equality. To make sense of new relationships within and outside the group and to legitimize their positions, various sections of the intellectual strata of the group articulate their contestations in the language of tradition and ethnicity. This approach illustrates how competing groups vie for political prominence by reconstructing the past in order to redefine the moral nature of group membership. Conceptions of civic virtue although constructed for specific purposes can develop their own logic and may therefore operate autonomously from sectional and material interests and act to modify or provoke behaviour (Lonsdale 1992).

This approach to citizenship allows us to relate participation in development to other forms of social activism and locate it in social organization, social practices and institutions. It reveals how a range of indigenous development actors conceptualize their participation in development by relating it to other forms of communal activism. It provides a conceptual framework to analyse how institutions and social practices are harnessed for and transformed by development and reveals the bases on which the process of development is regulated and contested. As illustrated in the following case study, this approach can help to resolve the seeming paradox of how social practices that appear to be tyrannical are governed by relatively egalitarian norms and can have progressive outcomes.

The Sebat Bet Gurage and GPSDO[1]

GPSDO is the oldest and most successful indigenous development association in Ethiopia. Its predecessor, the Gurage Road Construction Organization, was established in 1961 in Addis Ababa as a federation of seven community-based development associations representing the seven houses of the western Gurage. Members of the urban elite, at the request of rural elders, founded the organization to activate urban–rural linkages within the Sebat Bet Gurage communities to mobilize communal resources to connect Gurageland with the national highway system. Later GPSDO expanded its activities to encompass a range of rural development activities and its achievements have included the construction and maintenance of over 500km of all-weather roads, six high schools, seven adult literacy centres and several primary schools. GPSDO has also provided several towns and villages with access to drinking water, electricity and telephone services. In addition it has facilitated the transcription and 'modernization' of Gurage customary law and runs programmes on AIDS awareness and improving farming techniques. With the exception of a 35 per cent government subsidy for road construction, these activities were funded exclusively from within the Sebat Bet Gurage communities.

Gurageland is located in the southernmost part of the central Ethiopian plateau approximately 150–250km south of Addis Ababa. The population of Gurageland is estimated at between 3 and 5 million with around 2 million being Sebat Bet Gurages (Gabre 1997). The majority of Gurages now reside outside Gurageland and they constitute one-fifth of the population of Addis Ababa. Gurageland is one of the most densely populated areas of Ethiopia, varying between 200–300 people per square kilometre. The sexual division of rural labour and proximity to Addis facilitates cyclical migration, and since the 1950s virtually all male Gurages have migrated outside Gurageland to generate income, usually through trade. In the absence of hard data, there is a widespread perception that the economic survival of rural households is dependent on migrants' remittances.

Gurage migration and citizenship discourses

> Being a Gurage you cannot say, 'I can live by myself and I do not want any contact with the other members of the society'. If you are born a Gurage, if you are a member of the Gurage you have to assist your family. The shoe-shiners are young kids but they assist their families in the rural areas. If you do not help your immediate family you will be outcast. This is a strong social obligation. Having a child is an investment, as their lives are partly dependent on their children in Addis. (GPSDO activist)

Contemporary Gurage notions of citizenship are materially rooted and driven by discourse and social practice around migration. Since the imposition of land taxation in 1929, the social adaptations to migration have become embedded within Gurage cultures, social organization and value systems. They have become 'institutionalised to such an extent that without careful historical analysis one cannot tell that they are new' (Nida 1996: 143). However, the dominant discourse on migration is rooted in understandings of the past, particularly the 1960s and 1970s, and is a response to the challenges and opportunities in contemporary Ethiopia and changes in the Gurage communities. These factors include political instability caused by ethnic federalism, the saturation of economic spheres associated with Gurages and delinking by young urbanites from Gurage institutions and identities. Hence, migration is a central part of Gurage social life and the expectation that young men will support the parental household is embedded in their cultures. In addition to paying land tax, Gurage men must amass capital to marry, establish a household and to discharge obligations to relatives and finance festivals. Until recently, most Gurage men began migration at an early age with the archetypal migrant beginning his career as a shoe-shiner, progressing to street trading and then on to more formal forms of trade.

Gurage households have adapted to the socioeconomic conditions created by incorporation into the Ethiopian economy and operate as economic units that span geographical divides and harness the resources of different generations. Unmarried and, to a lesser extent, married men are expected to support the parental household. Power relations within households structure how people participate in the social affairs of the group. The head participates on behalf of the household in the web of institutions and social practices that constitute the Gurage communities. As discussed later, this has important implications for how people conceptualize the nature of community and who is expected to participate in development. The gender implications are particularly important; unlike other hometown associations in Africa that have women's wings (Denzer and Mbanefoh 1998), there is little evidence of female participation in GPSDO or other areas of urban associational life.[2] This suggests that a traditional form of civic republicanism underpins notions of civic virtue among the Gurage, as is arguably the case with ethnic citizenship in Africa more broadly (Ndegwa 1997). The gendered 'public–private' divide that this entails has been criticzed by recent feminist theories of citizenship (e.g. Lister 1997), who argue for a broader conception of the public that recognizes and validates the often informal and less visible forms of participation and 'civic' action undertaken by women (see Chapter 4).

Through their migratory survival strategies, Gurage migrants engage with and reconstruct a social world based on interdependence between migrants and rural dependence on remittances. The rights and obligations embedded in Gurage migratory survival strategies vary over time and expand with age and financial capacity. Participation in the social affairs of groups such as clan and house defines one as Gurage. Returning to the village for festivals and contributing to the parental household are seen as essential aspects of Gurage masculinity. In particular, one must demonstrate commitment through discharging the obligations of group membership in order to activate the rights inherent in being a Gurage.

For youths, migration takes place in the context of village and kinship networks of existing migrants and peers. Upon arrival in Addis most migrants stay with relatives who are expected to provide accommodation, assist in finding employment and secure access to credit. Youths also use village-based networks to provide similar forms of socioeconomic support. This village-level mutual interdependence is institutionalized through participation in *Ikube* (rotating credit associations) and village-level *Idirs* (burial societies). Prominent men from the village often assist through providing employment, dispensing advice on business opportunities or acting as guarantors in *Ikube*. These institutions and networks provide a range of benefits for the youths and are an arena in which to discuss business opportunities. These groups are bound by a strong sense of mutual obligation and are underpinned by expectations that peers will support each other in economic hardship.

Although parochial kinship and village level contacts continue, the migrants' social worlds expand as their network diversifies and becomes based on varied business and social contacts. When youths marry and establish a household, they are admitted into the domains of heads of household such as clan and house-based institutions. The rights and obligations embedded in these forms of identity are complex and based on informal and subconscious social expectations rather than formal laws. While maintaining links with Gurageland remains a constant obligation, other elements of these expectations vary between groups, ages and individuals. Clan obligations and rights are rooted in dispute settlement, although they and house connections have been extended to social insurance related to illness, bereavement and bankruptcy. Informants suggested that although institutions such as *Idir*, *Ikubes* and friendship networks were often formed on the basis of clan, house and ethnic affiliations, they did not affect economic advancement. This contradicts the findings of other researchers (Gedamu 1972; Baker 1992) and personal observations that members of the different Gurage houses and clans often filled specific occupational niches.

Outside the extended family and institutions, there are few binding obligations on Gurages to provide mutual assistance. Social rights come with citizenship and are not granted automatically by virtue of being born Gurage. For example, rights inherent in clan membership are activated only if one demonstrates commitment to the clan, usually through membership of *Idirs*. Members of *Idirs* can expect some form of support from other clansmen in times of crisis, although for non-members this assistance is not automatic. Instead, it is determined by elders on the basis of the extent to which they believe the concerned individual has demonstrated commitment to the clan in the past. This recurred across the different layers of Gurage identity including village, clan, house and ethnicity, revealing a perception that the rights embedded in membership of Gurage communities are not automatically granted but must be earned by demonstrating commitment to Gurage citizenship through fulfilling the obligations inherent in being a Gurage man.

This brief review of Gurage migration and citizenship has illustrated that economic necessity forced Gurage men to migrate in large numbers and construct a social world based on urban interdependence and rural dependence on remittances. For many migrants economic and social survival and the provision of welfare are all dependent on support from other migrants and more established contacts. In this process the household acts as an economic unit and also as a basis of participation in social affairs. However, the exercise of rights, inherent in Gurage citizenship, over people outside the extended family is dependent on demonstrating commitment to the values of citizenship either through institutionalizing one's obligations through membership of identity-based institutions such as *Idir* or as evidenced in daily interactions. In the next section I illustrate how Gurage citizenship, its obligations and rights and particularly the institutions that have become their concrete expression have become the backbone of Gurage development.

The process of participation

> If you have a shop, there will be a chain of shops owned by Gurages. If you contribute you tell the person in the next shop and all will contribute. If you have a good tie with your family or you are a member of an *Idir*, you will be told how much you have to pay and you will pay. Once we have access there is no way out but if there is no access or you are not a member of an *Idir* you will not be made to pay. (GPSDO official)

The form of participation constructed by GPSDO and the Gurage communities contradicts many of the assumptions underpinning the participation discourses as it is forced, passive and hierarchical. However, it has proved effective and is regarded as legitimate by most Gurages and has become central to Gurage citizenship (Henry 2001). For rural people, participation involves a web of institutions and social practices, which secure legitimacy, mobilize resources and demonstrate commitment. These institutions and practices are reconstructed in Addis as vehicles for participation in development. Here the resources mobilized include skills, contacts and organizational ability in addition to money. I will draw on data gathered in two areas of Gurageland, Moher and Enamor, relating to interventions over the last twenty-five years, including the construction of roads, high schools and a telephone station and electrification.

Development projects are initiated in Addis in negotiation with the urban elite, including high-ranking civil servants, prominent businessmen and activists in associational life. Once the association adopts a plan, it is discussed with the urban community, i.e. heads of household at urban clan and house *Idirs*. This secures acceptance of the plans and pledges of financial support and other resources from the urban community. Then activists visit prominent elders and state representatives in Gurageland for informal discussions. When the association has produced detailed plans, it consults the rural community at gatherings such as Peasant Association (PA)[3] meetings or indigenous institutions. The purpose of these consultations is to explain the benefits of the project, to outline the sacrifices the rural people would have to make, to ensure that the rural community support the ideas and to keep them abreast of progress. There is little scope for rural input into the planning process as the purpose of consultation is securing legitimacy and disseminating information downwards.

Once the community, i.e. those who participate in associational gatherings, accept the project in principle, the committee and elders negotiate issues such as its location and the contributions expected from rural households. The outcome of these discussions is then put to the house *Shango*.[4] If accepted, directives relating to the project are backed by customary law and a range of sanctions may be applied to non-participants. In theory all members of the community have the right to attend the *Shango* and decision-making is on the basis of consensus. In practice usually only male heads of household attend and the proceedings are dominated by prominent elders. Although some elders are highly influential in rural Gurageland, they do not impose their will on the community through the *Shango*. In developmental and other activities it is evident that they act as enablers allowing the community to take advantage of new opportunities by relating them to Gurage history and traditions.

The rural organizational structures of GPSDO vary over time and between localities with permanent sub-committees in some areas and ad hoc sub-committees activated for specific purposes in other areas. Although these structures may have the potential to balance urban dominance within GPSDO, their main purpose is to mobilize resources. In Moher the rural development committee stands at the apex of rural resource mobilization and is composed of PA leaders and prominent elders. This committee ensures that each PA mobilizes resources from rural households and acts as a point of liaison between the rural community and the Addis-based development association. If households did not contribute, the PA could take the case to the village, clan or house *Shango* and apply the sanctions discussed below.

Rural participation in development is limited to providing resources, which may appear an instrumental form of participation. There is little scope for rural input into decision-making other than negotiating and enforcing the levels of contribution. However, it was evident that there was little desire on the part of the rural population to become involved in decision-making. They deferred to the increased knowledge, resources and organizational capacity of the urban elite. This low opinion of rural capacity in development was shared by most informants and reflects the urban–rural power relationships that are embedded in Gurage migratory survival strategies.

Urban participation takes a similar instrumental form based on resource mobilization, usually in the form of cash contributions. However, members of the community with other attributes, such as skills, contacts and organizational ability, are also expected to contribute these resources to development. GPSDO contacts what it defines as the urban community through networks of friendship and employment and particularly *Idirs*. The clan and particularly house-based *Idirs* form the urban backbone of GPSDO and many have a 10 per cent development levy on monthly fees in addition to making ad hoc contributions to projects and acting as a point of access. GPSDO activists and elders use their knowledge of urban networks, urban associational linkages and rural kinship ties to access a large proportion of the urban Gurage population to mobilize urban resources.

Similar processes of participation have been observed in indigenous development associations elsewhere in Africa (Honey and Okafor 1998; Trager 2001; Woods 1994). However, these approaches do not critically evaluate participation beyond suggesting that these processes reflect communal power relationships. Furthermore, they rarely go beyond instrumentalist accounts of ethnicity when analysing the relationships between citizenships and collective action such as participatory development.

Sanctions underpinning participation

> Previously if someone came to me for a contribution there was no voluntary element ... you just pay an amount calculated from your income. Otherwise, you will be outcast. They would send people and go through processes and then nobody will come to your house if somebody dies. Then social life was very important, so people paid. Even for urban people, this was an important sanction. (Wealthy Gurage businessman)

Previous sections have hinted at elements of compulsion in development activities undertaken by GPSDO, and since the 1960s non-participating households have been liable to a range of sanctions. However, before discussing the use of sanctions in development it is important to add two qualifiers. First, non-participation in development is unusual due to its perceived benefits, the authority of *Shangos* and the trust vested in the associations. Second, the enduring power of these sanctions lies in their threat rather than their use.

When a house *Shango* accepts the legitimacy of a development project, disputes relating to it may be regulated by the Gurage customary law and can be enforced by a range of sanctions including *Yeka*[5] and *Zowa*,[6] expulsion from *Idirs* and ostracism. GPSDO and the state have used *Yeka* to ensure that all rural households contribute to development. When a party refuses to accept a *Shango* decision, *Yeka* is used to enforce compliance. In Moher, all *Shango* attendees become *Yeka*,[7] decamp to the transgressor's house and remain until he relents, causing stigma and expense. Those defying *Yeka* are cursed, ostracized and the matter is referred to a higher *Shango*.

Officially *Yeka* is used by GPSDO to ensure that people contribute sums they had previously pledged. However, many informants suggested that it was used, as in the past (Gedamu 1972), to compel households to contribute an amount fixed by the *Shango* to development or provide labour. It is used rarely and it is unusual for it to escalate beyond a single visit, which serves as a warning of more drastic sanctions. In Addis the institution evolved into a semi-permanent committee comprised of prominent urban dwellers, such as elders and *Idir* leaders, that enforces decisions taken by the General Assembly of the Development Association. It ensures that all urban households contribute to development and has encouraged other forms of participation such as providing professional skills and leadership.

Other sanctions are used more rarely and again their power lies in their threat rather than their activation. In the past *Zowa* was used consensually to remind people to pay *Idir* contributions or fines for minor transgressions. This practice is authorized only by the relevant *Shango* and is regulated by customary law. However, it contradicts government-protected property rights and is officially prohibited. *Zowa* is generally discussed in terms of how it is used by other groups in outlying areas. However, some informants suggested that it is used to ensure participation by confiscating and selling cattle in lieu of financial contributions to projects. Apparently this was done consensually; although, withholding consent would leave the person liable to more drastic sanctions.

Ostracism is the ultimate sanction in Gurageland, as when invoked it becomes impossible for households to function socially or economically. The household is expelled from the community and, unable to receive any form of communal assistance, is excluded from all rural social affairs, such as attendance at burial, which entails immense stigma and is considered the ultimate sanction. Due to its severity, this sanction is very rarely if ever used in the development process, as the threat of ostracism is normally sufficient to ensure compliance.

This web of social practices is regulated by customary law and is applied with discretion. Households with financial problems are often excused or are assisted by more wealthy members of the community. The impact of these sanctions varies between the urban and rural areas and between social groups. For those whose social and economic well-being is dependent on links with the Gurage communities, they are potentially devastating. However, their effect is limited on groups with alternative socioeconomic ties. This is recognized by GPSDO activists who apply sanctions according to their effectiveness and therefore do not use them on people with few connections to the Gurage communities. These sanctions are applied with greater vigour on those such as elders and hereditary clan heads who are expected to lead communal affairs and embody the characteristics I have labelled as Gurage civic virtue.

Volunteerism and leadership

> Elders came to my office and I tried to explain that I had no time and have a sensitive job. So they came again. One was the person who built my elementary school and said, 'You are my product, you have studied because we built the school and now you are in a position to serve the people in your area', so I had to accept and become an executive committee member. (GPSDO official and senior civil servant)

Any understanding of how Gurages conceptualize participation is incomplete without outlining how obligations to provide communal leadership are central to Gurage civic virtue. Positions in GPSDO are unpaid and time-consuming, involving regular meetings, designing and monitoring projects and maintaining relationships with associational activists and government officials. In Gurage notions of citizenship, communal leadership is a resource which is harnessed by institutions and underpinned by sanctions. Thus their dominant discourse regards activism in development as a willingly accepted sacrifice. This perception of leadership as an obligated burden is also apparent in other aspects of Gurage associational life such as leadership of *Idirs* and dispute settlement.

The obligatory nature of much of the participation by leaders became apparent in the 1990s when members of the Gurage elite decided to increase the capacity of GPSDO. In line with their ethos of self-help and citizenship, they professionalized the organization by shifting the criteria for leadership from associational linkages to technical and organizational skills. They identified and encouraged suitable people to accept leadership roles. In some cases a *Yeka* committee or other informal institution was used to encourage people to participate by visiting their homes and workplaces and applying moral pressure and threats of sanctions such as expulsion from *Idirs*. However, these practices are applied on the basis of their effectiveness as although elders visited people with few contacts they did not take sanctions against them due to their limited effectiveness.

If participation can be enforced, there are greater obligations for those with the greatest abilities. As the attributes deemed necessary for leadership are regarded as innate to the individual and divinely sanctioned, those with the greatest attributes also have the greatest responsibility to serve the community. The obligated nature of leadership roots the leadership's understanding of the nature of community participation in development.

Conclusions

This form of participation is radically different to that envisaged by the participation discourses and challenges assumptions about community, empowerment, democracy and 'volunteerism'. When related to indigenous agents of development, these contextual notions are best analysed by reference to the relationships between citizenship, social organization and cultures. The conception of citizenship as the moral basis of membership of political communities focuses on how the rights and obligations that underpin the social practices and relationships of citizenship can become embedded in institutions and developmental practices. This approach broadens the focus of citizenship beyond demanding rights from the state to include the interplay between and contestation of the rights and obligations inherent in membership of a community.

In the Sebat Bet Gurage communities citizenship is activated if one discharges the obligations inherent in group membership. The rights and obligations that are embedded in the contemporary dominant construction of Gurage citizenship have been extended to include participation in development. Specifically, obligations to contribute resources and the right to expect that other Gurages will assist the rural areas in the same way that they assist their families. This process of development can appear simultaneously tyrannical and transformative as it reflects the tensions inherent in the rights and obligations of an obligated and instrumental form of participation.

For GPSDO and the Gurage community, participation in development is primarily about increasing the effectiveness of the project. This reflects their conception of development as tangible outcomes rather than social process (Henry 2001). This instrumental understanding of the nature of development underpins the instrumental process of participation and challenges notions that participation is of itself empowering. The meanings ascribed to participation by the dominant Gurage development discourses emphasize contributing a range of resources to projects according to one's capacity and are seen as an integral aspect of wider obligations to the Gurage community. These discourses resonate with a sense of participation in development being a willingly undertaken sacrifice and a burden. This perception reflects their instrumental conception of development as tangible outcomes rather than as a process which could empower rural people.

In addition to increasing the effectiveness of projects by reducing overheads and becoming a marker of ethnic differentiation (Henry 2001), rural participation, as resource mobilization, is understood in two further ways. First, financial sacrifices vest the rural and urban communities with ownership of projects and increase sustainability. A GPSDO leader emphasized this point: 'Sometimes they [the rural people] do not invest their money in things that do not show immediate results ... if we tell them something [about long-term benefits] they may forget. We get them to feel ownership by forcing them to invest their own money so that they will take care of the project.' This paternalistic conception of the relationship between participation and sustainability was repeated by the chair of a PA: 'Activities in which the people take part are fruitful because the people will look after them. They will consider the project as their own, so they do not want to see it damaged.'

Second, rural participation demonstrates that they deserve assistance. Rural resource mobilization legitimizes the position of the rural population as recipients of assistance from the urban population by demonstrating their commitment to the project and to Gurage notions of citizenship. This dynamic reflects how urban and rural people understand the urban–rural relationships embedded in their migratory survival strategies and the discourses that underpin them. A statement by a farmer sums up the rural perception: 'It is not just development, we depend on our brothers in Addis for everything. If it was not for them we would not survive.' While rural informants expressed gratitude for the contributions that urban Gurages had made to rural development, they stressed that the urban people were only behaving in the way expected of them in Gurage culture and related this to their wider obligations to rural kin. They continually stressed the sacrifices that the rural people had made for development and how this justified their entitlement to development. Their participation in development was presented as their way of meeting social expectations, which required that both urban and rural people should make sacrifices for the benefit of the rural area.

Community participation in development is intimately entwined with urban–rural relationships within the Gurage communities, particularly the obligations on migrants to support rural kin, and also reflects the power relations in the countryside. Hence, it entails rural dependence, passivity and deference to the skills and knowledge of the educated urban sectors of the community. The dominant development discourses are underpinned by an assumption that community participation in development is an essential aspect of the process of development. However, while the dominant development discourses view this participation as being part of a process of empowerment, Gurages see participation as a burden that is a willingly accepted aspect of their wider communal obligations. The effectiveness and legitimacy of indigenous agencies is based on the ways they engage with and reconstruct indigenous social practices and institutions.

Notes

1 This is based on fieldwork conducted in Addis Ababa and various locations in the Gurage Zone during 1998, 1999 and 2000. Data were gathered through semi-structured interviews, focus groups and observation.

2 As a result, the voices of women are almost absent from this chapter. In one rural location it was almost impossible to contact local women and in the other area women were engaged in agricultural labour, which men were not permitted to observe. Only a few short interviews were possible. This limited evidence suggested that women shared the general perception that participation in development is a burden undertaken by the head on behalf of the household.

3 The lowest stratum of government administration.

4 A customary dispute settlement forum.

5 *Kayewa* in some Gurage dialects.

6 The practice of removing an item, such as agricultural tools or cattle, to remind a household to meet financial obligations.

7 In some Gurage areas its composition varies.

References

Baker, J. (1992) 'The Gurage of Ethiopia: Rural–Urban Interaction and Entrepreneurship', in P. O. Pedersen (ed.), *The Rural–Urban Interface in Africa: Expansion and Adaptation* (Uppsala: Scandinavian Institute of African Studies).

Cooke, B. and U. Kothari (eds) (2001) *Participation: The New Tyranny?* (London: Zed Books).

Cornwall, A. and J. Gaventa (2000) 'From Users and Choosers to Makers and Shapers: Repositioning Participation in Social Policy', *IDS Bulletin*, 31 (4).

Denzer, L. and N. Mbanefoh (1998) 'Women's Participation in Hometown Associations', in R. Honey and S. Okafor, *Hometown Associations: Indigenous Knowledge and Development in Nigeria* (London: IT Publications), pp. 123–34.

Gabre, Y. (1997) 'The Gurage Road Construction Organisation', in R. Poesschke (ed.), *Development Associations and Self-help in the Southern Region of Ethiopia* (Addis Ababa: GTZ Ethiopia).

Gaventa, J. (2002) 'Introduction: Exploring Citizenship, Participation and Accountability', *IDS Bulletin*, 33 (2): 1–12.

Gedamu, F. (1972) 'Ethnic Associations in Ethiopia and the Maintenance of Urban–Rural Relationships: With Special Reference to the Allemgana–

Walamo Road Construction Association' (Unpublished thesis, London School of Economics).

Henry, L. (2001) 'Doing Development and Being Gurage: The Embeddedness of Development in Sebat Bet Gurage Identities', unpublished PhD thesis, Open University.

Honey, R. and S. Okafor (eds) (1998) *Hometown Associations: Indigenous Knowledge and Development in Nigeria* (London: IT Publications).

Lister, R. (1997) 'Citizenship: Towards a Feminist Synthesis', *Feminist Review*, 57 (Autumn): 28–48.

— (1998) 'Citizenship in Action: Citizenship and Community Development in Northern Ireland', *Community Development Journal*, 33 (3): 226–35.

Lonsdale, J. (1992) 'The Moral Economy of Mau Mau: Wealth, Poverty and Civic Virtue in Kikuyu Political Thought', in J. Lonsdale (ed.), *Unhappy Valley: Conflict in Kenya and Africa* (London: James Currey).

Mamdani, M. (1996) *Citizen and Subject: Contemporary Africa and the Legacy of Late Colonialism* (Princeton, NJ: Princeton University Press).

Ndegwa, S. (1997) 'Citizenship and Ethnicity: An Examination of Two Transition Movements on Kenyan Politics', *American Political Science Review*, 91 (3): 599–616.

Nida, W. (1996) 'Gurage Urban Migration and the Dynamics of Cultural Life in the Villages', in G. Hudson (ed.), *Essays on Gurage Language and Culture in Honour of Wolf Leslau* (Weisbaden: Harrassowitz Verlag).

Trager, L. (2001) *Yoruba Hometowns: Community, Identity and Development in Nigeria* (Boulder, CO: Lynne Rienner).

Turner, B. S. (2001) 'The Erosion of Citizenship', *British Journal of Sociology*, 52 (2): 189–209.

Woods, D. (1994) 'Elites, Ethnicity, and Home Town Associations in the Côte d' Ivoire – an Historical Analysis of State–Society Links', *Africa*, 64 (4): 465–83.

FOUR | Realizing transformative participation in practice: state and civil responses

10 | Relocating participation within a radical politics of development: insights from political action and practice

SAM HICKEY AND GILES MOHAN

This chapter looks at how participation has been used in sites of participatory governance and development reform, and seeks to identify cases that have moved beyond the problems identified with participation as 'tyranny' and towards participation as transformation. Evidence is drawn from a selection of the fields of policy and practice within which participation forms a key element, namely participatory poverty assessments and poverty reduction strategy processes; participatory governance/decentralization; NGOs; and social movements.[1] It is argued that initiatives within each arena, aside from the first, have either gone or have the potential to go beyond the critical positions against participation to address broader issues of politics in ways that make change more embedded and thoroughgoing. The chapter then goes on to identify the factors that have underpinned these successes, which suggest that participatory approaches are most likely to achieve transformations where (i) they are pursued as part of a wider (radical) political project; (ii) where they are aimed specifically at securing citizenship rights and participation for marginal and subordinate groups; and (iii) when they seek to engage with development as an underlying process of social change rather than in the form of discrete technocratic interventions. To the extent that this broad finding holds across approaches to both participatory development and participatory governance, there are sound empirical reasons for repositioning participation within a radical political approach to development.

The pinnacle of participation? PPAs and PRSs

The World Bank's Participatory Poverty Assessments (PPAs) have come to illustrate the most explicit 'scaling-up' of the participatory methods advocated by Robert Chambers (Robb 2002). Although mixed, reviews of PPAs to date suggest that they have informed pro-poor policy changes in some cases, particularly those 'second-generation' PPAs (e.g. South Africa, Uganda and Vietnam) that emphasized the need to influence policy alongside the generation of data (Holland and Blackburn 1998; Robb 2002). However, the emphasis on participation within PPAs has remained on information extraction for macro- and sector policy analysis, and challenging policy-makers' attitudes towards poverty and civil society involvement in policy analysis as opposed to deeper participatory transformation (Norton 1998). For example, the 2002 round of the Ugandan PPA process had no feedback mechanism and no support for communities to work towards resolving the problems that were raised.

Towards the end of the 1990s, this in-country scaling-up of participatory approaches was further formalized through the Poverty Reduction Strategy Paper (PRSP) initiative. Theoretically, the PRSP is the output from a participatory strategy designed to include civil society in a process of analysing poverty, poverty reduction outcomes and key public actions towards these outcomes (McGee with Norton 2000). However, although there is some evidence to suggest that PRSPs constitute an innovation that leads to more inclusive policy processes, they appear to fall short of genuine inclusion and partnership.

Evaluations carried out for the Bank stress the problems of ensuring participation (Donnelly-Roark 2001), even in 'flagship' countries such as Uganda with its 'homegrown' PRSP. It is becoming apparent that conflicts are emerging between the PRSP process and the institutionalization of participation through Uganda's decentralization programme, a political reform that is central to the regime's project of transforming state–society relations and rebuilding state legitimacy (Regan 1998). Although the system of local government was designed to identify local priorities and administer policy interventions, the PRSP process has helped to ensure that an increasing proportion of central government funding for local government is conditional, with 85 per cent of the total local government income earmarked according to nationally determined priorities (Government of Uganda 2002). Compliance is ensured, in part, through a series of fiscal sanctions and penalties, which are closely linked to donor insistence that certain central funds should be ring-fenced. The input by the lowest political tiers into national policy-making processes has been virtually non-existent (e.g. Jeppsson 2001). The outcome is a disciplining of the local level rather than its liberation and empowerment in order to determine, as far as possible, its own priorities and actions. The participatory rhetoric of national poverty planning is thus implicit in circumventing the transformation of the local state, and effectively short-circuiting the establishment of more participatory forms of governance, to the extent that a recent study has noted 'the destructive effect on local governance of the financing and management arrangements accompanying PRSPs' in Uganda (Craig and Porter 2003).

The scope for participation to influence national poverty policy is closely circumscribed in general (see Brown, this volume), contrary to some rather optimistic claims (e.g. Brinkerhoff and Goldsmith 2003), in that key areas of national policy-making are not up for negotiation. As one critical agency notes, the wider macro-economic picture is sewn up before the voices reach the table (Wilkes and Lefrançois 2002). The result is that debates about alternative forms of 'pro-poor' or 'redistributive' growth are circumvented.[2] Here, the transformation aimed at by development alternatives is written out of the picture despite the rhetoric of 'dialogue' and 'openness'.

Although the high profile accorded to participation within PRSPs undoubtedly marks a victory for Robert Chambers's 'benign virus' of participation spreading through institutions, the problem remains that a change in individuals' attitudes does not guarantee the overthrowing of deeper institutional divisions or the forms of governance thrown up by uneven development. Indeed, it may simply ensure that the locus of 'transformation' is individualized at the centre rather than at the structural or the local. Such approaches are tied to the same limited conception of participation that has been complicit in the co-option and depoliticization of the concept, and may in practice short-circuit more genuine attempts at participation. PRSPs remain steadfastly part of the neo-liberal agenda and are simply a new 'technical framework' which does not address uneven power relations within countries and between them and donors. Importantly, underlying processes of development remain shielded from view.

Participatory governance and democratic decentralization

Democratic decentralization is a key aspect of the participatory governance agenda, and is associated with the institutionalization of participation through regular elections, council hearings and, more recently, participatory budgeting (e.g. Blair 2000). The devolution of power to local authorities creates incentives for increased local civil society activity, while the success of 'partnerships' as a form of participatory service provision may depend to a large extent on local authorities having genuine authority and resources. However, despite being lauded by international development agencies and theorists (across the political spectrum) alike as the key to state reform, popular empowerment and, more recently, poverty reduction (e.g. World Bank 2000), the track record of decentralization in developing countries has come under increasing criticism (e.g. Crook and Sverrisson 2001). In terms of participation, a key question concerns the extent to which the increased participation of marginal groups within local government has been merely tokenistic. For example, the '33 per cent quota rule' that seeks to ensure representation of marginal groups on local councils in both India (women and lower caste groups) and Uganda (women) has apparently failed to secure regular participation for these groups or to ensure that this participation overcomes power relations embedded within particular sociocultural structures (Kapoor 2000; Tripp 2000). More theoretically, Francis and James (2003) argue that the form of participation introduced by decentralization engages with, and is often subsumed within, more informal modes of patronage in ways that nullify its transformative potential.

However, certain cases of democratic decentralization stand out as having achieved both greater participation of and social justice for marginal groups and localities, as with the Indian states of West Bengal and Kerala. In both cases, decentralization has been credited with ensuring the participation of subordinate groups – such as women, landless groups, sharecroppers and small peasants – and being directly linked to the pursuit of redistributive policies that have had pro-poor outcomes (Harriss 2000: 15; Heller 2001: 142). The vested interests associated with 'elite capture' removed (Crook and Sverrisson 2001: 14–15), while democratic decentralization has also increased the 'political space' within which poor groups can mobilize themselves beyond the formal institutions of state power (Webster 2002).

The project of democratic decentralization within both Kerala and West Bengal has been clearly closely informed by the 'reinvention' of leftist politics. The failures of centralized rule and planned economies, and the need for parties of the left to maintain and increase their electoral constituency, provided the context within which participatory forms of governance became integrated within wider projects of redistributive politics and social justice. In Kerala, the project of institutionalizing democratic decentralization was termed 'the Campaign', and measures were adopted deliberately to emphasize the political rather than the technical significance of devolution (for example, the overnight devolution of large-scale resources to local authorities) (Heller 2001: 141). Of further importance is the extent to which a counter-elite was able to pursue a political project against the interests of economic elites, a key theme returned to below.

Similar findings also emerge from reviews of participatory budgeting in Brazil, with findings of increased popular participation (e.g. over 10 per cent of the electorate in the state of Rio Grande do Sul participate in budgeting); changed investment patterns in favour of progressive social sectors such as housing, education, sanitation and health; excluded slums and populations drawn into the political process; and also increased efficiency in terms of planning and implementation (Santos 1998; Schneider and Goldfrank 2002; Souza 2001). Patronage relations have been challenged (Heller 2001: 140), with people now able to make claims according to their status as citizens rather than as clients (Abers 1998; Souza 2001).

Once again, the agency for the success of these participatory reforms can be located within a wider radical political project. The most successful cases of participatory budgeting in Brazil have been in cities and states where the Workers' Party has been in power for prolonged periods (Schneider and Goldfrank 2002: 9). Further support has come from the Landless Movement, in alliance with the unions and progressive churches, and even from priests inspired by liberation theology (ibid.), marking a convergence between new approaches to participation and actors from earlier radical moments within participatory politics.

As argued by Schneider and Goldfrank (2002: 13): 'participatory budgeting articulates first and foremost the political project of excluded groups' who seek to promote a popular vision of democracy and a redistributive vision of development. Similarly, Heller (2001: 139) argues that the defining feature of both democratic decentralization in India and participatory budgeting in Brazil is that of 'a political project in which an organized political force – and specifically non-Leninist left-of-center political parties that have strong social movement characteristics – champions decentralization'. With reference to a case with less success, Barten et al. (2002) argue that any project of democratic local governance must adopt a development paradigm that directly challenges structural inequalities, a theme returned to below.

NGOs and participatory development

The forms of participation promoted by non-governmental organizations (NGOs) through discrete project interventions have been among the most vigorously pursued element of the critical backlash against participation (e.g. Fowler 1998; Townsend et al. 2002; Uphoff 1996). To a large extent, this chapter would concur that NGOs face severe limitations in seeking to be genuine agents of transformative development through participatory approaches. However, the vast range and diversity of agencies and activities within the transnational community of NGOs not only precludes sweeping judgements, but has also produced initiatives capable of promoting participatory development in ways that *do* involve transformation. Three such examples can be expanded on here, namely the 'REFLECT' approach to literacy generation; the growing focus on rights-based approaches to development; and the increasing role of NGOs in advocacy work. Although space precludes a full investigation of each initiative or process, we argue that each engages with issues of citizenship located within a wider project of achieving transformations at a number of levels.

REFLECT: Regenerated Freirean Literacy through Empowering Community Techniques

The REFLECT approach to literacy generation, originally piloted by ActionAid in the mid-1990s, is currently employed by 350 organizations in sixty countries, involving governmental and non-governmental agencies (ActionAid 2003). The key idea behind REFLECT is to merge the pedagogical and political philosophy of Paulo Freire (Freire 1972) with the techniques of participatory rural appraisal (see Waddington and Mohan, this volume). It is also theoretically informed by 'gender and development' thinking, and seeks to develop women's capacity to take on participatory roles at community level and beyond (Archer and Cottingham 1996). REFLECT proceeds by engaging participants in dialogical discussions of their socioeconomic problems, and uses visual graphics to structure and depict the discussion (ibid.). 'Keywords' emerge from these discussions, which then form the basis for literacy development. Participants are encouraged to devise means of solving the problems, beginning with 'action-points' to be addressed either by REFLECT groups or higher-level organizations.

The results of REFLECT in many cases to date have been impressive, with genuine transformation taking place with regard to gender relations, community–state relations, and between age groups within communities. Participants report self-realization, increased participation in community organizations, and increased community-level actions (Archer and Cottingham 1997: 200–1); female participants and REFLECT facilitators in particular have become key resource people for the communities (Kanyesigye 1998: 51–3). However, while REFLECT was constructed and is currently promoted by northern NGDOs, it has been noted that, 'radical adult education initiatives are unlikely to prove effective when carried out on their own. They must operate in relation to a social movement' (Mayo 1999: 133), a challenge we return to below.

NGOs and rights-based approaches

In broad terms, rights-based development attaches political rights and responsibilities to fundamental aspects of human needs and well-being (Maxwell 1999; UNDP 2000). For our purposes, the significance of a rights-based approach for NGOs lies in its capacity to locate NGO challenges to exclusion and poverty within a political response, which therefore holds the promise of empowerment. In some cases, it has transformed the way in which NGOs engage with marginal groups, relating to them as agents with claims rather than as victims in need of 'rescue and rehabilitation', with subsequent successes in terms of empowerment (e.g. Misra et al. 2000). Although the issue of 'universalism' needs to be problematized (see Chapter 4), the discourse of rights offers an ideological resource that marginal groups can draw on in order to situate their struggles within a broader democratic project with a 'universally' recognized and politically powerful framework (Hickey 2002: 853; Mohan and Holland 2001: 193–5; Wignaraja 1993). The relative autonomy and international recognition of rights-based approaches renders this discourse less malleable and this may open up spaces within donor agencies that cannot be so easily co-opted (Holland et al., this volume).

NGO advocacy

One of the key weaknesses of the project-based work traditionally favoured by NGOs is its inability to challenge wider structures of marginalization and impoverishment (Nyamugasira 1998: 297). The increasing shift towards advocacy work, however, contains greater potential for transformation by engaging with, and making claims for and with, excluded people in ways that (should) increase their capacity to demand their rights of citizenship and help them participate in wider arenas of decision-making. Significantly, it can be seen as one of the mechanisms by which the links between participatory development and participatory governance might be forged (e.g. PLA Notes 2002). For example, Harper (2001) argues for a participatory form of advocacy that both involves the grassroots in agenda setting through genuine partnerships and participatory methods, and opens up policy processes to a wider range of voices and stakeholders. In successful advocacy campaigns, however, participation is often a form of popular protest rather than a set of methods traditionally preferred by NGOs (Dechalert 1999).

NGO advocacy, then, involves the alignment of participatory approaches with a rights-based agenda, and brings together the key elements of a citizenship-based approach that stresses political engagement at local, national and international levels. However, important dangers remain apparent. For example, much global citizen action bypasses national governments in favour of applying direct pressure to global institutions (Edwards 2001: 148). As such, some transnational social movements may be undermining national citizenship, and seeking to replace it with a form of 'global citizenship' that remains unattainable to most people in poor countries. In failing to engage with states, global movements may end up circumventing the political processes that need strengthening in order for poverty and exclusion to be challenged. Furthermore, some advocacy campaigns reflect the current inequalities between northern and southern NGOs within the 'transnational community of NGOs' (Townsend et al. 2002), and are particularly open to growing charges concerning the problems of representation and legitimacy. One potential solution to this problem is to focus on those examples of 'horizontal solidarity', whereby South–South relationships form the basis of empowering advances in both livelihood strategies and policy change (Patel and Mitlin 2002).

This section has argued that participatory approaches promoted by NGOs can enhance citizenship, but they require linkage to more political forms of participatory action than has been the case until recently. Much of this activity increasingly requires moving beyond the locality with empowerment involving multi-scaled strategies and networks. Clearly, engaging with a more politicized and radical project will often entail heightened conflict with vested interests at multiple levels (e.g. Rafi and Chowdhury 2000). Issues of representation – whether of 'universalist' ideals within different cultural contexts or of 'southern' NGOs by 'northern' NGOs in various policy arenas – still abound (e.g. Hudson 2000). However, it might be that a clearer focus on the political is once again the way forwards here, with a shift in focus from issues of 'representation' and 'legitimacy' to one on 'political responsibility' at all levels of NGO work (Jordan and van Tuijl 2000). Here, NGOs can conduct their work and relationships 'with democratic principles foremost in the process' (ibid., p. 2053), with all actors having to respond to the demands of 'political responsibility' at each stage. This involves dividing different political arenas between different actors and empowering them to act therein, while monitoring the (potentially negative) impact that actions in one political arena might have in another (ibid., p. 2063).

Social movements

Development theory and practice has generally been wary of engaging directly with social movements as sites of popular participation and political projects, preferring the more orderly and 'makeable' world of NGOs. However, a number of theorists are realizing the potential of the former for radical change. This move towards social movements was initially premised on a thorough-going critique of the dominant 'left' position on civil society (e.g. Laclau and Mouffe 1985) but has more recently been influenced by post-modern interpretations of such developments (Escobar 1995; Esteva and Prakash 1998). This has tended to leave the debate around social movements polarized between cultural and political readings of their meaning and potential. In the developing world, social movements are frequently characterized as standing in resistance to development (e.g. Routledge 2001), or depicted by post-modern theorists as either 'post-' or even 'anti-' development.

However, we would argue that the importance of social movements in relation to participation and development cannot be captured in such terms, particularly in relation to the oppositions between 'culture'/'politics', and 'development'/'resistance'. Rather, the historical and contemporary role of social movements in using identity-based forms of mobilization to extend the boundaries of citizenship participation and rights to marginal groups (Scott 1990; Foweraker and Landman 1997), suggests that the cultural and the political are closely entwined (Castells 1997). Furthermore, we would argue that movements such as the Zapatistas are better understood as being located within a critical position *vis-à-vis* the ongoing project of modernity (e.g. Veltmeyer 1997), rather than being 'post-modern' alternatives to development.

The starting point for the Zapatistas is that the processes of state formation and political economy that have prevailed within Mexico, and which were accelerated as a result of globalization and the North American Free Trade Agreement, have led indigenous Indians to become 'a very inferior category of "citizens in formation"', forced to occupy 'the basement of the Mexican nation' (Marcos 1994). The Zapatistas have campaigned actively since 1994 to not only attain full citizenship for the Indians of the Chiapas region of Mexico, but also for wider political and economic reforms in Mexico. In terms of 'culture' as the basis of political claims, the Zapatistas reveal how a new form of (pan-ethnic) identity can be both forged and politicized through a struggle over a particular place (Castells 1997: 78). However, in attempting to claim citizenship for indigenous communities, there is no renouncement of the notion of Mexican citizenship, but of the exclusive way in which it has been forged. In a statement to mark seven years of activity by the Zapatistas, Marcos (2001) issued a demand that the government amend the constitution so as to 'recognise the indigenous as indigenous and as Mexicans'. The movement has challenged patronage politics in favour of genuine democracy at the regional level, within which people can actively participate as citizens.

What is arguably most significant about the Zapatistas is the ways in which their claims of 'indigenous rights' and 'cultural autonomy' are woven within a broader discourse of the familiar demands of modernity. Land, democracy, citizenship and development – all totems of the modern project – remain the key concerns of a number of 'new' social movements (Veltmeyer 1997). In so doing, they have articulated a mode of political action capable of imagining and generating alternative development futures not only for its immediate constituency, but also for a broader community of dispossessed and marginalized peoples. Citizenship has provided both the frame of analysis and the strategic way forward. This notion of social movements being transformative and radical within the modern is further supported by research with popular organizations in the Andean regions of Latin America (Bebbington and Bebbington 2001), further suggesting that the politics of cultural identity, material redistribution and social justice are not alternatives, but can be part of a single political project.

Identifying the politics of participation as transformation

This (selective) sampling of political and policy arenas demonstrates that participatory approaches to development and governance have, to some extent and in some ways, gone beyond the critique mounted against them, particularly regarding the failure to engage with issues of politics and power. Although we cannot claim that these developments are conclusive or will go on to achieve their ends fully, they have transcended the search for simple technical fixes and are demonstrably moving towards the more structural transformations suggested by the language of 'participation for empowerment'. Moreover, we argue that there are several threads of continuity that run throughout these initiatives, which can be drawn out as the key dimensions that underlie successful approaches to participation as transformation. We identify four key dimensions that emerge from this review.

First, the successes of participation within contemporary development policy and practice have depended upon being part of a broader project that is at once political and radical. By this we mean a project that seeks directly to challenge existing power relations rather than simply work around them for more technically efficient service delivery, as with PRSPs. The roots of this political radicalism vary. In the case of decentralization, the stage has recently been set in some contexts by a convergence between the growth of populist approaches to governance and development, and the need for organizations of the political left to find a means of both institutionalizing a politics of social justice in the post-welfarist, post-centralist era of governance and (re)connect with an electoral base. With NGOs, it has either formed around a rediscovery of the radical within participatory development history (REFLECT), and of efforts to transform the policy process and development discourse itself through advocacy work. What is key here is that there is an explicit articulation of a radical project that focuses primarily on issues of power and politics.

Second, each approach that can be said to have achieved transformations at an institutional or structural level has sought to direct participatory approaches towards a close engagement with underlying processes of development, rather than remain constrained within the frame of specific policy processes or interventions. New social movements form the clearest example of a close and critical engagement with efforts to reshape development – and the project of modernity itself. The political parties that have attained the greatest success with participatory governance re-forms have directly sought to alter patterns of inequality created by uneven processes of development. In terms of NGOs, the REFLECT approach addresses itself to the patterns of domination and subordination within developing countries, rather than those between development professionals and project participants. Moreover the underlying focus of NGO advocacy is 'an act of organizing the strategic use of information to democratise unequal power relations' (Jordan and van Tuijl 2000: 2052). In contrast, processes of immanent development remain obscured to participation within PRSPs.

Third, each approach is characterized by an explicit focus on and pursuit of participation as *citizenship*.[3] Each of the initiatives reviewed here seeks in different ways not only to bring people into the political process, but also to transform and democratize the political process in ways that progressively alter the 'immanent' processes of inclusion and exclusion that operate within particular political communities, and which govern the opportunities for individuals and groups to claim their rights to participation and resources. Among the key exemplars here are the Zapatistas' campaign for constitutional change in Mexico and the success of some participatory governance reforms in securing citizenship participation as an alternative form of inclusion to patron–client relations. As Waddington and Mohan (this volume) demonstrate, REFLECT is inextricably linked to citizenship formation, in that it focuses on 'people's ability to participate in civil society, enabling them to effectively assert their rights and assume their responsibilities' (Archer 1998: 101). It thus emphasizes that participation needs to be practised in the broader spaces of the political community beyond the project level, and recognizes the need to 'reconnect' populist methods of participation with more politicized understandings of social change. In such instances, citizenship is not being requested from a proscribed menu of rights and obligations, but actively defined and claimed on the basis of strengthened political capabilities.

The fourth commonality appears to be that, for participatory approaches to be successful in achieving transformation, a pre-condition is that the modes of accumulating political and economic power in the given context are structurally disentwined from each other. For example, the success of decentralization in West Bengal and Kerala has been predicated to a large extent on the fact that the political elite that gained power on a radical agenda were separate from and able to avoid being captured by the local economic (landed) elite. Hence, there is a need to examine the political economy of participation, particularly in contexts where the accumulation of political power and economic wealth are entwined and a focus on 'participation' may simply conceal ongoing patronage. However, the new forms of citizenship participation outlined here, and elsewhere in this volume (e.g. Gaventa, Cornwall), can arguably play a key role in challenging and reforming such 'dysfunctional' forms of rule.

Conclusion

This chapter has argued that recent advances within and across the several fields of development and governance where participation plays a major role have reaffirmed the empowering potential of participation. However, the conditions within which participation can be transformative, and the form of politics that underpins such approaches, need to be closely delineated and analysed. This work has been started here, but requires further elaboration from both empirical and theoretical perspectives. The intention has not been to suggest that there is no hope for participation unless carried out in this way. Elsewhere in this volume, there are strong arguments for a more realistic assessment of the potential of participatory approaches, and evidence of the incremental gains that they can achieve with political but perhaps less radical approaches. Rather, the aim here has been to connect the radical rhetoric of participation with radical transformatory practice in order better to understand the conditions under which such convergences are possible. From here it is possible to weave a theoretical and strategic coherence into the praxis of participation (Chapter 4), and move towards reconstituting it as a radical approach to challenging exclusion.

Notes

1 This follows the schema followed by Mohan and Stokke's (2000) review of the participatory turn within development, and is similar to Cornwall's approach in this volume, whereby she identifies three key strands within participatory literature that need to be brought together (namely deliberative democracy, participatory methodologies and popular mobilization).

2 This argument, based on recent research by one of the authors in Uganda, is pursued in greater depth elsewhere (Hickey 2003).

3 See Chapter 4 on the particular notion of citizenship that we understand to be mobilized in the developments cited above.

References

Abers, R. (1998) 'From Clientelism to Cooperation: Local Government, Participatory Policy and Civic Organising in Porto Alegre, Brazil', *Politics and Society*, 26 (4): 511–23.

ActionAid (2003) 'Our Priorities: Education: REFLECT'. At <http://www.actionaid.org> (accessed February 2003).

Archer, D. (1998) 'The Evolving Conception of Literacy in REFLECT', *PLA Notes*, 32: 100–8.

Archer, D. and S. Cottingham (1996) *The REFLECT Mother Manual: A New Approach to Adult Literacy* (London: ACTIONAID).

— (1997) 'REFLECT': A New Approach to Literacy and Social Change', *Development in Practice*, 7 (2): 199–202.

Barten, F., R. P. Montiel, E. Espinoza, C. M. Carbonell (2002) 'Democratic Governance – Fairytale or Real Perspective? Lessons from Central America', *Environment and Urbanization*, 14 (1): 129–44.

Bebbington, A. J. and D. H. Bebbington (2001) 'Development Alternatives: Practice, Dilemmas and Theory', *Area*, 33 (1): 7–17.

Blair, H. (2000) 'Participation and Accountability at the Periphery: Democratic Local Governance in Six Countries', *World Development*, 28 (1): 21–39.

Brinkerhoff, D. W. and A. A. Goldsmith. (2003) 'How Citizens Participate in Macroeconomic Policy: International Experience and Implications for Poverty Reduction', *World Development*, 31 (4): 685–701.

Castells, M. (1997) *The Power of Identity* (Oxford: Blackwell).

Craig, D. and D. Porter (2003) 'Poverty Reduction Strategy Papers: A New Convergence', *World Development*, 31 (1): 53–69.

Crook, R. C. and A. S. Sverrisson (2001) 'Decentralization and Poverty-Alleviation in Developing Countries: A Comparative Analysis or, is West Bengal Unique?', *IDS Working Paper*, 130 (Brighton: Institute of Development Studies).

Dechalert, P. (1999) 'NGOs, Advocacy and Popular Protest: A Case Study of Thailand', *C.V.O. International Working Paper*, 6 (London: LSE).

Donnelly-Roark, P. (2001) 'Mainstreaming Participation in the PRSP', Mimeo <www.worldbank.org> (accessed April 2001).

Edwards, M. (2001) 'Global Civil Society and Community Exchanges: A Different Form of Movement', *Environment and Urbanization*, 13 (2): 145–9.

Escobar, A. (1995) *Encountering Development: The Making and Unmaking of the Third World* (Princeton, NJ: Princeton University Press).

Esteva, G. and M. Prakash, M (1998) *Grassroots Post-modernism: Remaking the Soils of Cultures* (London: Zed Books).

Foweraker, J. and T. Landman (1997) *Citizenship Rights and Social Movements: A Comparative and Statistical Analysis* (New York: Oxford University Press).

Fowler, A. (1998) 'Authentic NGDO Partnerships in the New Policy Agenda for International Aid: Dead End or Light Ahead?', *Development and Change*, 29 (1): 137–59.

Francis, P. and R. James (2003) 'Balancing Rural Poverty Reduction and Citizen Participation: The Contradictions of Uganda's Decentralization Programme', *World Development*, 31 (2): 325–37.

Freire, P. (1972) *Pedagogy of the Oppressed* (London: Penguin).

Government of Uganda (2002) 'Fiscal Decentralisation in Uganda', Draft Strategy Paper, prepared by the Fiscal Decentralisation Working Group, March (Kampala: GoU).

Harper, C. (2001) 'Do the Facts Matter: NGOs, Advocacy and Research?', in

M. Edwards and J. Gaventa (eds), *Global Citizen Action* (Boulder, CO: Lynne Rienner), pp. 247–58.

Harriss, J. (2000) 'How Much Difference Does Politics Make? Regime Differences Across Indian States and Rural Poverty Reduction', *LSE Working Paper Series 1*, 1 (London: LSE).

Heller P. (2001) 'Moving the State: The Politics of Democratic Decentralization in Kerala, South Africa, and Porto Alegre', *Politics and Society*, 29 (1): 1–28.

Hickey, S. (2002) 'Transnational NGDOs and Participatory Forms of Rights-based Development: Converging with the Local Politics of Citizenship in Cameroon', *Journal of International Development*, 14 (6): 841–57.

— (2003) 'The Politics of Staying Poor in Uganda', *CPRC Working Paper*, 37 (Manchester: IDPM). <www.chronicpoverty.org>

Holland, J. with J. Blackburn (eds) (1998) *Whose Voice? Participatory Research and Policy Change* (London: IT Publications).

Hudson, A. (2000) 'Making the Connection: Legitimacy Claims, Legitimacy Chains and Northern NGOs' International Advocacy', in D. Lewis and T. Wallace (eds), *New Roles and Relevance: Development NGOs and the Challenge of Change* (CT: Kumarian Press), pp. 89–97.

Jeppsson, A. (2001) 'Financial Priorities Under Decentralisation in Uganda', *Health Policy and Planning*, 16 (2): 187–92.

Jordan, L. and P. van Tuijl (2000) 'Political Responsibility in Transnational NGO Advocacy', *World Development*, 28 (12): 2051–65.

Kanyesigye, J. (1998) 'REFLECT and Empowerment: Our Field Experiences', *PLA Notes*, 32: 51–3 (London: IIED).

Kapoor, N. (2000) 'Women and Governance', *Participation and Governance*, November (New Delhi: PRIA).

Laclau, E. and C. Mouffe (1985) *Hegemony and Socialist Strategy: Towards a Radical Democratic Politics* (London: Verso).

McGee, R. (2001) 'Poverty Reduction Strategies: A Part for the Poor?', *IDS Policy Briefing*, Issue 13 (April) (Brighton: Institute of Development Studies).

McGee, R. with A. Norton (2000) 'Participation in Poverty Reduction Strategies: A Synthesis of Experience with Participatory Approaches to Policy Design, Implementation and Monitoring', *IDS Working Paper*, 109 (Brighton: Institute of Development Studies).

Marcos (1994) 'The Long Journey from Despair to Hope', ZALN Communiqué, Supplement for the anniversary of *La Jornada* (22 September). <http://struggle.ws/zapatista.html> (accessed September 2001).

— (2001) '7 years from what we call "the other uprising"', ZALN Communiqué <http://struggle.ws/zapatista.html> (accessed September 2001).

Maxwell, S. (1999) 'What Can We Do with a Rights-Based Approach To Development?', *ODI Briefing Paper* (September) (London: ODI).

Mayo, P. (1999) *Gramsci, Freire and Adult Education: Possibilities for Transformative Action* (London: Zed Books).

Misra, G., A. Mahal and R. Shah (2000) 'Protecting the Rights of Sex Workers: The Indian Experience', *Health and Human Rights*, 5 (1): 88–115.

Mohan, G. and J. Holland (2001) 'Human Rights and Development in Africa', *Review of African Political Economy*, 88: 177–96.

Mohan, G. and K. Stokke (2000) 'Participatory Development and Empowerment', *Third World Quarterly*, 21 (2): 266–80.

Norton, A. (1998) 'Some Reflections on the PPA Process and Lessons Learned', in J. Holland with J. Blackburn (eds), *Whose Voice? Participatory Research and Policy Change* (London: IT Publications), pp. 143–6.

Nyamugasira, W. (1998) 'NGOs and Advocacy: How Well are the Poor Represented?', *Development in Practice*, 8 (3): 297–308.

Patel, S. and D. Mitlin (2002) 'Sharing Experiences and Changing Lives', *Community Development Journal*, 37 (2): 125–36.

PLA Notes (2002) *Advocacy and Citizen Participation*, 43 (London: IIED).

Rafi, M. and A. M. R. Chowdhury (2000) 'Human Rights and Religious Backlash: The Experience of a Bangladeshi NGO', *Development in Practice*, 10 (1): 19–30.

Regan, A. J. (1998) 'Decentralisation Policy: Reshaping State and Society', in M. Twaddle and H. B. Hansen (eds), *Developing Uganda* (London: James Currey), pp. 159–75.

Robb, C. (2002) *Can the Poor Influence Policy: Participatory Poverty Assessments in the Developing World*, 2nd edn (Washington, DC: World Bank).

Routledge, P. (2001) '"Our Resistance Will be as Transnational as Capital": Convergence Space and Strategy in Globalising Resistance', *Geojournal*, 52: 25–33.

Santos, B. S. (1998) 'Participatory Budgeting in Porto Alegre, Brazil: Towards a Redistributive Democracy', *Politics and Society*, 26 (4): 461–510.

Schneider, A. and B. Goldfrank (2002) 'Budgets and Ballots in Brazil: Participatory Budgeting from the City to the State', *IDS Working Paper*, 149 (Brighton: Institute of Development Studies).

Scott, A. (1990) *Ideology and the New Social Movements* (London: Unwin/Hyman).

Souza, C. (2001) 'Participatory Budgeting in Brazilian Cities: Limits and Possibilities in Building Democratic Institutions', *Environment and Urbanization*, 13 (1): 159–84.

Townsend, J. E. Mawdesly and G. Porter (2002). 'The Role of the Transnational Community of Nongovernment Organisations: Governance or Poverty Reduction?', *Journal of International Development*, 14 (6): 829–39.

Tripp, A. M. (2000) *Women and Politics in Uganda* (London: James Currey; Kampala: Fountain Press).

UNDP (2000) *The Human Development Report: Human Rights and Human Development* (New York: UNDP; Oxford: Oxford University Press).

Uphoff, N. (1996) 'Why NGOs are Not a Third Sector: A Sectoral Analysis with Some Thoughts on Accountability, Sustainability and Accountability', in M. Edwards and D. Hulme (eds), *NGOs: Performance and Accountability: Beyond the Magic Bullet* (London: Earthscan), pp. 17–30.

Veltmeyer, H. (1997) 'New Social Movements in Latin America: The Dynamics of Class and Identity', *Journal of Peasant Studies*, 25 (1): 139–69.

Webster, N. (2002) 'Local Organizations and Political Space in the Forests of West Bengal', in N. Webster and L. Engberg-Pedersen (eds), *In the Name of the Poor: Contesting Political Space for Poverty Reduction* (London: Zed Books), pp. 233–54.

Wignaraja, P. (ed) (1993) *New Social Movements in the South: Empowering the People* (London: Zed Books).

Wilkes, A. and F. Lefrançois (2002) *Blinding with Science or Encouraging Debate? How the World Bank Determines PRSP Policies* (London: Bretton Woods Project/World Vision).

World Bank (2000) *World Development Report 2000/01: Attacking Poverty* (Washington, DC: World Bank).

11 | Securing voice and transforming practice in local government: the role of federating in grassroots development

DIANA MITLIN

The recent political and economic situation in Zimbabwe has created many difficulties for the urban poor. Nevertheless, some new opportunities have also emerged. This chapter describes how a locally-based grassroots organization has been able to use its links with national and international federations of the urban poor and its own strategies to secure land and lobby for changes in local authority regulatory practice, thereby facilitating the affordable development of land, services and housing. As argued below, the opportunities reflect both the declining legitimacy and effectiveness of the central state and the anxiety on the part of local councillors to maintain power in a context of increasing electoral competition. This chapter describes how grassroots organizations have been able to make the most of emerging opportunities due to their membership of a national federation of similar organizations and associated relationship and resource benefits. The discussion shows how grassroots organizations have secured political inclusion and material benefits for their members and offers an opportunity to assess the advantages of federating strategies in terms of securing higher levels of both 'voice' and 'responsiveness' (see Gaventa, this volume).

Beyond developmental NGOs: the power of federating

In 1998, when the Zimbabwean Homeless People's Federation was formed, there were very few opportunities for the urban poor to secure land.[1] Through setting unaffordable building standards and regulations, the state maintained spatial exclusivity in urban areas. In 2000, organized community groups in Victoria Falls secured 565 plots which they developed with the active participation of the community in infrastructure installation and with an acceptance by the local authority that one-room houses may be all that is affordable in the near future. These experiences add to our understanding of the potential role of civil society groups and how they might be strengthened.

Development theorists and practitioners have placed emphasis on the contribution of civil society groups both as a direct provider of services and as a force for pro-poor advocacy (e.g. Van Rooy 1998). However, much of this literature (e.g. Edwards and Fowler 2002) tends to focus on professionalized development NGOs with relatively little attention given to the strategies, functions and roles of grassroots organizations and self-help groups. The experiences considered here relate particularly to empowerment-based notions of people's participation and people-centred development (Oakley 1995: 6). Crucially we analyse the potential of grassroots organizations and their federations to be agents for participation and a voice leading to citizenship and inclusion for the urban poor.

Recent evidence suggests that federation can have significant benefits for grassroots organizations in terms of their capacity to secure political inclusion and poverty reduction for their members. In a review of membership organizations, Howes (1997: 601) argues that federating offers 'obvious advantages in representing members' interests in wider fora and providing access to external resources'. This is developed in Bebbington's (2002) research into federated groupings of Ecuadorian grassroots organizations, or 'supra-communal organisations'. Although not particularly successful in securing economic benefits for members, federation here was successful in supporting the direct move of members into local politics, securing more participatory forms of governance and, at a national level, defending the land rights of indigenous people and promoting bilingual education (ibid., p. 6–11). Overall, the success of federating has been such that: 'Authors of all stripes share the view that the community enablement that has occurred in Ecuador would not have occurred had there not been the emergence of local and later national federations ... To the extent that enablement (of community or markets) is about a shift in power relationships, federations were the primary vehicle through which this occurred' (ibid., p. 16).

Further benefits from federating have also been noted. A study of grassroots organizations in Bolivia, Ecuador and Peru shows how federations that link together community-based groups around 'shared economic, political and cultural interests' are important in strengthening both bonding and bridging social capital (Bebbington and Carroll 2002: 4, 8).[2] Moctezuma (2001: 121) notes, in an analysis of grassroots organization in Mexico City, that linking to other organizations helps groups focus on appropriate issues and reduces their isolation. The experiences of an international NGO in supporting local organizations in Nepal, Mali, Haiti and Peru shows how federations can help develop strategic capacities within grassroots organizations (Petit 2000). More generally, federation shows that for the poor organizations are the primary basis for empowerment. Work in Mumbai suggests that federating is a:

> reminder that groups (even at the level of families) that have a claim to political agency of their own have chosen to combine their political and material power. The primacy of the principle of federation also serves to remind all members ... that the power of the Alliance lies not in its donors, its technical expertise or its administration but, rather, in the will to federate among poor families and communities. (Appadurai 2001: 32)

Hence, the emerging experience is that federating grassroots organization can strengthen the capacity of individual organizations to address the needs and attain the rights of their members. While federating is not closely defined within this literature, it appears to be characterized by a number of common elements: the coming together of leaders and/or members of grassroots organizations of the poor at regular periods to work together to further their objectives within an organizational structure that they perceive to be their own.

What explains the success of federative action in securing the objectives associated with participatory development and governance? In Ecuador, the key factors underpinning the emergence of successful federations were support from NGOs, the church and (on occasions) state agencies; the redistribution of land and educational opportunities to indigenous groups; and strategic alliances with other groups (Bebbington 2002: 15; Bebbington and Carroll 2002: 26). A genuine membership base is also important (Howes 1997: 603). Credit projects may be significant in building the capacity of self-help groups although in the latter case the authors also note that such strategies may result in problems of exclusion and accountability (Pettit 2002: 64; Bebbington and Carroll 2002: 29). These explanations highlight the significance of NGO support strategies, a theme returned to in the concluding section.

Transforming models of urban development: Victoria Falls 1999–2002

Political conflict and violence, legal uncertainties and economic decline have characterized Zimbabwe since 1999. In that year, Zimbabwe was experiencing serious economic difficulties, in part due to the country's involvement in the war in the Democratic Republic of the Congo, and inflation rose to 60 per cent by October. The invasion of white-owned farms by 'ex-combatants' was followed by a state-sanctioned resettlement policy that has resulted in the transfer of a considerable number of farms to government supporters. The continuing fall in agricultural production, lack of foreign currency, shortage of essential goods and declining real incomes (as inflation rose to 200 per cent in 2002) have further reduced economic activity.

During the 1980s, the government introduced measures to support decentralization, although this was limited by the lack of financial autonomy for lower levels of government, the centralizing tendencies of some ministries and a dominant single party (Stewart et al. 1994: 7). In 1998, the government introduced measures to seek the wider participation of civil society in decision-making with Thirteen Principles to Guide the Decentralization Process. Matovu (2002: 4) argues that there has been some response from civil society groups, although such groups may represent very specific organizations' interests rather than the 'concerns of the grassroots'. It is into this unfavourable context of limited citizen voice and government responsiveness that a grassroots initiative seeking pro-poor development in Victoria Falls emerged.

Community organizations in Zimbabwe and the catalyst for change In 2000, there were an estimated 40,000 residents in the town of Victoria Falls, close to the border with Zambia and a famous tourist destination with one million visitors each year. Many residents lived in or alongside Chinotimba, the low-income area. Some had been allotted formal concrete-block houses, typically 40 sq. m., two bedrooms with a living area, small kitchen and bathroom. However, over 3,000 families live in backyard shacks and squatter settlements, some with wooden and corrugated-iron shacks, others with simple shelters (called 'bagdads') made from waste material and plastic sheeting. On average, one toilet serves 507 shack-dwellers, while one water tap serves 1,350 people. These 'informal settlement dwellers' pay Z$4 million per annum in rentals to their landlords (Dialogue on Shelter 1999).

In 1995 a group of community members from the South African Homeless People's Federation (SAHPF) visited people living in Chinotimba, starting the chain of critical events that led to processes of federative action in urban Zimbabwe (see Box 11.1). The group had been working for some years to strengthen communities in their own country (Baumann et al. 2001). They discussed development options with the Zimbabweans that they met. At that time, the residents were organized within Zanu-PF, the political party that had dominated Zimbabwean state and government activities since independence in 1981. The approaches encouraged by the South Africans were very different from those with which the shack-dwellers in Chinotimba were familiar. SAHPF had emerged from savings groups of women who got together to save money to buy access to land, services and housing. The women had learnt about this from a grassroots federation in India, the National Slum Dwellers' Federation, and the women's collective that they worked with, *Mahila Milan* (Appadurai 2001). The focus on saving encourages women's participation as they quickly see the relevance of this activity. The focus on housing and secure tenure has emerged in both South Africa and Zimbabwe because it is a priority. In Zimbabwe, the saving schemes were everything that fosrmal party structures were not: participatory, emphasizing self-reliance, not dependent on the state, establishing relationships of accountability between leaders and members, and dominated by women.

THE FIRST SAVINGS SCHEMES, 1995 AND 1996 In Victoria Falls, ten savings schemes were immediately formed around district wards and existing Zanu-PF groups. Due to Zanu-PF's involvement, council officials dominated discussions and this resulted in a monthly 'required' savings contribution (which effectively excluded the poorest). To address their housing needs, the groups tried to register as a housing cooperative to

Land development in Victoria Falls

1995:	Savings schemes started in Victoria Falls following visit of South African Homeless People's Federation
1997:	Formation of Dialogue on Shelter
1998 (November):	Enumeration in Victoria Falls
1998 (December):	Formation of the Zimbabwe Homeless People's Federation
1999 (July):	Promise of land (approximately 400 plots) to the Federation at visit of the South African Homeless People's Federation
2000 (January):	Indication of the land that would be made available
2000 (May):	Federation community centre completed in Victoria Falls
2000 (March):	General election
2000 (November):	Agreement on layout, submission of plans to Department of Local Government
2001 (January):	Ground-breaking ceremony with local politicians
2001 (February):	Visits of community members and council officials to Namibia and Zimbabwe to study community management
2001 (April):	First families move on site. Basic water provision and no toilets
2001 (August):	Dialogue on Shelter offers Gungano funds for site development
2002 (March):	Presidential election
2002 (June):	Infrastructure begins
2002 (December):	Infrastructure 90 per cent completed

obtain subsidized building society loans. However, this solution was far from ideal. The societies would not recognize many shack-dwellers as viable borrowers because they were not formally employed.

In 1996, the South African Federation invited a group of community leaders from Victoria Falls together with two local councillors to a celebration of the first five years of savings schemes in South Africa. The meeting brought together federations of community organizations from Brazil, Cambodia, India, Namibia, Thailand and Zimbabwe and they collectively agreed to launch Shack or Slum Dwellers International (Patel et al. 2001). This international network would strengthen members' activities, offering support as required. The Zimbabwean community members participated in events but the community leaders were unclear about how the activities described by other community groups might be realized within their own country.

THE GROWTH OF THE FEDERATION IN ZIMBABWE, 1997–98 During 1997 and the first half of 1998, savings schemes spread to other towns in Zimbabwe. An NGO was formed, Dialogue on Shelter for the Homeless in Zimbabwe Trust, to support local activities. A national meeting of savings schemes took place in December 1998 and the Zimbabwe Homeless People's Federation was launched. Dialogue on Shelter was anxious that local activity should be prioritized. Together with the Victoria Falls savings schemes, they organized a community enumeration in November 1998. A community exchange came from South Africa to show local savings scheme members how to develop a questionnaire, go from house to house collecting information, and how to collate the information.

Nationally, the young Federation faced a changing political situation. The hegemony of Zanu-PF was weakening; inflation was rising; questions about Zimbabwe's involvement in the war in the Democratic Republic of the Congo and the constitutional reform process offered a constant if low-key challenge to state control and legitimacy. However, in Victoria Falls, there was an opening political environment. By July 1999, just six months after the council had been presented with the results of the enumeration, the Federation had its first indication that the council might be prepared to offer land.

In 1999 Federation groups were offered land in Beitbridge (Chitekwe and Mitlin 2001: 93), a small town on the border with South Africa. This resulted in Dialogue on Shelter and the Federation establishing a revolving loan fund for housing, the Gungano Fund. By the second half of 1999, Dialogue on Shelter decided to use this finance to catalyse innovation in urban development without expecting members to repay at an interest rate sufficient to cover inflation (then running at 60 per cent a year). The commitment was to identify and support processes that worked for the poorest members. This was not an easy decision, because the Federation set great pride by its financial self-reliance. Subsidizing loans would limit the scale of lending and would mean a continuing need for external donor finance. But without subsidies, the poor could not afford to participate. Irrespective of the loan policy, by 2000 the development impetus in the Federation had switched back to Victoria Falls.

The changing political situation in Victoria Falls and the offer of land, 1999–2000 The local authorities and government agencies that had been indifferent or hostile to the urban poor for so long now appeared to be increasingly responsive. During the early months of 2000, the council followed up on its earlier promise with a firm offer of an area of land with 565 stands relatively well located on the periphery of Victoria Falls.

A layout had been prepared by the Department of Local Government. Savings scheme members wished to reduce the size of plots and increase affordability. However, the town engineer argued that amendments would cause delays. After discussions, community members agreed that the unchanged plans should be submitted to the appropriate national authorities.

By March 2000, political conditions in the country resulted in nearly all savings schemes temporarily abandoning activities. The general election was being contested by an opposition party, the Movement for Democratic Change (MDC) and Zanu-PF felt its majority was threatened. In low-income settlements, any organizing became fraught with danger: at worst, meetings would be broken up with violence; at best, vying political parties would pressurize community leaders to make a commitment to support that party. In this context, the party political neutrality that the Federation sought was impossible. Savings schemes stopped meetings and activities slowed considerably.

In Victoria Falls there was little political violence; most people are Ndebele and there was relatively little genuine support for the Shona-based Zanu-PF. Here, the Federation took advantage of the forthcoming election and declared its willingness to construct a community centre in Chinotimba. The council offered a plot of land and election candidates were generous with materials, and, with Federation groups sourcing a builder from among their members and making their own blocks, the centre was complete within a month and ceremoniously opened by the newly elected MDC MP.

Development for whom? control, selection and affordability, August 2001 to August 2002 However, progress on the land development proved to be slow, particularly during the key planning stage (August 2000 to August 2001), due to divergences between the key institutional interests at work (those of the community and town planners) and related contextual constraints (both financial and political).

Experiences in other Federation groups demonstrated that formally installed conventional infrastructure for urban settlements was too expensive.[3] The Chair of the Housing Committee in Victoria Falls agreed with the Federation Groups and Dialogue on Shelter Group about the possibility of an bottom-up, community-managed approach, and sought a low-cost construction approach, involving Federation members offering their labour as 25 per cent deposit and repaying the remaining costs over several years. Initially preferring a 'traditional' approach to municipal planning, the town engineer was persuaded to amend the plans into a more incremental and affordable approach following a series of planned international exchanges whereby other members of SDI demonstrated the effectiveness of their strategies.[4]

Entering negotiations with the council and USAID, the Federation was also able to influence the decision-making processes concerning funding modalities for the settlement and the waiting list for plots. Through a mixture of formal engagements and direct action (e.g. temporary land occupation), various threats to the process were averted, particularly a move by central government to remove the 'unsightly' shacks to beyond the periphery of Victoria Falls for reasons of tourism, a suggestion mirrored by USAID. Federation members would occupy the site rather than housing waiting list applicants taken in order from the list.[5] Having held off the challenges, members had to move fast in developing the land allocated to the Federation; as one of the women explained, 'We just picked up everything and brought it here. The council threatened eviction, there was nowhere else to go.' Using council materials and Federation labour, a ground-breaking ceremony to confirm the settlement was held in January 2001. By August 2001, this sense of agency gained by the Federation and Dialogue on Shelter in these negotiations led them to circumvent USAID and instead use Gungano Funds to provide a loan to the community to undertake the infrastructure development. This effectively shifted the pattern of organizational relationships surrounding the Federation further away from those of vertical patronage and towards those of horizontal solidarity.

Through most of these negotiations, the Federation found support within the council. As noted by the Chair of the Housing Committee: 'You have to remember that the councillors, they now have only two years before the election ... they want to see something happening.' Moreover, the present councillors differed from the previous group, who had not been sufficiently skilled and tended to allow staff to dominate decision-making. The new council reflected the entrance of entrepreneurs into town politics, with greater management experience and an eagerness to secure efficient services, not only to protect their business interests but also in recognition that they had to deliver in order to be re-elected.

By June 2001, the national economic situation was deteriorating. In April, Victoria Falls had been without fuel. In the country as a whole, the lack of foreign exchange and the general lack of confidence had reduced output and halted investment. Within communities and local government, there was an increasing scepticism about the ability of central government to manage the situation. In order to maintain credibility in the community and continue to negotiate with the municipality, the Federation remained explicitly non-partisan, and opted to work with any state agency or politician that would advance its cause. Despite a degree of suspicion surrounding the previous political affiliations of some Federation leaders, most in the Victoria Falls Council believed that the Federation was primarily interested in serving the poor.

Emerging results and constraints, April–December 2002 By July 2002, 300 Federation members were living on the school site and the infrastructure installation had begun. To reduce costs, the Federation had cleared large areas of the site themselves and participated in digging ditches, although those with young children found it particularly difficult to contribute their labour. The making of building blocks that started with the community centre in 2000 continued. Five to eight members were employed, earning a basic wage making blocks that were sold commercially to customers throughout Victoria Falls. There were also other livelihood benefits: members living on the new site benefited from not having to pay rent and many grew their own food. Moreover, when the council tried to claim that the firewood on the area was council property, members were successful in securing the timber for themselves (to use and to sell).

However, despite these gains – both in terms of livelihoods and political capital – new problems have emerged. A surprising issue was that the group struggled to find members for all the plots. There was a huge uncertainty about the cost of the development as inflation was high and continuing to rise, despite the Federation agreeing that the Gungano Fund would lend money for infrastructure and one room plus bathroom. Federation leaders and Dialogue on Shelter assessed that, with the pressure of the development, leaders and members had found it difficult to meet to identify problems and solutions. The recurrence of AIDS led to the deaths of a number of members and leaders, weakening leadership within the savings groups. There was a need to return to basic discussions and communications about members' needs and how they could best be met.

Reflecting on achievements and emerging lessons

Overall, federating in Victoria Falls has involved regular working relationships at three levels:

1. Between savings schemes in Victoria Falls. Members and their leaders meet regularly to share ideas, plan new strategies, gain skills and information from each other, and support work within each other's savings schemes.
2. Between Victoria Falls and other towns and cities in Zimbabwe. The national Federation realizes its identity through regular exchanges between communities and through meetings that consider national issues. This reduces the isolation of individual groups and ensures that individual successes can consolidate and expand advantages for others.
3. Groups in Zimbabwe are linked to other community groups through Shack Dwellers International. This international link has proved to be important in adding legitimacy to local groups and helping ensure they are heard. Great importance is given to international connections although there is relatively little direct interface between members in Victoria Falls and other members of SDI.

For the urban poor in Zimbabwe (as elsewhere), securing access to land and housing offers much more than just the physical assets. It is a process of securing inclusion as equal citizens in society. What can we understand about the strategies that have made this possible? This discussion focuses on the significance of federating.

The Zimbabwe Homeless People's Federation and Dialogue on Shelter have been working in Victoria Falls at a time of immense political change. Despite real problems, they have embarked on their own change process. To secure widespread inclusion, new standards and conventions for urban development, the recognition of their rights and access to state resources, new relationships needed to be secured and new capacities developed. A high level of political capability (Williams, this volume) was required for this negotiation to be successful, with community leaders relying on a strong local membership, persistence and the ability to compromise.

On the 'other side of the equation' (Gaventa, this volume), local authority officials and politicians also needed to change. Council officials needed to understand what the organized poor could offer to the development process, to recognize the value of incremental housing development, and to learn how to use their own resources more effectively. Advocacy by professional groups and exposure to the actual contribution of savings group members contributed to their acceptance of such change. The ability of state and civil society to work together in a context of changing activities in which grassroots organizations took on increasing responsibility contradicts the suggestion of Evans (1996: 1123) that for the bureaucracy and local citizens to work well together requires a well-defined division of labour.

Belonging to a federation emerges as a significant factor in the successes that have been achieved. What did federating mean for the savings schemes in Victoria Falls? The discussion below highlights four key benefits.

Reducing isolation Regular meetings within local groups, with other federation groups, with international groups through Shack Dwellers International and with their professional support agency, have reduced the isolation of the local communities. When one leader is frustrated with the lack of progress, another can take up the struggle. When members argue that house-building will be impossible, they can see where groups have done it elsewhere. When council officials lack confidence in incremental development and community management initiative, the community could demonstrate how it works elsewhere. This network of horizontal support and solidarity has offered fertile ground for the cross-fertilization of ideas and institutional learning, and has given both the community and the council confidence to move forwards on processes of innovation and change.

Building local capacity Saving has helped to build relationships of trust between members as well as developing skills in financial management. This corresponds to broader findings concerning the importance of credit in building local organizational capacity (Pettit 2000: 64; Bebbington and Carroll 2002: 29). At the same time, the emphasis on savings of any amount rather than credit has helped to reduce the problems of inclusion for poorer members. With high inflation, the willingness of the Federation to offer a subsidized interest rate on loans has also been important.

Securing political inclusion Over the last few years, officials and politicians have come to recognize savings groups as a potential resource able to assist in urban development. The Federation has also become a local political force because of its evident support among people in Chinotimba and hence its perceived potential to influence community decisions in this low-income settlement (e.g. concerning votes or leaving shacks). Such relationships have been crucial in persuading the council to compromise on standards and procedures. The multitude of contacts, including those with other councils, have given the council the confidence to take on the perceived risks involved in working with the poor, and the Gungano Fund also helped to persuade the council to take the Federation seriously.

A further benefit of a national network is that Victoria Falls represents a moment of learning within a broader process of securing voice and responsiveness in Zimbabwe. The model developed at Victoria Falls is, the Federation now believes, unaffordable for the poorest urban residents. The present challenge is to persuade local authorities to agree to communal infrastructure. A new development of 1,500 plots in Mutare (in eastern Zimbabwe) offers such an opportunity. The Federation provides a structure through which the gains achieved in one place can be transferred to others, scaling-up the benefits.

Knowledge The solidarity offered to local groups when they federated has strengthened their knowledge and confidence. The poor in Victoria Falls, as elsewhere, have many ideas about their problems and how they might be addressed. All too often, residents lack the collective confidence to come together, plan a solution and strategize how it can be achieved. The Federation offers a framework through which their knowledge can move from being passive to active, with community exchanges between more and less active settlements providing an impetus to start again. Members can suggest analysis or proposals for action at meetings, starting a process of political learning through which confidence is built. Through their involvement in development projects, community leaders have similarly gained a high degree of political literacy concerning the practices of powerful groups and institutions, particularly professional urban development specialists and the council. Previously denied insider access to municipal development plans, the increased understanding gained through multiple contacts and continual pressure has been key in securing both material benefits for the poor and their greater inclusion in policy processes.

As has been broadly recognized, NGO support for the federation of NGOs has been important (Bebbington 2002: 15; Bebbington and Carroll 2002: 26; Howes 1997: 601). Appropriate professional support in working with councils and raising donor funds has been essential. In their interaction with officials and politicians, grassroots organizations need professional credibility, and such links have enabled the community to gain legitimacy in a context in which the poor had not had a voice.[6] With appropriate professional support, new technical options in construction have been explored.

Conclusion

Solidarity, relationships, confidence and knowledge have been embedded into the local groups of the Zimbabwe Homeless People's Federation. As argued by Bebbington and Carroll (2002: 13), in Ecuador, factors such as these have contributed to the 'thickening' of civil society and have assisted in securing development. At the same time, the crisis in Zimbabwe has itself provoked recognition of the need for change. Political and economic tensions have resulted in what might be considered to be a 'thinning' of the central state. As central government has lost credibility, local municipal staff and politicians have become willing to innovate and experiment with new partners. In this new political space, councillors perceive that their success lies with addressing the needs of the electorate rather than pleasing central government. As Evans (1996: 1127–8) argued, political competition has been an important contributing factor to their increased responsiveness to the electorate.

What does this experience tell us about relations between civil society and the state? A comprehensive survey of the literature is beyond the scope of this paper, but reflecting on Evans's (1996) discussion on 'state–society synergies', we can see that civil society institutions (in this case NGOs and people's organizations) have successfully shifted the institutional direction of grassroots organizations and public agencies towards achieving greater voice and responsiveness. Critical to this has been an increase in 'embeddedness' as, with the support of the Federation, local community leaders have increased the depth and scope of their lobbying activities with the council. However, in contrast to Evans's examples, in this case it is civil society rather than the state that has been the catalyst. This suggests that federating offers a way in which synergy between the public and private sectors can be constructed by innovative civil society without initial state interest (ibid., pp. 1125–6).

Finally, we should recognize that the shack-dwellers in Victoria Falls have not solved all their problems. For those participating in the development, finance remains a major issue. While there have been some income-generation activities, these are too few for the large numbers in need. Without the more widespread adoption of incremental infrastructure and housing development, developments will appear unaffordable to the poor. Second, there are many shack-dwellers who remain in Chintotimba. What options are being developed for them? Construction has taken the time and energy of community leaders in Victoria Falls and little attention is being paid to the needs of those who are still without land and who are not presently members of the Federation. (Although the interests of the broader Federation are in membership growth and new activities.) Third, there are continuing and very significant economic and political problems that the group has to face. However, despite these issues, federating has added considerably to the opportunities and choices open to the poor and disempowered. Unlike isolated participatory events, federations provide an institutional form for the poor themselves to learn, strategize, consolidate to address their own needs, secure their rights of citizenship and press for greater government responsiveness. As such, federations constitute a key strategy in securing the objectives of participatory development and governance, particularly in contexts where significant shifts in the field of power relations between state and its citizens are underway.

Notes

This chapter reflects an ongoing process of learning with the Zimbabwean Homeless People's Federation and Dialogue on Shelter for the Homeless in Zimbabwe Trust. The support of WaterAid is gratefully acknowledged. The author has been visiting the development discussed here on a six-monthly basis over the last three years.

1 To be a legal landowner in a Zimbabwean town in the period following Independence required an income sufficient to purchase 300 sq. m. of land, full services and a two-room concrete-block house; the building standards were revised downwards in 1993 but many authorities were reluctant to sanction lower-standard developments (Kamete 2001, 129–30).

2 Bonding social capital refers to the horizontal links between members of the same community and bridging social capital is that between the community and more powerful individuals (Woolcock 1998).

3 This had been anticipated by the NGO but experiential learning was considered by the professional staff to be important for the community members.

4 These took place in 2000; one exchange was to Windhoek (Namibia) to visit a council willing to allow incremental development and the second was to the Orangi Pilot Project (Pakistan) to see sanitation installed by residents.

5 Many councils have waiting lists for housing even if there is little new provision. Families generally pay an administration fee to join the list. Many of the poorest do not join the list as they cannot afford the fee, lack the required documentation and/or do not believe housing will be provided.

6 In one council meeting, a silent Federation member was asked by the Deputy Mayor to leave when the individual came and sat at the back of the meeting to observe proceedings. Federation leaders noted that a few years ago none of them would be allowed to sit down in council discussions.

References

Appadurai, A. (2001) 'Deep Democracy: Urban Governmentality and the Horizon of Politics', *Environment and Urbanization*, 13 (2): 23–44.

Baumann, T., J. Bolnick and D. Mitlin (2001) 'The Age of Cities and Organizations of the Urban Poor: The Work of the South African Homeless People's

Federation', *Poverty Reduction in Urban Areas Series*, Working Paper 2 (London: International Institute for Environment and Development).

Bebbington, A. (2002) 'Organization, Inclusion and Citizenship: Policy and (Some) Economic Gains of Indigenous Peoples' Organizations in Ecuador', Mimeo.

Bebbington, A. J. and T. F. Carroll (2002) 'Induced Social Capital and Federations of the Rural Poor in the Andes', in C. Grootaert and T. van Bastelaer (eds), *Social Capital And Poverty: An Empirical Assessment* (Cambridge: Cambridge University Press), pp. 234–78.

Chitekwe, B. and D. Mitlin (2001) 'The Urban Poor Under Threat and in Struggle: Options for Urban Development in Zimbabwe, 1995–2000', *Environment and Urbanization*, 13 (2): 85–102.

Dialogue on Shelter (1999) *Victoria Falls Enumeration*, Unpublished Report, Victoria Falls.

Edwards, M. and A. Fowler (eds) (2002) *The Earthscan Reader on NGO Management* (London: Earthscan Publications).

Evans, P. (1996) 'Government Action, Society Capital and Development: Reviewing the Action on Synergy', *World Development*, 24 (6): 1119–32.

Howes, M. (1997) 'NGOs and the Institutional Development of Membership Organizations: The Evidence from Six Cases', *Journal for International Development*, 9 (4): 597–604.

Kamete, A. Y. (2001) 'US AID's Private Sector Housing Programme in Urban Zimbabwe: Examining the Terrain from the Terraces', *Environment and Urbanization*, 13 (1): 125–36.

Matovu, G. (2002) 'Africa and Decentralization: Enter the Citizens', *Private Sector and Infrastructure*, 211 (Washington, DC: World Bank).

Moctezuma, P. (2001) 'Community-based Organization and Participatory Planning in South-east Mexico City', *Environment and Urbanization*, 13 (2): 117–33.

Oakley, P. (1995) 'People's Participation in Development Projects', *INTRAC Occasional Papers Series*, 7 (Oxford: INTRAC).

Patel, S., S. Burra and C. d'Cruz (2001) 'Shack/Slum Dwellers International (SDI): Foundations to Treetops', *Environment and Urbanization*, 13 (2): 45–60.

Pettit, J. (2000) 'Strengthening Local Organization: "Where the Rubber Hits the Road"', *IDS Bulletin*, 31 (3): 57–66

Stewart, F., J. Klugsman and A. H. Helmsing (1994) 'Decentralization in Zimbabwe', Occasional Paper 15 (Zimbabwe: UNDP Human Development Office).

Van Rooy, A. (ed.) (1998) *Civil Society and the Aid Industry: The Politics and the Promise* (London: Earthscan).

Woolcock, M. (1998) 'Social Capital and Economic Development: Toward a Theoretical Synthesis and Policy Framework', *Theory and Society*, 27 (2): 151–208.

12 | Participatory municipal development plans in Brazil: divergent partners constructing common futures

GLAUCO REGIS FLORISBELO AND
IRENE GUIJT

As the development debate on participation shifts from a community development perspective to that of wider governance processes such as decentralization, the question of who 'does' democracy becomes critical. Where many participatory development efforts often ended up creating artificial mechanisms and structures that ran parallel to the state systems (cf. Cleaver 2001), the governance debate includes the state as a key partner in democracy. In this chapter, we discuss one case of democracy-in-action in Brazil, involving non-government organizations (NGOs), trade unions and municipal administrations. The example offers a realistic and encouraging perspective on the roles that these three partners can play to strengthen the space in participatory municipal planning processes in favour of poor and marginalized groups and alternative approaches to development.

When participatory governance is discussed in relation to Brazil, many people think of the innovative participatory budgeting example from Porto Alegre. A less well-known example is that of decentralization to municipal levels, the lowest level of government in Brazil, a process primarily set in train by the Workers' Party (the PT). PT-affiliated politicians are now in power in around 200 municipalities besides leading at the federal level via President Lula, who was elected in October 2002. In current Brazilian politics, municipalities now represent a critical focus for state and civic action on local development processes with respect to formulating and implementing public policies, and also the forging of strategic alliances between these key state and civic agents. The implementation of Municipal Councils for Sustainable Rural Development and the elaboration of municipal development plans are already pre-conditions for receiving certain resources from national or state-level policies, such as PRONAF.[1] With the growing presence of the political left at all levels of decision-making, such trends are expected to accelerate and expand.

One organization that has pioneered participatory municipal planning is the Centre for Alternative Technologies (CTA), a local NGO working on alternative futures for and with rural smallholders in the Zona da Mata of Minas Gerais, Brazil. Founded in 1987 by marginalized farmers, their trade unions (the STRs),[2] and a handful of committed agricultural professionals, CTA's core programme is the Local Development Programme (LDP) that focuses on participatory municipal planning. The LDP is active in three municipalities of Minas Gerais: Araponga, Tombos and Acaiaca. This chapter will focus on the experiences of Araponga and Tombos, which offer more compelling stories of political change. The change process has involved steady efforts by multiple partners in local analysis and participatory planning, community mobilization, strategic reflection on political processes, and holding local government to account. Critical has been the focus on local political actors who are embedded in their own social movements and pursue often radical political agendas.

Local development plans as social innovation in Brazil

CTA's story The Zona da Mata of Minas Gerais covers 143 municipalities, 128 of which have a population of less than 20,000. A largely agricultural economy, smallholder agriculture represents a large proportion of production and of properties, though not of total land area given the skewed land tenure relationships.[3] The region is marked by chronic and deteriorating environmental degradation, with a lack of sufficient clean water and ongoing loss of agro-biodiversity, leading to a situation that represents several threats to food security for poor households. Smallholders generally have low expectations of support from public administrations as traditionally, in most municipalities, mayors and secretaries have been large landholders or their supporters and most voters are more interested in urban issues than rural problems.

It is in this context that CTA has been active as a local NGO for fifteen years, working on developing sustainable livelihood options for, and with, smallholders. CTA's work has always been ideologically inspired by the political left, notably the Workers' Party (PT), and it has tended to work with leftist social movements and organizations such as rural workers' unions and their smallholder members (CTA 2002: 3). Legally a non-profit civil association, the organization has a threefold mission: to strengthen small farmer organizations to work towards alternative futures; to promote social equity within these associations and in development processes; and to promote public debate on conservation, sustainable agriculture and local development.

Since its inception in 1987, CTA has worked through a series of distinct phases in its work, starting from initial information-gathering and sensitizing work in support of discrete project-based activities, through to a regional development focus that culminated in its Programme of Local Municipal Development Plans (CTA 2002: 5; Marcondes de Moraes 2002: 3). This trajectory has involved a cumulative process of developing strategic alliances with key state and civic agencies, and entailed an increasingly political role for CTA. Importantly, each phase has brought shifts in how the team has 'wielded' the notion of participation, with new aspects of participatory thinking and practice added en route.

Whereas some critiques of participatory methodologies tend to see PRA (participatory rural appraisal) as the only vehicle for participatory development, and caricature it as both a quasi-religious and mechanical approach to project work (cf. Leeuwis 2000; Francis 2001), the practice of CTA shows a more elaborate and evolving way of dealing with participatory development. Although always steeped in a political perspective, CTA has clearly shifted from a practical focus working only with economically marginalized groups to sophisticated alliances with diverse political actors in order to influence policy processes. In this transition, it has maintained a core partnership with the workers' trade unions that had helped form the NGO, and who still govern its overall directions through the board and general assembly. This transition has evolved as part of the continual self-critique of the staff and affiliates of CTA and has happened without knowing about the 'tyranny of participation' critique (cf. Cooke and Kothari 2001) that some deem to have been so instrumental in furthering the thinking on participatory development.

CTA therefore considers participatory methodologies as useful, as long as they are part of a longer-term change process that enables the methodology to act as a political catalyst. It started working in 1987 with a solidly politically-informed change agenda, without any participatory toolkits. When PRA emerged, CTA skilled its members in it after seeing its potential to aid collective analysis of problems and proposal identification. Other methodologies have also contributed, depending on the issues at hand. CTA's methodological evolution represents an ongoing expansion of its understanding of and skills in social change, always maintaining a strongly political focus. This mirrors what some in western academia refer to as a convergence of participatory development and participatory governance (e.g. Gaventa, this volume).

THE MAIN PLAYERS Throughout this methodological trajectory, the main players have always been CTA's technical team, the rural workers' unions (STRs) and other organizations they have spawned, and farmers' groups. It is important to become acquainted with these players in order to understand how the municipal planning process works to bridge these two forms of participation, before discussing the character of the public administration that these actors have engaged with, and the broader social movements to which they relate in terms of institutional alliances and wider political objectives.

The rural trade unions, STRs, are central to CTA's work. STRs are membership organizations, operate at the municipal level (and are federated at state/national levels), and are the most accepted, democratically elected bodies that represent smallholder agriculture. From a traditional focus on legal rights and political struggles, the engagement with CTA has expanded the unions' activities to include an agro-ecological perspective. However, the STRs are affected by limitations in capacity, with a few dedicated unionists taking on the bulk of the work, and of physical access, with low funds not permitting mobility other than by foot or motorcycle. Mobility is not insignificant as the type of political dialogue discussed in this chapter requires many meetings in all corners of the municipality to break the urban domination of municipal policies and politics.

The farmers and their groups tend to focus on technical agricultural issues of personal interest, such as animal production or agro-forestry (CTA 2001). Within the LDP, they play the role of researchers and implementers. Without them, there would be no critical mass of citizens to push the debates on rural development in the municipal councils.

INVITED AND CLAIMED SPACES: PUBLIC ADMINISTRATIONS AND SOCIAL MOVEMENTS Two other groups are particularly important for understanding the municipal processes of governance: the public administrations themselves and the social movements that are political homes to organizations such as CTA, the unions and farmers' groups. Each offers a very different type of political space within which the NGO, unions and groups can assert their agency and voice.

Public administrations at municipal level in Brazil are not, by and large, 'community' spaces for the marginalized. Leaving aside the two well publicized examples of participatory governance in Porto Alegre and Curitiba, the remaining 5,000 municipalities in Brazil are generally driven by a political culture of paternalism and centralization. '*Partidismo*'(polarization along political party lines) generally splits municipal residents in 'pro' and 'anti' groups that avoid collaboration once election results are known. Few pro-poor candidates get far in these elections and hence rarely play a strong role in municipal-level implementation. Instead, local policies are implemented in part by civil servants with fixed jobs whose mediocre energy levels are matched by mediocre outputs. The other group in public administration is the elected office-holders, or career politicians, who often have bad relationships with civil servants, particularly if they are from opposing political parties. At times of transition, when pro-poor politicians enter office, sabotage by outgoing officials is not uncommon.

Animosity among the ranks of public administration is aggravated by a decentralization of responsibility towards municipalities that is not matched with appropriate levels of funding. Growing numbers of tasks and fewer resources perpetuate the continual disputes among municipal councillors, and only when a councillor fighting for issues related to a specific community is particularly assertive, is there a chance of success. It is in this fraught space of internal division that marginalized communities are seeking to exert their voices and influence how public monies are allocated.

Social movements constitute the 'claimed' spaces (Cornwall, this volume) for marginalized groups. Within the context of CTA's municipal planning work, three movements play a role: the STR or labour movement, associations and the women's movement. Each movement has its own form of governance, with more or less democratic tendencies. For example, the labour movement has far less of a participatory democratic culture at state than at municipal level. At the municipal level, the internal governance of social movements is strongly determined by social relations of individuals. Hence, where a community group has frequent interactions and shared activities, a more cohesive movement and community agenda are likely to be present; but as social relations also need to be preserved, this can create tensions when different agenda priorities arise.

Three points are significant concerning the relationship between social movements, as potential advocates of community interests, and public administrations, as potential spaces for these interests.

1. *The relationship with public administration varies for each movement.* Each movement has its own formal policy on the relationship: one of proximity, distance or opposition. For example, in municipal councils, the labour movement (CONTAG/CUT)[4] will opt to use that political space while MST, the famous landless movement, will stay outside to avoid the risk of being co-opted. Hence, the interests of marginalized communities will either emerge within the domain of public power or stand alongside it, depending on the social movement to which these interests are aligned.
2. *Ideological difference defines differences only to a certain extent.* Personal relationships – family and friends – are critical and can override voting preferences. Having a brother-in-law from an opposing political party who is mayor means there are limits to the demands one can put on him

to push through a certain agenda item related to the pro-poor alliance that one is affiliated to oneself. Hence one's personal allegiance to two communities, that of kinship and that of politics, regularly vie for space.

3. *Each relationship has its own evolution and dynamics, so space for community interests to be addressed is continually being (re)negotiated.* The STR of Araponga always had a distant, sometimes tense relationship with the municipal council. However, after two years in which the STR sought proximity to the council, the current (right-wing) mayor has now invited one of the STR leaders to consider a more formal alliance, already anticipating the votes this may bring in the next elections. In Tombos, the labour movement had open conflicts with the council, then won the elections and subsequently lost them along with the gains made during its brief period of influence. Thus, space for community interests has had a rollercoaster ride.

These essentially political details are critical in order to understand the extent to which citizens are able make use of the opportunities created with CTA and the STRs in fora of participatory governance where social movements and public administration meet.

The origins of the LDP idea

In this context and with these players, from 1996 onwards, the CTA slowly developed the idea of municipal-level development plans as its central intervention strategy for effecting alternative development futures in the region. This came neither from a critique of PRA nor from a reinforcement of Freirean roots, but rather from an understanding of the importance of formal government as a vehicle for larger-scale changes. The NGO's main objective was to accumulate methodological experiences that could be used by municipal players elsewhere – for which it needed some reasonably successful experiences. It wanted to show how a participatory process of political dialogue and negotiation could provoke municipal-wide improvements in the use of productive agricultural resources, job/employment creation, and general improvement of the living conditions of citizens.

Elections played a varied but defining role in catalysing this process in both municipalities. In Araponga in 1996, the STR candidates stood for but lost the municipal council elections. This provoked an analysis of the limitations of the elaborate union-driven local development plan (LDP) that had focused their efforts to date (Fária 1994). The STR of Araponga concluded that political isolation had limited the impact of development initiatives, and dropped their categorical resistance to working with the public administration because of party policy differences in order to work towards realizing a local development plan. On the other hand, in Tombos, where the Workers' Party won after a strong showing by the STR-affiliated candidates, a region-wide discussion about public policies and the role of municipal administrations was stimulated, supported in part by union-organized courses for rural leaders on this theme. Two years later, the LDP process started in Tombos. The municipal council, now including several STR leaders, earmarked many funds for the first time to be devoted to smallholder issues. Also a 'first' was the creation and resourcing of a Municipal Secretary for Agriculture, Livestock, Supplies and Environment. The same year CTA signed a convention with the municipal council and farmers' organizations to facilitate the formulation and implementation of an MRDP and to provide technical assistance to farmers.

CTA's local development work is based on a deep-rooted political vision of rights and citizenship, the value of societal debate, environmental sustainability, and the urgency of practical options for smallholders. Working initially with participatory rural appraisal and farmer participatory research approaches to facilitate understanding and planning and to develop innovations, CTA and partners had perceived a limit to the impact they were having. Waiting for the correct political party – one that favoured marginalized rural smallholders – to win council elections was proving to be an uncertain strategy for scaling up impact. This factor, plus the excessive workload for a limited number of dedicated rural union activists, led CTA and its union-based partners to invest in 'municipal rural development planning' based on wider partnerships. Today, the municipal planning work as facilitated by CTA has developed into elaborate processes of continual consultation and strategic realignment in which PRA is but one of several processes critical for the emergence of participatory development and governance.

Comparing Araponga and Tombos

The uniqueness of local context Although the political processes that underpin participatory development and governance in Araponga and Tombos continue to be unique, the processes have three features in common. First, both started with an elaborate analytical exercise that laid the basis for the collective formulation of a Municipal Rural Development Plan, which itself involved three phases: citizen mobilization; problem appraisal and survey of options using PRA; and analysis and proposal of priorities. The process and the results are documented in a Municipal Rural Development Plan (MRDP), which becomes the official agreement between civil society organizations and the public administration. Importantly, this lengthy process can take a year, and is led by the more political civil society organizations with some methodological support from the NGO. Moreover, the plan that emerges has an officially negotiated status.

A second common feature was the establishment of a Municipal Council for Sustainable Rural Development (MCSRD) after the plans were documented. The councils are legally established under municipal law and are constitutionally responsible for implementing the plan by monitoring the process and thus holding the partners accountable to their commitments. They are also the entity where all aspects of municipal rural development policies and proposals for rural investment are discussed. The council is composed of representatives from the town council, councillors, agricultural/forestry extension and research services, CTA, STR and any women's groups or smallholder cooperatives that might exist. Following guidelines set by the National Council on Rural Sustainable Development, at least 50 per cent of the members represent smallholder agriculture (although this advice is not followed in all municipalities where councils are established).

The third commonality was the strong support given to farmers' organizations (the STRs and associations) by CTA. During all phases, CTA and the STRs and/or associations were in constant communication to ensure a strategy that would build local citizens' capacity to act as effective local protagonists in municipal debates and thus to use local government mechanisms to further pro-poor agendas. Various strategies were adopted to enable community representatives, with CTA financial support for transport in some cases, to participate in meetings. The participatory methodologies used were constructed to facilitate access by farmers to information and enable them to express their concerns in public fora. As an NGO, CTA is not providing information or doing the lobbying itself. Nor is it making the mistake of many NGOs of providing a parallel service to the poor by implementing development that should be the responsibility of the state. Instead, CTA has worked on trying out methodologies for planning and holding government accountable and encouraging cooperative relationships between government and citizens.

Despite these similarities, the differences were considerable between Araponga and Tombos in terms of their initial conditions and evolution. The initial motivation varied as did the number of initial partners. The catalytic moment and timing of each of the PRAs and subsequent municipal plans also varied. Local conditions and capacities moulded its role in each process.

These differences resulted in quite unique relationships between the STR movement and the public administration. In Araponga, where union leaders never held public office, conflict had marked the communications between the union and various administrations, interspersed with short-lived moments of convergence and dialogue. Overall, a cold silent distance had prevailed. Tombos, by contrast, had seen great highs and lows. Historically, the union had experienced intense conflicts with the public administrations. However, with the victory of the Workers' Party in 1998, the STR entered the municipal council, which coincided with the start of the LDP. This was short-lived, as the next elections in 2001 saw the Workers' Party removed from office. Relations were initially polarized but the union movement had gained considerable experience in governance and organizational issues. This enabled it to evolve towards a more responsible, less radical type of opposition that decreased antipathy and resistance between the municipal council and STR/APAT.

A second key difference is the unique identities of the plans. The MRDP of Araponga was viewed by the union movement mainly as an opportunity to hold the public administration accountable to earlier promises of policies and actions. The critical mass of ten years of experience with agro-ecological innovations played an important role in debates and in formulating concrete proposals. These self-help examples had enhanced smallholders' sense of independence from the vagaries of municipal policy and sense of the possible. The language was clearly one of communities conquering the odds to carve out better futures. Thus, during the LDP implementation farmers no longer accepted excuses such as 'This can't be done' or 'There isn't enough money' from public office holders.

Tombos did not have the benefit of years of agro-ecology. There, the municipal plan was grasped as an opportunity by the union movement to translate its flagship issues into public policies. Each of the sectors was considered in detail, although in the implementation more was achieved in agriculture than elsewhere, particularly in transport, processing and marketing.

KEY IMPACTS The key gains from the MRDP in Araponga begin with the valuable experience gained by the STR and CTA in working with divergent partners in the context of public policy formulation, an involvement that allowed CTA to show that it was more than a radical political group. Over the years, the STR has gained in respect and is now considered a legitimate civil society partner, hence the invitation in 2001 from the municipal council to participate in making a municipal plan and the STR as a key driver of the MCSRD. However, the implementation of the plan saw some impasses, particularly concerning state-level grants for farmers, and debates intensified on issues that the STR now dared to take on, such as alternative medicine.

Nevertheless, successive gains have been made in terms of alternative development approaches (e.g. the widespread adoption of organic agriculture) and initial data are showing the greater flexibility, autonomy, productivity and food security of the organic systems (Ferrari 2002). More generally, this opening of the policy process has encouraged a variety of further agencies to engage in this growing municipal partnership, including both state agencies such as agricultural research institutes, and a regional university through its work on environmental education in the municipal schools. In turn, organizational changes that permit more community voice to define policies and practices have been catalysed in these institutions.

Tombos experienced an entirely different trajectory, shaped by the decision to prioritize the creation of appropriate structures and partnerships and then formulate and implement the plan. As a first step, an Executive Committee was formed, with the STR, APAT (the local smallholder cooperative), CTA, Emater (state agricultural extension agency) and the Secretary of Agriculture. Rural development was prioritized over urban development issues, and thus the plan got its first focus. However, as implementation started, internal conflicts of interest within the public administration emerged that left many non-agricultural proposals in the municipal plan untouched and undebated. As a second term in office for the pro-STR councillors was looking increasingly unlikely, CTA successfully submitted a funding proposal to the InterAmerican Foundation so that the pro-poor municipal plan could continue to be implemented without the support of the incoming municipal council, who would not be favourably inclined towards the pro-poor agenda.

In 2000, a Convention was signed between the council (then still of the political left) and APAT, in which material resources were given by the council in exchange for services provided to smallholders. Although this mutual help relationship was to be of short duration, ending with municipal elections in 2001, it was exactly the support needed to kick-start the existence of APAT. The association took on a key leadership role in the LDP. APAT committee members quickly gained the capacity to deal with conflicts and complex political negotiations, mobilize political support strategically, and manage a commercial enterprise. This institutional growth gave it increasing credibility as a civil society partner in Tombos. In 2000, the women's municipal STR committee founded the Association of Women Farmers and Rural Workers in Tombos which also took up an important role in the LDP by focusing attention on women's income generation and training opportunities, and rural women's rights and political engagement.

As mentioned above, the 2000 municipal elections did not extend the term of the Workers' Party. The new mayor failed to respect the promises embedded in the formal municipal plan and annulled the agreements with CTA and APAT. While causing great anxiety at the time, current analysis by farmer leaders sees it as an opportunity to mature politically and focus on local development strategies that did not rely so heavily on the fragile seat of formal power. Since then (between September 2000 and June 2002), twenty-five new jobs have been created and the livelihoods of 682 farmers have been improved, in part through the establishment of a farmers' market (offering fair prices and a chance to sell what would otherwise have been lost). Moreover, in Tombos, the civic organizations involved have greatly increased their capacities, engaging with successively increased activities at each stage.

At a general level, the process of building partnerships, dealing with conflicts, appraisals and planning have built the political and methodological capacities of participants. Identifying municipal-level problems, acknowledging challenges and needs that afflict each community and organization, the debates resulting from confrontations between different interests and needs, and defining priorities represented a unique form of political education. This form of capacity-building, while not skill- or issue-specific, has been critical in ensuring continuity of the participatory spaces needed to implement the MRDP, as well as strengthening the management of and effectiveness of organizations involved in these participatory processes. There has arguably been an enhancing of political maturity in and between agencies of political and civic society, beyond the narrow party-bound perspective pervasive throughout Brazil, making viable what were hitherto unlikely partnerships, making the municipal council accountable, developing a collective vision, and increasing the scope of community-level action.

Nevertheless, key challenges remain. As with any political process, the road towards alternative development futures through governance reform is bumpy. Both municipalities continue to deal with political, organizational/institutional and financial challenges, although these are, by and large, recognized as a shared responsibility between previously divergent partners. The key political challenge in both cases examined here is to fulfil promises and to maintain alliances (despite the difficulties) and partnerships established during the planning process, and in so doing maintain a political space within which alternative development can be discussed and implemented. In Tombos, the movement is now facing the dilemma posed by the concentration of decision-making power and knowledge in the hands of a select group of very capable farmers' leaders and the reduction of opportunities for others to participate and develop strategic capacities. The main organizational challenge is to maintain the mechanisms by which households can continue participating in decision-making processes. Financially, Araponga and Tombos struggle with ensuring sufficient resources for the ongoing implementation of the plan.

One move that CTA has taken towards meeting these challenges has been to address concerns over the local embeddedness of the social change processes catalysed by the municipal development plans. CTA staff and some STR leaders were conscious of the ease with which an NGO-supported process could be perceived as 'not ours' by the smallholders in Tombos and Araponga. The shift in the mid-1990s from having STR-specific plans to a

TABLE 12.1 Lessons identified by CTA staff regarding LDP processes

Theme	Lessons learned
Municipal planning	• Initial conditions: it is critical to have a clear strategy for how farmers' organizations can influence the elaboration and implementation of municipal public policies that will be embodied in the plan. • Plan elaboration methodology: under different conditions of public power relations, the participatory methodology defines the autonomy of organizations and the continuity of the plan. • Leadership capacity-building: the training of leaders, specifically but not solely on public policy issues, can enhance the participation of their organizations.
Agro-ecology	• The existence of concrete experiences greatly facilitates its inclusion as a priority issue in the development plan. • The challenge and opportunity of an LDP process is the amplification of agro-ecology, as the plan makes existing experiences more visible. The opportunity lies in greater dissemination while the challenge hinges on finding a viable means to communicate this to a larger public and to integrate it into public policies. • Each municipality has its trajectory for initiation and amplification. In Tombos it was the farmers' market; in Araponga it was through common property use.
Partnerships	• It is critical to distinguish between tactical and strategic partnership alliances, and who is a partner and an ally. • Within an LDP process, it is essential to enlarge the partnership but also to ensure a cohesive partnership core. This nucleus guarantees continuity given the inherent uncertainty of public office holders and their processes. • Establishing partnership is a process of construction that hinges on trust, ideas and joint action.

development plan carried by a much larger group of municipal actors was precisely to increase the ownership base. The STRs and CTA were keen to avoid the LDP being seen as an artificial construction to obtain resources for short-term development, hoping instead it would be viewed as a long-term vision to guide local initiatives. To try and secure this, CTA staff facilitated meetings in each of the municipalities over three months and prepared an exchange weekend in Araponga with STR members. This collective reflection with municipal councillors and STR and other local leaders has worked towards developing a shared sense of what LDP represents and a broader sense of ownership. Investing in the collective understanding of participatory municipal planning helps to value the unique differences of each process, and thereby avoids the idea that there is a single formula or model that can be followed.

Conclusions

Participatory municipal-level planning in the municipalities of the Zona da Mata of Minas Gerais as discussed here is shaped by the dynamics of political process and the existing social and historical patterns of communication and domination. Of course, one says! But this is significant for those trying to standardize the experience into a set of steps, as will inevitably happen as efforts to scale up such localized experiences emerge. It cannot be 'methodologized' nor can a model be set down for others to follow. It thus confirms the critique that grew in the late 1990s about the routine, mechanical application of participation as a bag of tricks rather than as political awareness.

Nevertheless, the experiences in Araponga and Tombos have helped the CTA team to consolidate their understanding of how participatory development and strategic partnerships can support processes of democratic governance and alternative forms of development (see Table 11.1). Methodologies such as PRA that can drive 'visioning', problem appraisal and solution identification can contribute to participatory governance when given sufficient time, prepared well and embedded in an ongoing planning and implementation process. The embedding of any resulting plans in a supervisory and decision-making body in which formal government is one member alongside civil society in all its diversity gives it a public visibility that is hard to ignore. These components require the ongoing capacity-building of leadership, facilitation and negotiation skills. If an external organization is involved in capacity-building, it can take an example from CTA and aim at making itself a methodological or technical adviser, at most, thus leaving the process firmly in local hands.

The contribution of participatory methodologies to this process has been important but only to a degree. Any gains in formal political power should also not be overrated. For CTA and the STRs of Tombos and Araponga, occupying existing or self-created spaces of participation (cf. Cornwall 2002) does not necessarily mean that there is meaningful 'participation' that improves the lives of the poor. As Geovani, the STR leader in Tombos, commented on the new potential in Brazil for rural workers to have access to municipal-level structures and resources: 'We don't think that the municipal council will resolve our issues. It should be an instrument but if we don't fight then even Jesus Christ can't solve it.' Such fights must be pursued by the more political elements of civil society such as unions and social movements that are so often marginalized in international development debates. Development NGOs can support such processes with long-term investment in local capacities, but cannot do the fighting themselves.

Participation, including in Tombos and Araponga, is about conflict and learning. Dissent forms an opportunity for negotiation and therefore creative inputs in identifying actions. Not everything can be resolved by consensus. The LPD, with PRA as a critical ingredient alongside debate and capacity-building of young leaders, and strong alliances between civil and political society, confirms the original Freirean idea of democracy as fundamentally a pedagogic process. The learning is institutional – in people's organizations and in the seat of municipal power.

Notes

1 National Programme to Strengthen Smallholder Agriculture.

2 Sindicato dos Trabalhadores Rurais (Rural Workers' Union).

3 In Zona da Mata, 91.31 per cent of properties are between 0 and 100ha, corresponding with 140,748 properties, while 8.69 per cent of properties are larger than 100ha, with a total of 6,700 properties (IBGE 1997).

4 National Confederation of Agricultural Labourers/Central Workers' Union Confederation.

References

Cleaver, F. (2001) 'Institutions, Agency and the Limits of Participatory Approaches to Development', in B. Cooke and U. Kothari (eds), *Participation: The New Tyranny?* (London: Zed Books), pp. 36–55.

Cooke, B. and U. Kothari (2001) *Participation: The New Tyranny?* (London: Zed Books).

Cornwall, A. (2002) 'Making Spaces, Changing Places: Situating Participation in Development', *IDS Working Paper*, 170 (Brighton: Institute of Development Studies).

CTA (2001) 'Relatório do Diagnóstico Participativo do Município de Acaiaca, Viçosa, MG', in I. Cardoso, I. Guijt et al., 'Continual Learning for Agro-forestry System Design: University, NGO and Farmer Partnership in Minas Gerais, Brazil', *Agricultural Systems*, 69: 235–57.

— (2002) *Revista 15 Anos CTA* (Viçosa: CTA), p. 26.

Fária, A. A. d. C. (1994) *Uma Visão do Município de Araponga, Minas Gerais. Informações sobre o diagnóstico realizado* (Viçosa: CTA), p. 41.

Ferrari, E. A. (2002) 'Monitoramento de impactos econômicos de práticas agroecológicas', presented at a Workshop on 'Métodos e Experiências Inovadoras de Monitoramento de Projetos de Desenvolvimento Sustentável', Brasília.

Francis, P. (2001) 'Participatory Development at the World Bank: The Primacy of Process', in B. Cooke and U. Kothari (eds), *Participation: The New Tyranny?* (London: Zed Books), pp. 72–87.

IBGE (Fudação Instituto Brasileiro de Geografia e Estatística (1997) *Censo Demográfico, 1996* (Rio de Janeiro: IBGE).

Leeuwis, C. (2000) 'Reconceptualizing Participation for Sustainable Rural Development. Towards a Negotiation Approach', *Development and Change*, 31 (5): 931–59.

Marcondes de Moraes, M. S. (2002) 'Closure Report: Projeto de Desenvolvimento Rural Sustentável para o Município de Tombos (MG), baseado no fortalecimento da Agricultura Familiar (Agreement BR-778)' (Rio de Janeiro: InterAmerican Foundation), p. 15.

13 | Confrontations with power: moving beyond 'the tyranny of safety' in participation

UTE KELLY

A key problem that critiques of 'participatory development' have highlighted is its potential to reinforce rather than challenge power relations, and thus to fall short of its own declared goal of 'empowerment' (Cooke and Kothari 2001). Analyses have drawn attention both to the wider context – the depoliticization that accompanies the valorization of the personal, the local and 'the community' – and to the dynamics of particular instances of participation that reinforce existing privileges and discourage an articulation of subordinate perspectives.

This chapter suggests that in order to understand and move beyond this failure, we need to look at what I call 'the tyranny of safety'. What might an approach that avoids this particular tyranny look like? I will argue that it is worth looking for clues in the work of the School for Peace in Neve Shalom/Wahat al-Salam in Israel, which explicitly focuses on power relations within participatory processes of engagement between opposing factions. To further support this argument, I will consider the UK Commission on Poverty, Participation and Power as an example of how an analysis derived from the School for Peace may resonate more widely. Drawing on these practical examples, I will suggest a number of ways forward for transformatory forms of participation, while also noting potential problems for further reflection.

The focus in much of this chapter on the micro-level of participation is not meant to suggest that this is the only level at which repoliticization can or should take place. Instead, it should be read within the context set in Part II of this volume, particularly the insistence that participation be linked to broader political projects. And yet, if we are interested in transformation, an understanding of 'micropolitics' (Connolly 2002: 20) is crucial. What happens (and what does not happen) at the micro-level has implications for broader structural processes (Kothari 2001). This chapter, then, is intended as one response to Cornwall's (2002: 28) suggestion that '[m]ore micro-level research is required if we are to understand which forms of participation work in which kinds of spaces to provide people with opportunities to realise inclusive, active citizenship'.

'The tyranny of safety'

Many instances of 'participation' are attempts to create spaces for discussion that feel 'safe' for participants. Sometimes, this is explicit: clear ground rules, for example, seek to encourage an atmosphere of mutual respect and to preclude potentially offensive statements. A concern for this kind of 'safety' is understandable, and questioning its desirability may seem counter-intuitive. After all, the intention is to create an atmosphere in which people feel free both to express and to change their views. And yet, the unease that Cooke and Kothari (2001) identified is also being felt by people who have organized or participated in 'safe spaces'. Perhaps most seriously, there is a feeling that the emphasis on safety discourages precisely the kind of open, honest discussion that it attempts to facilitate.

To understand why and how this happens, it is worth considering a more implicit desire for 'safety': consciously or otherwise, people collaborate to sustain particular discourses, identities and self-images, even if they privately know that these are problematic (Goffman 1990a, 1990b; Cooke 2001; Kothari 2001). This tendency is part of everyday life, shaping individual personalities and social interactions as well as social structures (Goffman 1990a). In terms of social interaction, 'playing it safe' means sustaining performances, roles and 'definitions of the situation' that participants have got used to. Views at odds with the accepted parameters are unlikely to find expression, particularly in situations where participants are expected to avoid offending each other's sensibilities. This collaboration to 'save face', however, is not necessarily equally desirable for all participants. At the level of personal identity, people may privately adopt a range of positions in relation to their public performances (Goffman 1990a, 1990b). I would suggest that 'safe' social interactions are likely to be most comfortable for participants whose self-image and attitudes overlap with their publicly-performed roles, and most dissatisfactory for those who experience a dissonance between the two. For the former, the emphasis on safety allows them to maintain their self-image and the roles they are used to playing. For the latter, it is likely to be frustrating precisely because it encourages stability rather than change. At this point, the level of social structure becomes significant. As Goffman (1990a: 235) suggests, social interactions can also be interpreted as a test of the legitimacy of the wider social units that individuals or groups represent. While 'successful' performances reinforce wider social structures, disruptions may have consequences that go beyond the immediate context in which they occur.[1]

This brief outline of how 'safety' can impede transformation raises an important question: are these problems inherent in participation generally? Or can we envisage forms of participation that manage to avoid 'the tyranny of safety' and allow the disruptions that are arguably required to effect transformations at any or all of the levels of social interaction, individual identity and social structure?

The School for Peace approach

It is worth looking for clues in the work of the School for Peace in Neve Shalom/Wahat al-Salam. Founded in 1979 to facilitate encounters between Jewish and Palestinian[2] Israelis, the School for Peace started with an approach that had two main features: it was psychologically oriented, and it focused on exchanges between individuals (Suleiman 2001). This had significant effects. Most importantly, it depoliticized encounters. As long as the latter focused mainly on inter-personal relationships, it was relatively easy to avoid political discussions, a problem characteristic of the methodological individualism of many participatory approaches (Francis 2001). This observation, moreover, has to be viewed in the context of a second recurring dynamic: '[T]he Palestinian participants usually attempt to bring group-specific and political themes to the discussion ... On the other hand the Jewish participants generally react to the attempt to provoke a political dialogue with rejection; for their part, they try to direct the attention of the group to themes related to personal, individual experiences' (Suleiman 2001: 39–40)

It is worth considering the dynamics of such encounters from the perspective of 'safety': among the dominant Jewish group 'the willingness to open up personal experiences for discussion, to admit personal deficits and to express doubts' – all forms of behaviour that proponents both of 'safe spaces' and of PRA (Chambers 1997) are trying to encourage – 'is much stronger' (ibid., p. 40). The same participants, however, tend to 'shrink back from current political topics that they see as explosive or disturbing to the dialogue' (ibid.) – in other words, from forms of interaction that they do not experience as 'safe'. For Palestinian participants, the reverse is the case. While they are more likely to bring up political issues at the inter-group level, they are less likely to admit any differences between themselves to the other group (ibid.). For the members of less powerful minority groups, then, it is not 'safe' to break ranks or show uncertainty.

As Suleiman (2001: 37) suggests, the dynamics of such groups 'represent a kind of "microcosm"' of wider society, and thus of the structures and processes that reinforce existing power relations. It was precisely this conclusion that prompted staff at the School for Peace to start experimenting with a different approach. Today, their work is based on the following premises (Halabi and Sonnenschein 2001: 55–8):

- The conflict between Palestinians and Jewish Israelis is a conflict between groups, not between indsividuals. The encounter emphasizes the inter-group rather than the inter-personal level. This is reflected, for example, in the encouragement given to all participants to speak in their own languages, and in the practice of 'uninational forums', in which each group meets separately to understand and react to the inter-group process, and to air internal differences that it does not want to share with the other group (Sonnenschein and Hijazi 2001).
- The convictions that shape people's identities and behaviour – including their feelings of superiority/inferiority – are deeply rooted, largely subconscious, and relatively resistant to change. The encounter aims to make these deep-seated ideas visible to the participants to enable them to examine and ultimately transform them. All encounters are accompanied by a Jewish and a Palestinian facilitator, who have previously experienced the encounter process themselves, and who help participants to understand what is happening.
- The group encounter is a microcosm of wider reality, the basic patterns of which are reflected in small-scale encounters and individual identities. The encounter does not, however, simply replicate reality. Instead, it encourages processes among the participants that increase their awareness of this reality, and of what needs to happen more widely if real change is to take place.

These ways of working have significant effects. Typically, encounters go through different phases (Halabi et al. 2001; Halabi 2001a):

- In phase 1, participants 'play it safe'. They are careful, polite, and trying to work out what to expect. The Jewish participants favour interactions at the inter-personal level and attempt to resist the idea of an inter-group encounter.
- In phase 2, the Palestinian group becomes stronger. It starts to raise political issues, on which it tends to express common positions. The style in which these issues are raised is confrontational – demanding rights rather than asking for favours. For the Jewish participants, this is a difficult experience. The accusations of oppression directed at them challenge their liberal self-image. They feel threatened and sense a loss of control over the situation.
- From this feeling of frustration, the Jewish group attempts, in phase 3, to regain its dominant status. It does this through various means: steering the interaction back to the inter-personal level, pointing out the complexities of the conflict, and questioning the Palestinians' ethics and humanity. As a result, group dynamics change: it is now the Palestinians

who feel undermined, while the Jewish group seems to have regained control.

- In phase 4, the encounter seems to have reached a deadlock. Both groups feel pessimistic about continuing the dialogue.
- Phase 5 sees a breakthrough. This becomes possible when some of the Jewish participants acknowledge their own powerful position and thus respond to the earlier challenges from the Palestinian group. From this point, the dialogue becomes more honest. Power relations between the groups are out in the open and, on the basis of this recognition, a new kind of political dialogue becomes possible. Differences within each group are more openly discussed, and participants genuinely engage with the conflict.
- While dynamics within the encounter change in this final phase, however, participants are acutely aware of the reality outside. Both Jews and Palestinians 'have become more conscious. But the Jews are happy and proud of their consciousness, while the Arabs have become quite pessimistic in the light of this consciousness' (Jewish participant, in Halabi et al. 2001: 81). For the Palestinian participants, after all, it is the reality outside that needs to change, and that remains unaffected by what has happened in the encounter.

This last observation makes it necessary to be realistic about the nature and scope of this type of work. School for Peace staff know that 'in the end, one can only change reality through social and political action. Our encounter group is an educational process and as such limited in its potential to change the face of society' (Halabi and Sonnenschein 2001: 61).

The educational process does encourage transformations, but those transformations are changes in individuals. At the same time, however, the process that happens between the two groups exemplifies what needs to happen if the wider reality of the conflict is to be transformed: '[A]n essential change in Arab–Jewish relations will occur only when the Arabs are sufficiently empowered to assertively demand their rights. The majority – in the room as well as in society – will not surrender its position of strength simply on the basis of good will, generosity or liberal ideas' (Halabi 1999).

The necessary transformations are not 'safe' at any of the three levels of the individual, social interactions or social structures: at the individual level, the process causes 'pain, frustration and disappointment' (Halabi and Sonnenschein 2001: 63) and involves 'working through guilt and shame' (Zak 1999) and 'emotional distress' (Shahar 1999). It demands that participants confront aspects of their own identities that are normally safe from examination. At the level of social interactions within the encounter, 'safety' is undermined by the suspension of 'normal' mechanisms of control. The more dominant group is denied the powers it is used to: 'The power to dictate the essential nature of the interpersonal connection; the power to legislate the rules that would say what was forbidden and what permitted in a relationship; the power to dictate the agenda for the relationship' (Shahar 1999). The less powerful group, on the other hand, needs to break out of a 'safe' mode of interaction, to stop censoring itself, and to become assertive and even aggressive in its demands (Halabi et al. 2001; Halabi 2002). Nor are the implications for the wider social structures 'safe': the conclusion that powerful groups 'will not surrender [their] position of strength simply on the basis of good will, generosity or liberal ideas' implies the need for far greater – and far less manageable – transformations than dominant groups may be prepared to countenance (Halabi 1999, 2001a).

The Commission on Poverty, Participation and Power

The School of Peace's attempt to move beyond the 'tyranny of safety' within dialogical encounters offers a basis for reflection on participatory processes more generally. The following shows how one innovative experiment in bridging the gap between people experiencing poverty and the processes of decision-making that affect them mirrored processes observed at the School for Peace. The Commission on Poverty, Participation and Power was set up by the UK Coalition Against Poverty in 1999 and supported by Oxfam and the Joseph Rowntree Foundation. It brought six 'grassroots' and six 'public life' commissioners together over a period of nearly a year and gave them the task of 'examin[ing] why people experiencing poverty do not influence decision-making and policy' (de Tufo and Gaster 2002: 1).

It is worth looking at what happened in the commission in the light of the issues raised above. The commission, of course, was never intended as an encounter between groups in conflict. On the contrary: the twelve commissioners were described as 'people with different kinds of expertise and knowledge all sharing the same commitment and passion' (ibid., p. 1). And yet, they were seen as representing two different groups of people: people with direct experience of living in poverty on the one hand, and people 'recruited for ... their practical, political and theoretical knowledge of poverty' (ibid., p. 3) on the other. At a second viewing, this is not dissimilar from participants at the School for Peace, where the people who are most likely to take part in encounters – especially on the Jewish side – identify themselves as liberal and on the political left, 'so that for a moment it looks as if there is no conflict at all. In the further development of the conversation, though, it becomes clear that the situation is more complex' (Halab et al. 2001: 72). The evaluation of the Commission on Poverty, Participation and Power suggests that it, too, was more complex.

Initially, commissioners from both 'groups' felt uncertain about the nature of the process they were about to be involved in. In this first phase, several interesting things happened: although a 'commitment to working in a participatory and inclusive manner' had been one of the criteria for the selection of commissioners, the efforts of an Oxfam facilitator to run a participatory exercise were resisted by a public life commissioner. A grassroots commissioner who suggested informal seating arrangements 'was snubbed', and the group adopted a formal layout (de Tufo and Gaster 2002: 24). After this first meeting, a public life commissioner suggested that staff should *'[l]et the commissioners decide how to tackle the agenda and workload and whether to use facilitators once we've agreed'* (ibid.).[3] Commissioners subsequently agreed to work in plenary sessions and asked one of the staff members to act as a 'neutral' chair. Chairing, however, proved difficult, and '[s]ometimes grass roots commissioners were ignored and were aware of this' (ibid.).

Arguably, this first phase of the commission parallels the first of the phases typical at the School for Peace: uncertainty about what to expect, but also subtle, and not necessarily conscious, attempts by members of the dominant group to set the framework (ibid., p. 34). The suggestion that the setting was unequal is also supported by the observation that 'the grass roots people had to learn public life commissioners' "language", and feared that they were losing touch with their roots in the process', while '[n]o "public life" commissioner made a similar comment' (ibid.). At the same time, some public life commissioners consciously held back, with the result that, ironically, they themselves *'felt quite silenced by some of the more assertive "grass roots" members'* (ibid.). The experience of the early meetings, then, was unsatisfactory for most participants.

Reflecting on this early phase, several grassroots commissioners commented that it had made them *'angry that the real problems were not being discussed'* (ibid., p. 34). At the third meeting, 'a grass roots commissioner felt so strongly that the public life commissioners did not understand where she was coming from that she made a presentation about the situation in her area and her own experience'. This included an attack on a group of people that the public life commissioners probably fell into: 'The cabs ... are jammed in the evening with people who work there, but who don't live there, going home. We have lost confidence in people coming in and driving out again' (ibid.).

At the next meeting, 'there was a "cathartic" confrontation between a grass roots and a public life commissioner' (ibid., p. 38). These confrontations, in turn, generated angry responses by at least some of the public life commissioners (ibid., p. 36). At the same time, however, they produced reflections on the differences between the two groups. One public life commissioner realized at this point that

> these meetings couldn't be 'done' in the normal way ... I had to put the whole of myself into the process and be willing to challenge others – not to be an unemotional academic or professional ... I realised that there was a big difference between myself as a public life commissioner and the grass roots: I can go back to a comfortable home and, if the Commission fails, it won't affect my life. This is totally different from [the grass roots commissioner]'s position. (ibid., p. 37)

Again, what happened can be interpreted against the background of processes observed at the School for Peace: the second phase involved the less powerful group coming together to confront the dominant group. This happened after some of the grassroots commissioners had discussed the situation among themselves and found that they were '*all talking the same language*' (grassroots commissioner, ibid.). The open confrontation, which clearly put people into two categories, was not an easy experience for either group: '*People were shattered*' and '*quite battered in both groups*' (ibid., p. 37). And yet, 'painful though it was at the time, the air was cleared. Grass roots commissioners became less "careful" and more willing to speak their mind. The public life commissioners were perceived as changing, the power balance moved and the group came together more' (ibid., p. 38).

Perhaps some of the phases that typically occur at the School for Peace – the reassertion of power by the dominant group and the feeling of deadlock – were not as pronounced in the commission, but the overall process looks remarkably similar. The most significant aspect was a shift from a situation of inequality towards one that, if not perfect, came closer to an equalization of power relations within the encounter: an equalization of respect, of the chance to speak and the obligation to listen, of opportunities to influence the agenda. This shift, moreover, could not have happened without a confrontation that was painful and that did not feel 'safe'. Lastly, however, and even though a shift in power did occur within the group of commissioners, it is important to recognize that outside realities had not changed. Public life commissioners could '*go back to a comfortable home*' (ibid., p. 37), while grassroots commissioners had no choice but to keep facing the realities of poverty, participation and power.[4]

It seems to have been partly the experience of the commission itself that led its members to conclude that: '[T]he main problem is that too often people experiencing poverty don't feel respected. Too often they aren't respected. And what is the ultimate disrespect? Being involved in phoney participation, by people who don't listen, when things don't change. Phoney because it doesn't lead to a shift in power' (Commission on Poverty, Participation and Power 2000b: 1).

Shifts in power are not 'safe'. They are difficult processes, both for those who attempt to 'empower' themselves, and for those who have to surrender some of their power. They are difficult for individuals because they entail profound and potentially threatening challenges to their identities. They are even more difficult – and no more 'safe' – in their implications for wider social structures. And yet, if we do not challenge 'the tyranny of safety', participation is likely to remain 'phoney'.

'Non-phoney' participation: some pointers

A series of insights can be drawn from the above discussion that offer clues concerning how to develop forms of participation that are not 'phoney' or, put positively, that are consistent with a commitment to the transformation of conflict and inequality.

First, I would suggest that we perceive inequality as a form of asymmetrical conflict: a conflict that is located at the structural rather than the inter-personal level, and a conflict in which power is unevenly distributed.

If participation is to be emancipatory rather than tyrannical, conflicts and inequalities need to be expressed openly and honestly, even if this means confrontation rather than consensus-building, even if it implies the destruction of an initially cooperative atmosphere, and even if, in the short term at least, it seems to lead to a breakdown in communication.

In terms of the level of transformation, a serious examination of structural power relations is unlikely to happen at the level of inter-personal interactions, or if only one 'side' of the conflict participates. Treating individuals only as individuals – and 'people [only] as people' (Chambers 1997: 188) – depoliticizes their experiences and ultimately favours members of more powerful groups (Commission on Poverty, Participation and Power 2000a: 10). At the intergroup level, however, systematic power relations become visible and thus potentially open to transformation, especially if participants are encouraged to reflect on the group dynamics that drive the processes they go through without escaping from what is happening (Halabi and Philipps-Heck 2001).

A focus on the intergroup level also implies rethinking the common format of professional individuals facilitating group discussions among 'local people' – a format that is likely to protect facilitators and the groups they belong to from critical interrogation. As the experience of the Commission on Poverty, Participation and Power demonstrates, the participation of professionals as a group has important effects for the kinds of issues that are likely to be problematized. The School for Peace's work, moreover, suggests that to create an atmosphere in which greater equality becomes possible, it is helpful to have facilitators who are not 'neutral outsiders' but who have experienced the tensions and unequal power relations being explored.

Encounters designed to confront unequal power relations take longer than the brief engagements that typify much of what passes for participatory practice. Confrontation seems to be necessary in order to do so, but giving up when reaching a deadlock would be destructive. The goal, after all, is to get to a situation in which serious, meaningful dialogue becomes possible. For groups in asymmetrical conflict, there do not seem to be shortcuts to this situation.

Overall, these findings support the emerging finding that a key danger for discourses of participation, dialogue and empowerment is that they claim more than they can deliver and thus risk being criticized for not doing what they cannot be expected to do (see Williams, this volume). While this is not necessarily a reason to abandon them, it is a reason to be realistic about what they can and cannot achieve. Particular instances of participation, by themselves, cannot change an unequal reality, and '[t]he crucial transformative dimension requires more than just arguing' (Kohn 2000: 424). The transformatory potential of approaches to participation, then, is related to the extent to which they encourage a serious engagement with power relations, both by those who have the highest stakes in their transformation and by those who benefit from their maintenance – and this is something they can and should do.

Remaining questions

I have argued for the exploration of a different approach to participation. If such an exploration is to be serious, it also needs to consider potential problem areas. At the end of this discussion, therefore, I would like to share some tentative reflections on what these problem areas might be. These are meant to be not an exhaustive list but some pointers to stimulate further discussion.

The complexity of power One of the conclusions of *Participation: The New Tyranny?* was that the starting-point for efforts to 'rescue' the idea of non-tyrannical participation should be 'a more sophisticated and genuinely reflexive understanding of power' (Cooke and Kothari 2001: 14–15). Arguably, the approach I have suggested would contribute to the self-examination of participation professionals that Cooke and Kothari called for. It would go beyond the comfortable assumption of the 'harmony model of power' (Mohan and Stokke 2000: 249) and challenge the reassuring idea that 'disempowerment', after all, is fun even for those who experience it (Chambers 1997: 235–6).

It is less clear, however, whether it fits as easily with the recognition that power relations are complex and multi-layered. Focusing on clearly identifiable groups is ambiguous: it inevitably makes some power relations visible while hiding others. On the other hand, over-emphasizing complexity can be an avoidance mechanism that distracts attention away from inequalities that do exist. The School for Peace tries to balance the two through its mechanism of 'uninational forums', in which conflicts, differences and inequalities among members of 'the same group' can be problematized (Sonnenschein and Hijazi 2001). Even the 'uninational forum', of course, is part of the overall focus on the one main conflict; it is hard to see, however, how power relations could be challenged if the idea of groups in conflict is deconstructed to such an extent that all that is left are individuals (and thus the dynamics of inter-personal interactions that can prevent an examination of power). A pressing issue remains, then, concerning how to encourage an examination of power that is neither simplistic nor paralysing and escapist (see Masaki, this volume).

The ambiguity of strengthening group identities Strengthening group identities appears to be a necessary stage on the way towards greater equality (Halabi 2001a, 2001b). It is not easy to reconcile this emphasis on group identities with the recognition that no 'community' is homogeneous, and that some identities are themselves part of the problem rather than the solution. Nor is it clear whether a model developed in the context of a conflict between two ethnic/national groups is equally appropriate to the conditions of material inequality that pervade development contexts. For example, (how) do inter-group dynamics change when the identities concerned are based on class or gender? Are the desired transformations of such identities comparable or fundamentally different?

The power of facilitation The School for Peace's work accords a central role to facilitators who structure encounters in ways that encourage transformation. This in itself is a form of power – the power to pre-determine, to some significant extent, what will happen in the encounter, with all the consequences this has for participants. It is important to keep examining the implications of this power. Perhaps the only way forwards, though, is the recognition that it is impossible to escape to a pure space beyond power (Foucault 1977; Kesby 2003; Bennett and Shapiro 2002). If this is true, 'we have no choice but to draw upon *less* dominating forms of power to destabilize and transform *more* dominating frameworks of power'. The key question, then, 'is not whether participation is a form of power and hence should be resisted, but whether participation is a form of power that might also be able to frame and organise resistance' (Kesby 2003: 15) – a question with which advocates of participation must continually engage.

'The tyranny of safety'... Lastly, it is worth remembering that 'the tyranny of safety', which appears to pervade much participatory practice, militates against experiments with more confrontational approaches (although see Waddington and Mohan, this volume). Who, in the field of development and elsewhere, would dare to try approaches that are deeply challenging to members of privileged groups – including many development practitioners and advocates of participation themselves? Are we willing to take the risks, and to accept that transformatory approaches are much more likely to be painful and difficult than safe and enjoyable?

In this context, it is worth remembering that, to the extent that participatory approaches have been mainstreamed, 'the dominant approaches in the field have for the most part been created by researchers belonging to the ruling side. It seems reasonable that these people would try to construct a world-view that would make things easier for them and help them sustain the society's status quo' (Zak 1999).

At present, too few participatory encounters bring together groups from across the divisions of power that sustain exclusion and subordination with the explicit aim of challenging these unequal power relations, despite the likelihood that it is in such encounters that the basis for transformation can be found. What, then, would a re-emphasis on truly transformatory practices imply for the fields of development and participation themselves? Who is prepared to move beyond 'the tyranny of safety'?

Notes

1 For some examples, see Sanderson (1999).

2 A note on terminology: in Israel, Palestinians with Israeli citizenship are often referred to as 'Israeli Arabs'. This is also apparent in much of the literature by and on the School for Peace – as reflected in quotes used in this paper. Here, I use the term 'Palestinian', in line with the actual approach and goals of the School for Peace.

3 I have used italics in this section to indicate comments from commissioners rather than evaluators.

4 This last observation indicates that if we are genuinely interested in transformation, we need to go beyond shifts in power that are made possible by, but then remain limited to, 'fleeting formations' (Cornwall 2002: 19).

References

Bennett, J. and M. Shapiro (eds) (2002) *The Politics of Moralizing* (London: Routledge).

Chambers, R. (1997) *Whose Reality Counts? Putting the First Last* (London: ITDG Publishing).

Commission on Poverty, Participation and Power (2000a) *Listen Hear. The Right to be Heard. Report of the Commission on Poverty, Participation and Power* (London: Policy Press/UKCAP/Joseph Rowntree Foundation).

— (2000b) *Listen Hear. Summary* (London: Policy Press/UKCAP/Joseph Rowntree Foundation).

Connolly, W. (2002) *Neuropolitics. Thinking, Culture, Speed* (London: University of Minnesota Press).

Cooke, B. (2001) 'The Social Psychological Limits of Participation?', in B. Cooke and U. Kothari (eds), *Participation: The New Tyranny?* (London: Zed Books), pp. 102–21.

Cooke, B. and U. Kothari (2001) 'The Case for Participation as Tyranny', in B. Cooke and U. Kothari (eds), *Participation: The New Tyranny?* (London: Zed Books), pp. 1–15.

Cornwall, A. (2002) 'Making Spaces, Changing Places: Situating Participation in Development', *IDS Working Paper*, 170 (Brighton: Institute of Development Studies).

de Tufo, S. and L. Gaster (2002) *Evaluation of the Commission on Poverty, Participation and Power* (York: Joseph Rowntree Foundation).

Foucault, M. (1977) *Discipline and Punish. The Birth of the Prison* (London: Penguin Books).

Francis, P. (2001) 'Participatory Development at the World Bank: The Primacy of Process', in B. Cooke and U. Kothari (eds), *Participation: The New Tyranny?* (London: Zed Books), pp. 72–87.

Givon, S. and O. Ighbariya (1999) 'Aspiring to Equality in an Unequal Reality', *The School for Peace Web Article Series*. <http://www.nswas.com/sfp/articles/equality99.htm>

Goffman, E. (1990a) [1959] *The Presentation of Self in Everyday Life* (London: Penguin Books).

— (1990b) [1963] *Stigma. Notes on the Management of Spoiled Identity* (London: Penguin Books).

Halabi, R. (1999) 'Working with Conflict Groups: The Educational Approach of the School for Peace', Neve Shalom/Wahat al-Salam: *The School for Peace Web Article Series*. <http://www.nswas.com/sfp/updates/confgrps.htm>

— (2001a) 'Arab–Jewish Relations Since the Intifada', Neve Shalom/Wahat al-Salam: *The School for Peace Web Article Series*. <http://www.nswas.com/sfp/articles/reality.htm>

— (2001b) 'Die Ausbildung der Begleiter', in R. Halabi and U. Philipps-Heck (eds), *Identitäten im Dialog*, pp. 85–105.

— (2002) 'First Findings from the Research Institute', Neve Shalom/Wahat al Salam: *The School for Peace Web Article Series*. <http://www.nswas.com/sfp/articles/research.htm>

Halabi, R. and U. Philipps-Heck (eds) (2001) *Identitäten im Dialog. Konfliktintervention in der Friedensschule von Neve Schalom/Wahat al-Salam in Israel*, trans. M. Weiß and U. Philipps-Heck (Schwalbach: Wochenschau Verlag).

Halabi, R. and N. Sonnenschein (2001) 'Wie wir an unsere Arbeit herangehen', in R. Halabi and U. Philipps-Heck (eds), *Identitäten im Dialog*, pp. 52–63.

Halabi, R., N. Sonnenschein and A. Friedman (2001) 'Universitätskurse zum jüdisch-arabischen Konflikt', in R. Halabi and U. Philipps-Heck (eds), *Identitäten im Dialog*, pp. 64–84.

Hijazi, A. (2001) 'Working While Arab', Neve Shalom/Wahat al-Salam: *The School for Peace Web Article Series*. <http://www.nswas.com/sfp/articles/working.htm>

Ighbariya, O. (1999) 'Between a Rock and a Hard Place', Neve Shalom/Wahat al-Salam: *The School for Peace Web Article Series*. <http://www.nswas.com/sfp/articles/between_a_rock_and_a_hard_place.htm>

Kesby, M. (2003) 'Tyrannies of Transformation: A Post-Structural and Spatialised Understanding of Empowerment Through Participation', Paper presented at the conference 'Participation: From Tyranny to Transformation? Exploring New Approaches to Participation in Development', Manchester, IDPM, February 2003. <http://idpm.man.ac.uk/partconfKesby.pdf>

Kohn, M. (2000) 'Language, Power, and Persuasion: Toward a Critique of Deliberative Democracy', *Constellations*, 7 (3): 408–29.

Kothari, U. (2001) 'Power, Knowledge and Social Control in Participatory Development', in B. Cooke and U. Kothari (eds), *Participation: The New Tyranny?* (London: Zed Books), pp. 139–52.

Mohan, G. and K. Stokke (2000) 'Participatory Development and Empowerment: The Dangers of Localism', *Third World Quarterly* 21 (2): 247–68.

Sanderson, I. (1999) 'Participation and Democratic Renewal: From "Instrumental" to "Communicative Rationality"?', *Policy and Politics*, 27 (3): 325–39.

Shahar, G. (1999) 'The Politics of Emotional Distress in a Jewish–Arab Group', Neve Shalom/Wahat al-Salam: *The School for Peace Web Article Series*. <http://www.nswas.com/sfp/articles/politics_of_emotional_distress.htm>

Sonnenschein, N. and A. Hijazi (2001) 'Das uni-nationale Forum', in R. Halabi and U. Philipps-Heck (eds), *Identitäten im Dialog*, pp. 177–98.

Suleiman, R. (2001) 'Vorstrukturierte Encountergruppen mit jüdischen und palästinensischen Israelis – ein Mikrokosmos', in R. Halabi and U. Philipps-Heck (eds), *Identitäten im Dialog*, pp. 33–51.

Zak, M. (1999) 'Working Through Guilt and Shame', Neve Shalom/Wahat al-Salam: *The School for Peace Web Article Series*. <http://www.nswas.com/sfp/articles/working_through_guilt_and_shame.htm>

Zak, M. and R. Halabi (2001) 'Das Begleiten von Begegnungen gemeinsam mit einem Partner', in R. Halabi and U. Philipps-Heck (eds), *Identitäten im Dialog*, pp. 157–76.

14 | Failing forward: going beyond PRA and imposed forms of participation

MARK WADDINGTON AND GILES MOHAN

Over the past few years, approaches to participatory development and appraisal, especially Participatory Rural Appraisal (PRA), have come under concerted critique (Richards 1995; Cooke and Kothari 2001). This chapter outlines the way in which Village AiD,[1] a small UK NGO, is attempting to move beyond these critiques. In particular we show how they are attempting to go beyond the limited realm of imminent development interventions and discussion of methodological innovation to wider questions of immanent development and the ways of challenging embedded structures of exclusion (Hickey 2002; Mohan 2001). This bridging is being achieved in different ways through the exercise of citizenship via, wherever possible, indigenous institutions. Like any institutions these are not static and 'traditional', but embroiled in processes of ongoing modernity and exchange, of which Village AiD is but one actor.

This chapter outlines and analyses approaches to participation, political literacy, and citizenship building in Village AiD's programmes in West Africa. It begins with a sympathetic critique of PRA by showing how the political economy of development generates systemic inequalities in NGO management and how they shape more specific limitations around its cognitive assumptions, the management of information and the role played by facilitators. We argue that these problems undermine the value of PRA and, with it, the effectiveness of participatory development. We then go on to describe and analyse a number of programmes led by Village AiD in Ghana and Sierra Leone which work within a PRA paradigm, but place far greater emphasis on local facilitation methods and decision-making systems. We outline the evolution of these approaches, assess their impacts in terms of transformatory empowerment, and critically reflect on their strengths and weaknesses. We conclude by looking briefly at the ways in which the insights generated by these experiences – that the exercise of citizenship rights is a potent means of addressing poverty – can be taken forward.

The disappointments of participation and PRA

In the past five years, plenty has been written on the potentials and pitfalls of participatory learning and development (Mohan 1999; Nelson and Wright 1995; Chambers 1997; Blackburn and Holland 1998; Cooke and Kothari 2001). Our argument is twofold. First, that participation as circumscribed intervention is unlikely to yield sustainable benefits due to wider processes of economic and political exclusion (Kumar and Corbridge 2002). Furthermore, the political economy of the aid industry has tended to reflect these inequalities by treating those in the South as junior partners. This ultimately disempowers people and groups as a force in preventing the realization of active citizenship. Second, while we are broadly sympathetic to the use of PRA, the weaknesses largely stem from the broader management structures in which participatory development occurs. From these systemic issues further problems emerge – the cognitive assumptions of PRA tools and the political role of the facilitator. These can be self-reinforcing, but the lesson is that any attempt at transformatory participation needs not simply to tamper with the methodologies, but look at ways of challenging these broader structures through a range of political strategies across different scales. It is these evolving strategies that are discussed in the case study.

Systemic problems in the political economy of development The problems of using PRA within participatory development stem from the nature of both immanent and imminent development, although there is no singular causal link between these two realms of material and political power. Ngunjiri (1998) and Hintjens (1999) have raised questions regarding the political economy of development institutions and looked at how this structures imminent interventions. Hintjens (1999) examined the way in which aid and, more broadly, charitable conditionality structures the poor out of decision-making by defining them as beneficiaries in the worst sense of the term. Taking this to the micro-level, Ngunjiri (1998) argued that most participatory development begins by stigmatizing local communities as having a 'problem' as opposed to seeing communities endowed with many positive assets. The strong forces that push people and their communities into accepting their weak and impotent location is a fundamental driving force in shaping relationships and partnerships with the development organizations that work with them. Dependency rather than empowerment is the inevitable outcome.

In this way, the purpose of participation, almost unconsciously, is used to legitimize what development agents can offer rather than allowing people to exercise their own decision-making powers. Such development management affects the recruitment of facilitators, the pedagogy of the training paradigm, the nature of planning and monitoring, and the criteria, conditions and policies of funders. In the remainder of this section we want to unpack a little more the effects of these processes on the development interface.

Being able to stand back from reality and generate new perspectives is fundamental to PRA. But it is implicitly assumed that such processes do not occur in communities – otherwise why bring such a process to them? Imported participatory exercises often override existing and potentially legitimate forms of decision-making. Such assumptions inevitably make any PRA process an imposed means of facilitating participation in knowledge construction, analysis and decision-making. Likewise, the way in which information, analysis and decisions are communicated among people, as well as to external development agents such as NGOs, is constrained by the tools that are brought and imposed upon people.

SNGOs often recruit facilitators from the community, or even recruit them externally and impose them. Because the SNGO is providing financial support to facilitators, they are empowered to make the choices, lay down conditions and so on. The community must acquiesce to these conditions. This not only constrains the power of the communities, but the focus of participation is then upon the facilitator. The facilitator, paid by the SNGO, then takes his/her orders from that SNGO. In PRA terms, the process is fundamentally influenced by the nature of the relationship between the NGO and the facilitator, which ultimately serves to exclude people in the communities from the political process. As has been the experience with extension models, facilitators will in time settle into working most frequently with those most receptive to PRA. This is unlikely to reach the most excluded and marginalized, and is more likely to establish a clique, even a new local development elite and, therefore, another force of exclusion. The obvious consequence is that local people's priorities are not fed into the policy process.

In criticizing certain approaches to participatory development, we imply an alternative form of empowerment. For empowerment to be transformatory it cannot be given to a less powerful group by a more powerful one, but has to be fought for. This is fundamentally about altering the status quo and will be conflictual so that any intervention around empowerment must be able to work productively with, and simultaneously manage, conflict (Bebbington and Bebbington 2001). Crucially, this process entails access to both institutional power, in this case the local state, and popular bases of collective action such as social movements and traditional authorities. It is about new forms of citizenship which are beginning, albeit tentatively, to address processes of immanent development and challenge systemic exclusion.

Empowerment, however, is not just about group struggle, institutional capacities and alliance-building, but also about personal development around identity and confidence. As Edwards and Sen (2000: 609) stated: '[I]t is rarely possible to generate sustainable changes in human behaviour simply by altering the rules and institutions that govern our lives. The missing ingredient is personal change, which acts as the wellspring of change in all other areas.'

The process we describe addresses this inner basis of change, but not in isolation as in Chambers's 'primacy of the personal'. Rather the development of political consciousness and confidence, what we term 'political literacy', is inseparable from the institutional level and power structures governing access to it. The link between the individual and the institutional is mediated by local cultural practices, which is where Village AiD's approach differs from mainstream participatory practices that tend to import alien methodologies into local decision-making contexts. This chapter outlines how Village AiD worked within local cultural norms to transform institutional structures and relationships in favour of the marginalized. That is, they attempted to move beyond the constraints outlined above while retaining the ethos of participatory development. By this, we mean that the principles of reversal, flexibility and sharing underpin much of what is practised by Village AiD.

Rights, citizenship-building and 'deep' political literacy

So far we have identified the systemic causes underlying the disempowering (ab)use of participation in so-called participatory development interventions. The programmes we analyse below utilize innovative participatory methods in an approach to development that combines rights, citizenship and political literacy.

Political literacy and rights A key focus for rights-based interventions comes under the general heading of legal and political literacy. Most generally this means that, 'At the local level, people need a clear understanding of what particular rights mean in terms of concrete entitlements in order to be able to claim them' (DFID 2000: 8). In policy terms ,'Technical assistance can ... strengthen civil society initiatives which enhance the skills and capacity of poor people to participate in decision-making processes' (ibid., pp. 18, 20). If one of the priorities for NGOs and donors is political literacy, how might it be conceived and implemented?

One danger is that political literacy is conceived in limited terms. For example, Cassell and Lo opt for a definition of political literacy as 'knowledge of basic political concepts and facts' (Cassell and Lo 1997: 321). This approach tells us little about how people actually conduct politics, which is located within their social contexts, and so it is not clear how such concepts can translate into an arena such as rural Africa where 'forms of grass-roots political participation are often different and more varied than their counterparts in the Western liberal context' (Von Lieres 1999: 140). This points to approaches more attuned to both local culture and the prevailing political economy.

Approaches to political literacy within participatory development have been most honed with the REFLECT paradigm, developed initially by ActionAid (Cottingham 1998; Cottingham et al. 1995). REFLECT stands for REgenerated Freirean Literacy through Empowering Community Techniques. The reference to 'regenerated Freirean literacy' acknowledges that Freire's ideas have been misused or not adhered to in previous attempts to generate more empowering approaches to literacy. 'Through empowering community techniques' refers to the use of PRA tools to generate literacy from within the community itself rather than through the use of externally imposed primers.

Freire concluded that if learning to read and write is to constitute an act of knowing, then the learners must assume from the beginning the role of creative subjects. It is not a matter of memorizing and reporting, but reflecting critically on the process of reading and writing and the significance of *their* language. The REFLECT framework uses participants' own language and shared analysis of *their* problems. Literacy and numeracy are generated through the discussion of these problems and issues, and the identification by participants of keywords for reading and writing. Ideally, discussion leads to agreement on action, thereby linking literacy to practical development.

Towards locally meaningful participation In analysing Village AiD's efforts towards rights-based transformatory empowerment we begin at the end, so to speak, before returning to the start of the process and show how their experiential learning moved them along. In reconstructing any historical narrative there is inevitably a certain amount of smoothing over what would not have been a neat unfolding of events, but rather a multi-stranded process operating in different spaces and times. What we have done is to extract the essence of this complex process. Like any political process there was significant conflict and negotiation over the direction and purpose, both within Village AiD and between Village AiD, its partners and the communities in West Africa. What it shows is a learning trajectory moving from discrete interventions to a realization that not only are NGOs structurally part of the problem, but that local people possess significant agency. From here the next step was towards a revitalized citizenship in which institutional channels at and across political scales were utilized to realize this agency and seek to alter the structures of immanent development.

In Sierra Leone, Village AiD has adopted an approach called *tabotsaneh*, which starts from the premise that indigenous processes of facilitating participation, based on local values that people can easily relate to and make sense of, already exist; something which Masaki and Henry also discuss in this volume. *Tabotsaneh* is a Temne word that literally means a 'hanging of heads', sitting around in a group and bending forwards to listen to each other, speaking to each other and guiding each other. Its meaning is based on values of sharing and learning, influencing and advising, not exclusion, imposition and control. It seeks to build on the way that people already facilitate participation within their own communities and so establish the opportunity to address local economic, social and political injustices for themselves. However, this does not equate with an unproblematic consensus since change entails altering power relations and the conflicts this unleashes. We will see how gender relations and the power of 'traditional authorities' were contested in the process. But how did Village AiD get there? As we will describe, they got there because they were led there, with much of the critique and innovation emerging from the people themselves, though this requires an organization that is willing to learn and adapt. Most importantly, it requires a development agent to relinquish some of its power through robust negotiation and in such a way that it cannot simply be reclaimed when the discomfort of confrontation with newly empowered people emerges.

Adapting REFLECT: Village AiD's experience of Arizama in Northern Ghana

The use of *tabotsaneh* represents the learning garnered through a decade of work in four West African countries. The key to this learning process occurred in the Ghana programme where PRA was robustly questioned. So, the first step to Village AiD's citizenship and rights building was the recognition that PRA and other participatory methodologies often involve an imposed form of cognition and decision-making. This recognition emerged from difficult experiences with more conventional project approaches to local development and led to an approach called *Arizama*,[2] a process of development designed and managed by the people themselves. Arizama sought to deconstruct PRA and rebuild an alternative, which has underpinned subsequent programmes.

In its early days, Village AiD had a project focus which although relatively successful in some communities tended to increase the dependency of these communities on the NGO. From this realization Village AiD sought to engage in more political processes through which communities or sections of them could make demands on a range of public service providers. A key to this was enhancing political literacy as this was thought to give individuals and some groups within communities the ability to engage with power-holders and political processes.

For Village AiD literacy is a tool which people use to construct their own knowledge as well as lever in knowledge from outside, on their own terms, in order to change their lives. It is about being able to 'write their lives and read their world'. In practical terms this means maintaining rights and guarding against marginalization and exploitation. It is, therefore, a crucial component within rights-based development and for Village AiD paralleled Freirean ideas about consciousness and education (Freire 1970).

This saw the emergence of Arizama, which is a Dagbani word for 'meaningful discussion' but which came to characterize an alternative approach to participatory development for Village AiD in Northern Ghana. As the shift towards a more substantive immanent approach to development occurred, Village AiD came to the conclusion that a deeper sociopolitical awareness and ultimately political literacy were absent. An investigation of various approaches to literacy development was undertaken, which identified REFLECT as a possibility. It was the reshaping of REFLECT that drew in Arizama.

Within Arizama are processes of consultation, research and analysis, decision-making and participation, which are informed by local cultural values, practices, ethics and norms. Unlike PRA, which brings with it a framework of communication and analysis, Arizama seeks to generate the framework for participation from within the people themselves. In the early period, the key was to strengthen the grassroots' communication framework by identifying how local communities actually communicated and then building upon this. Having done this, it was hoped that the communities would 'have a greater capacity to negotiate their relationships with NGOs and Government on their own terms' (Village AiD 1998b: 24).

However, there is clearly a danger in that, when using such systems, existing inequalities, say around gender and age, may be entrenched. To negotiate such dangers the process did not simply involve taking these systems and letting them run, but was an iterative one in which consciousness-raising, discussion and decision-making occurred through local institutions and in so doing also transformed them. This was most clear in the chief's conference we discuss below. A further danger is that in this model of 'co-opting' local decision-making systems, an NGO may simply re-establish a new and inflexible approach to participation that plays to its own organizational needs. Village AiD was aware of this and attempted to circumvent it by gaining a deep appreciation of local needs and contexts so that each intervention was subtly different. Most importantly, new approaches to participatory monitoring and evaluation, which fundamentally informed planning and decision-making at all levels, promoted increased accountability of the organization to its partners and communities.

Arizama and citizenship-building It became clear that what was envisaged as a communication framework had been taken much further into an embedded political tool. During a workshop in February 2000, Arizama was distinguished from *yatoga,* which means discussing a problematic issue without it necessarily being linked to action, whereas Arizama is action-oriented. A key part of this was learning to appreciate other people's views and perceptions which was, in part, enabled by the coming together for meetings since different peer groups had previously met separately. So, there was a subtle and not always smooth tension between using indigenous decision-making structures and, at the same time, bringing in innovations that challenged these structures. Crucially, these innovations were not in terms of diagrams and maps, but concrete fora for discussion.

Beyond this general feeling, there were a number of positive changes identified by the communities. The first related to gaining confidence in expressing their needs. Arizama brings people together in an open and flexible space, allows them to raise sensitive issues and 'get to know one another very well'. In Cornwall's schema (this volume), the aim was to collapse the distinction between an 'invited' and a 'claimed' space in so far as the space was in many senses externally generated but filled with locally legitimate representatives. The longer-term effects are of building confidence and trust which generate further openness and shared problem-solving. Second, and leading on from this, there is clear evidence of the primary stakeholders of this project strengthening their capacity to identify and solve problems, as well as to mobilize funds to resource solutions.

An example of this came from a man from the village of Sabare (Zabzugu Tatale District) who indicated that a project benefit for him was that he now had the right to agricultural extension service provision. It was not only that he had a right, but that he had the capabilities to claim that right. It is this process that reflects the coming together of personal consciousness, the formation of locally meaningful political organizations and the leveraging open of hitherto unresponsive state structures. Baseline information collected on this issue at the outset of the project saw people from the village of Buglan (Tolon Kumbungu District) asking what extension actually was as they had not been visited by anyone from the Ministry of Agriculture in nine years. During the course of this most recent project year, four visits by extension officers were arranged by the project team and a further three by representatives of the community itself.

The Arizama project has contributed to these networks in terms of learning. Visits by representatives from each community to other villages were facilitated by the project team. These representatives were both social and economic entrepreneurs who had an interest in learning from others, and who were inspired in their willingness to convey their own ideas and learning on issues that were familiar to all the communities involved in the programme. In Zabzugu Tatale District, the networking undertaken among the four Arizama communities became the hub of mobilization which saw community representatives from across the district protest against corruption within the District Assembly and thereby held the District Chief Executive accountable for infringement of their rights. This issue was taken up by one of the local MPs who has since levered in investment through the District Assembly Common Fund.

Traditional authority and citizenship Debates around ethnicity and citizenship (see Chapter 4 and Henry, this volume) suggest that ethnicity need not be a force of exclusion, but can provide a meaningful basis for positive social change. However, blanket calls for revitalizing the role of traditional leaders (Owusu 1991) can be dangerous unless historical forces, such as Kwame Nkrumah's attempts to control the chiefs in Ghana, and concrete circumstances are take into consideration. Possibly the most important benefit has been the full recognition of traditional leaders at an innovatory chiefs' conference, which represented a scaling-up of the insights of Arizama. Convened at Dalun in the heart of rural Tolon Kumbungu, the conference brought together senior chiefs from two key districts within Dagbong. The purpose was to map the key development issues facing people in Dagbong, identify who these people are, share learning concerning how these issues are being tackled, agree the constitutional responsibilities of traditional leaders in helping to address them, and how they should engage with the state and civil agencies to support their efforts. Out of this they developed a new leadership mandate in which the role of *Malgu Naa* (Chief of Development Issues) is officially institutionalized within traditional society. This will be piloted at district level with the possibility of appointing people to such an office at village level. This recognizes a crucial leadership vacuum and provides the necessary institutional machinery to deal with issues that have continued to be neglected by traditional authorities.

Gender and citizenship The baseline research undertaken at the outset of the project indicated that information exchange networks were fractured along lines of gender. Men dominated decision-making through structured sociopolitical hierarchies and information exchange broadly followed established channels throughout traditional structures. Women, however, operated a much more informal network that is actually more encompassing in terms of the number of communities, different ethnic groups and interests. The Arizama fora on a community level have enabled men and women to explore how these information exchange and sociopolitical structures engage, where they conflict, and where they disempower.

The chiefs' conference also addressed the exclusion of women. The role of women and the security and development of their rights, especially those of young women, were widely acknowledged by the chiefs attending the conference as reflecting the attitudes among traditional leaders as well as senior administrators at district level. Senior chiefs (*Ya Naa* skins) and their village-level sub-chiefs from Tolon Kumbungu and Savelugu Nanton Districts met with NGO representatives, women's chiefs and local opinion leaders to discuss the role of women in traditional society and the problems they face. In each case, these issues were taken back to the communities through village-based workshops to drive the momentum of discussion and awareness-raising at village level for the need to take up responsibility to promote change for themselves. Some concrete outcomes were the emergence of localized cartels (e.g. groundnut price fixing) as a result of women being recognized as competent business people. There was also a relatively sudden increase in the mobility of women across several communities who began pursuing their businesses from market to market. One successful and mobile trader contributed to the building of the school because she had begun earning money.

Local NGOs and empowerment Given that Arizama sought to transform relations within communities and between communities, SNGOs, NNGOs and the state, one of the most important issues to emerge was that the assumptions upon which the NGO sector within civil society has been constructed can be clearly challenged. These are, first, that NGOs are assumed to be more efficient, cost effective and flexible compared to state institutions as agents of development (Allen 1997). Second, that they are formally apolitical, serving as more appropriate advocates of the interests of their grassroots' constituencies (Bebbington and Riddell 1997). Third, because of the above, they are positioned to play a significant role in holding state agencies to account.

There is an expanding body of evidence throughout Village AiD's work to suggest that these assumptions are tenuous and have major implications for the way in which it functions, which is primarily through partnerships with other NGOs and local state agencies. Some of the NGOs lack efficient and effective management structures and systems. With some exceptions, their fieldworkers are of low capacity, and decision-making is often autocratic and centralized. A conscious dependency on projects serves to foster uncoordinated management, while they lock themselves into a culture of dependency on funder criteria and interests, which are often socially and politically inappropriate to the needs of their development constituency (Mohan 2001). In some cases, senior NGO managers have openly used their position to mobilize grassroots support to secure a political mandate. This inevitably contaminates their NGO's position as a check and balance on local governance and, therefore, as a vital contributor to local democracy.

When some local NGOs are challenged on these issues, they often use the formula: 'You don't understand local custom, these are our people, we know what it is they need and it is our job to protect their rights.' In some cases, and ironically, they have ignored local customs themselves and exploited the very rights they are claiming to protect. This formula is a way for NGOs to protect themselves against a perceived dilution of their power base and legitimacy, which runs contrary to the aim of empowering the disempowered.

Although a major challenge, this realization and the learning that came with it informed Village AiD's own approach to organizational development as well as wider processes of institution-building. For example, much organizational development work focuses on the interface between NNGO and SNGO. In response to this, Village AiD began to focus on the relationships between partner communities, between Village AiD and communities, and on how their relationship with communities affected partners. A case here was with SLYEO who, as we shall see, have adopted an Arizama-style approach as an internal protocol. This form of organizational development takes time, trust and many visits to the villages with local NGO partners, but is the basis on which empowering development can be fostered.

Monitoring and evaluation On the basis of learning from this project, Village AiD's management structures and systems have been comprehensively reviewed. Although process-based, and so opening up more space for participation by key stakeholders, it was clear that the centrally conceived and prescriptive nature of these management structures ensured that the organization's information needs were being serviced at the expense of a loss of power among the primary beneficiaries. The learning concerning local approaches to communication, analysis and decision-making within this project were used to pilot a new approach to evaluation that was driven by upward learning mechanisms. This combined indigenous approaches with externally developed approaches such as participatory rural appraisal and social drama, but in a new configuration that attempted to locate evaluation as a structural component of empowerment in itself, rather than simply as a means to service accountability or extract learning (Waddington 2001).

For example, in Gbanga in Northern Ghana, Village AiD conducted PRA work, during which the community claimed that their priority was based on the need for a small ruminant project. The project was supported and gradually the relationship grew. Village AiD and partner staff spent nights there and discussed informally what Village AiD and the partners stood for. Eventually they felt confident enough to explain that they prioritized a small ruminant project only because they had heard from other communities that this is what Village AiD *did*. It transpired that, in fact, there was a mosaic of priorities. The linear prioritization that PRA encourages – high, medium, low – was compatible with standard log-framing and convenient in terms of a project-focused framework, but ignored the dynamic and complex realities. Conversation would constantly lift away from two-dimensional graphic representations towards relationships and the people involved in them that could not be easily explored by PRA-style tools. Walking around the village, taking food together and so on became the way in which these issues were presented, reflected upon and analysed.

This allowed Village AiD to open up the conversation with them about their interactions with more than one agency and how they might be able to achieve their objectives through a web of relationships, and what they believed was stopping them from doing this. Crucially, Village AiD applied this logic to itself and explored its own role in these relationships. This exercise led to a review of how they managed themselves and ultimately, their relationship with their partners.

Deep political literacy and transformation: EKANAK in Sierra Leone

As we mentioned earlier, Village AiD is currently using *tabotsaneh* in Sierra Leone within a political literacy framework to monitor changes in the lives of young people. Here Village AiD was able to build EKANAK, which involved REFLECT and Arizama in a process of politicizing marginalized groups within and between their communities. This was made possible by constructing PRA, which everyone had heard of and wanted to learn how to use, and then, through role reversal, enabling them to see for themselves how it would feel to have PRA applied to them. This served as the basis upon which to deconstruct PRA within the very local context of young people and their sub-cultures. *Tabotsaneh* emerged from this process. By leading them through role-playing and such like, SLYEO were able to see that wider, more powerful structures needed to be engaged with. From this point EKANAK began to grow as a process of confrontation, negotiation, awareness-raising and decision-making with the wider structures that its grassroots constituencies, as well as an organization, needed to engage with. Political literacy was seen to be vital within this and so Village AiD deconstructed REFLECT in the same way it had with PRA, and cultivated this within EKANAK.

EKANAK incorporates the REFLECT process of word identification and construction, but seeks to politicize this process through *tabotsaneh*. EKANAK is an acronym for the Temne, *Ekara ma naneh mami kaderu; ekara deru kama naneh ma mi* (Bringing what I have in my mind into the world, and bringing the world into my mind). This might involve drawing in local resource people to facilitate the unit, thereby using literacy as a means of passing on skills and knowledge. Very often reference will be made to proverbs on an issue of importance. Transcribing the proverbs generates useful literacy materials while providing a means whereby participants can stand back from reality and view it in a different way. The intention is to ensure that literacy is more relevant and useful to the circumstances that people live in, and so is more empowering and sustainable.

However, EKANAK is not merely literacy, it is intrinsically political. Each unit, which participants develop and explore for themselves, is grounded in their own sociopolitical realities. Overlaid on this sociopolitical platform are local interpretations of the judiciary, administration and legislature. Using *tabotsaneh* as a means of facilitating the participation of learners within the EKANAK framework, local understandings and interpretations of the constitution of the state, their ethnic-based constitution, and accepted roles, responsibilities and rights at household and community levels can be explored. The literacy process helps to capture their understanding of their rights and responsibilities by recording them, looking at them in new ways, and exploring their meaning. Through discussion, these can be assessed against people's own aspirations, capabilities and restrictions. As this broadens and deepens, units explore the practical things that people can do to effect change, while the need for change can be exported beyond the groups to their communities.

Conclusion

We have argued that in our experience, and to an extent that of others, PRA-based approaches to participation can weaken communities politically and undermine development. This realization prompted Village AiD to attempt a different approach based on indigenous communication methods in order that the communities' voices could be heard. In practice, the pro-cess went well beyond this and has been taken on by local communities as a potent political device that is bringing about deeper transformations than were envisaged.

As we said at the outset, this approach is in the spirit of PLA. A more overarching transformation involved awareness that people had certain fundamental rights. This is important as it moves away from passivity regarding the development agencies – either state or NGO – towards a more confident and proactive stance. Here, the process of empowerment leads towards an agenda around rights such that the abuse of rights is widely seen as a primary cause of poverty. So, a key benefit is assisting people to tackle their poverty for themselves. However, while people have identified this need there may still be a lack of awareness and skills about how an individual or group might secure their rights. It is here that political literacy becomes important as a strategy for citizenship formation.

Notes

We would like to thank all those people who have been a part of this process. To mirror the processes discussed in the chapter they are mentioned more or less chronologically. The architects of Arizama in Ghana were Coleman Ageyomah (GAS Associates, Ghana), James Ayikade (Community Water and Sanitation Agency, Ghana) and Dr Edward Soyiri. This was taken up by programme managers across West Africa. In Ghana these were Sam Salifu and Saeed Bancie; in The Gambia these were Pierre Mendey and Kate MacDonald; in Cameroon these were Mbah Grace, Caroline Nfi, Musa Ndamba, Nuhu Salihu, Duni Jedo, Emmanuelle Fomba and Robert Fon; and in Sierra Leone Charles Lahai and Sammy Stober Taylor.

1 Village AiD was established in 1989. Its initial activities were in The Gambia with programmes in Sierra Leone, Ghana and Cameroon added over the next seven years. Village AiD is a registered charity operating from Lumford Mill, Riverside Works, Buxton Road, Bakewell, Derbyshire, DE45 1GJ, UK. Website: <http://www.villageaid.org>

2 Much of the work around Arizama and its subsequent adaptions has been supported by the Community Fund.

References

Allen, C. (1997) 'Who Needs Civil Society?', *Review of African Political Economy*, 73: 329–37.

Bebbington, A. and D. Bebbington (2001) 'Development Alternatives: Practice, Dilemmas and Theory', *Area*, 33 (1): 7–17.

Bebbington, A. and R. Riddell (1997) 'Heavy Hands, Hidden Hands, Holding Hands? Donors, Intermediary NGOs and Civil Society Organisations', in

D. Hulme and M. Edwards (eds), *NGOs, States and Donors: Too Close for Comfort?* (Basingstoke: Macmillan), pp. 107–27.

Blackburn, J. and J. Holland (1998) 'General Introduction', in J. Blackburn with J. Holland (eds), *Who Changes? Institutionalizing Participation in Development* (London: IT Publications), pp. 1–8.

Cassell, C. and C. Lo (1997) 'Theories of Political Literacy', *Political Behavior*, 19 (4): 317–35.

Chambers, R. (1997) *Whose Reality Counts? Putting the First Last* (London: IT Publications).

Cooke, B. and U. Kothari (eds) (2001) *Participation: The New Tyranny?* (London: Zed Books).

Cottingham, S. (1998) 'How Can REFLECT be Used Widely without Diluting the Participatory Nature of the Process?', *PLA Notes 32: Participation, Literacy and Empowerment* (London: IIED).

Cottingham, S. et al. (1995) *Evaluation of the Reflect Methodology in the Africa Pilot Project* (Uganda: ActionAid).

DFID (2000) *Human Rights for Poor People* (London: DFID).

Edwards, M. and D. Hulme (1996) 'Too Close for Comfort? The Impact of Official aid on Non-Governmental Organizations', *World Development*, 24 (6): 961–73.

Edwards, M. and G. Sen (2000) 'NGOs, Social Change and the Transformation of Human Relationships: A 21st-Century Civic Agenda', *Third World Quarterly*, 21 (4): 605–16.

Freire, P. (1970) *The Pedagogy of the Oppressed* (New York: Seabury Press).

Hickey, S. (2002) 'Transnational NGDOs and Participatory Forms of Rights-Based Development: Converging with the Local Politics of Citizenship in Cameroon', *Journal of International Development*, 14 (6): 841–57.

Hintjens, H. (1999) 'The Emperor's New Clothes: A Moral Tale for Development Experts?', *Development in Practice*, 9 (4): 382–95.

Kumar, S. and S. Corbridge (2002) 'Programmed to Fail? Development Projects and the Politics of Participation', *Journal of Development Studies*, 39(2): 73–103.

Mohan, G. (1999) 'Not So Distant, Not So Strange: The Personal and the Political in Participatory Research', *Ethics, Place and Environment*, 2 (1): 41–54.

— (2001) 'The Disappointments of Civil Society: NGOs, Citizenship and Institution Building in Northern Ghana', *Political Geography*, 21 (1): 125–54.

Nelson, N. and S. Wright (1995) 'Participation and Power', in N. Nelson and S. Wright (eds), *Power and Participatory Development: Theory and Practice*, (London: IT Publications), pp. 1–18.

Ngunjiri, E. (1998) 'Participatory Methodologies: Double-edged Swords', *Development in Practice*, 8 (4): 466–70.

Owusu, M. (1991) 'Democracy and Africa – a View from the Village', *Journal of Modern African Studies*, 30 (3): 369–96.

Richards, P. (1995) 'Participatory Rural Appraisal: A Quick and Dirty Critique', in IIED (ed.), *Critical Reflections from Practice*, PLA Notes, 24 (London: IIED), pp. 13–16.

Village AiD (1996) *Beyond PRA: A New Approach to Village-led Development*, unpublished business plan, Andrew Kingman (Executive Co-ordinator) and Mark Waddington (Africa Programme Co-ordinator), Village AiD.

— (1997) *Application Summary: Growing from Within*, Mark Waddington (Africa Programme Co-ordinator), Village AiD.

— (1998a) *Application Summary: Empowering Dagomba Women Through Social and Cultural Change*, Mark Waddington (Africa Programme Co-ordinator), Village AiD.

— (1998b) *Ghana Field Report*, 7 March, Village AiD.

Von Lieres, B. (1999) 'New Perspectives on Citizenship in Africa', *Journal of Modern African Studies*, 25 (1): 139–48.

Waddington, M. (2001) 'Upward Learning within Monitoring and Evaluation as a Means of Social Empowerment', in P. Oakley (ed.), *Evaluating Empowerment – Reviewing the Concept and Practice* (London: INTRAC), pp. 137–51.

FIVE | Donors and participation: caught between tyranny and transformation

15 | Participation in poverty reduction strategies: democracy strengthened or democracy undermined?

DAVID BROWN

This chapter is concerned with public participation in the poverty reduction strategies (PRSPs) which are currently a favoured instrument of international concessional and grant aid. It asks whether the notion of participation has contributed positively to international policy development in relation to PRSPs, and whether it has done so in innovative ways, considered from the perspective of southern 'ownership'. It will consider what support this aid instrument offers for the view that participation might function as a constructive adjunct to international aid processes, and a reinforcement of the structures of democracy.

The rise of PRSPs provides a major test of the claim that participation can act as a transformative and radical force. With the advent of the PRSP, the participatory approach is presented with an institutional vehicle of near universality in the developing world, and one which can be judged against fairly concrete standards of pro-poor change. Thus, when it comes to assessing the transformative potential of participation, poverty reduction strategies commend themselves strongly as a test case.

The theoretical basis for participation in PRSP development

PRSPs are viewed by the IMF and the World Bank as a new framework for poverty reduction involving the development of nationally-owned and participatory poverty reduction strategies. Since 1999, they have been mandatory for recipients of funding under the enhanced Heavily Indebted Poor Countries' (HIPC) initiative,[1] as well as the World Bank's Poverty Reduction and Growth Facility (PRGF), and all other forms of concessional (IDA) finance. They have become the main vehicle to implement the Comprehensive Development Framework (CDF) – the focus of the World Bank's attempts to tackle poverty and inequality, and achieve the Millennium Development Goals.

The CDF advocates, and the PRSP is intended to implement, a holistic long-term strategy in which the recipient country owns and directs its development agenda, under the leadership of the government. The Bank and other development partners are expected to work in a coordinated manner, in association not only with the government but also civil society, the private sector, and other development stakeholders, united in a shared vision of the country's future development. Poverty alleviation is a central element, by definition and obligation. The challenge posed for the PRSP is thus to convert a political interest – the well-being of the poor – into a technocratic dimension of public administration.

An interesting aspect of the management of the poverty reduction process has been the way in which it has given new life and strength to contentious concepts and strategies. Concepts which were formerly of value largely in a project frame of reference have now taken on a role in macro-economic transformation. Under the World Bank/IMF guidelines, 'participation' is presented as one of the core elements of the PRSP, and central to the achievement of the principles underlying the approach.[2] This is one of the crucial dimensions differentiating the PRSP from previous generations of aid instruments, such as 'structural adjustment' conditionalities.

The rationale is clear. PRSP preparation is to be a country-driven process based upon a partnership between the government, its domestic stakeholders and its international donors. Country ownership of the strategy cannot be imposed off-the-shelf, but depends on ensuring the broad involvement of all elements of the domestic constituency. In such a context, language which might otherwise be criticized for its ambiguity and imprecision comes into its own, in that it favours a flexible process, responsive to the country conditions under review. In this way, it is argued, donor and western cultural bias can be avoided in deciding the forms that local democracy should take. Other terms which have hitherto looked to be prone to vagueness, depoliticization and cultural bias – such as 'stakeholders' and 'civil society' – can be construed in a similarly respectful way, as indicative of the inclusion of the previously marginal, and the integration of the institutions through which their voices can be heard.

There is an intuitive plausibility to the notion that aid should be concentrated on societies which can use it most effectively for the purposes of poverty reduction. It makes sense for donors to focus their efforts on rewarding countries that perform well in these terms, by virtue of their genuine willingness to improve the well-being of their weakest citizens. This contrasts with the tendency of former aid regimes to withdraw aid from the good performers, but maintain it for the bad.

A similar intuitive logic underlies the idea of widespread participation by all major stakeholders, particularly the vulnerable and marginalized. Few would question the argument that an effective poverty reduction strategy requires that the views of the poor be incorporated into the diagnosis of poverty, that appropriate tools be used to discern those views, that policy choices be influenced by them, and that they should be included in public monitoring, as the main intended beneficiaries.

One must also sound a cautionary note. First, all this occurs in the context of a system of aid delivery whose rentier characteristics inevitably distort political relationships.[3] Concessional aid flows are arguably inimical to 'national ownership' in any meaningful sense of the term, and can hardly be viewed as a good starting point to attain it (Bretton Woods Project 2002). Second, there is the question of who is to participate, and at the behest of whom? I have elsewhere questioned the class dynamics of participatory approaches, particularly the view that they lead to a new professionalism whose moral superiority is ensured by a more socially inclusive orientation (Brown 1995, 1998; Brown et al. 2002). I have suggested that participatory processes could well prove less socially inclusive, as well as less transparent, than the alternatives. This is of particular concern given the claims of the new approach to address important questions of governance. The linkages between participatory management and increased accountability and transparency, the twin foundations of sound governance, are clearly central to an assessment of the worth of this aid instrument.

I now investigate these questions from two perspectives. The first is an examination of the guidelines on participation contained in the World Bank's *PRSP Sourcebook* (2000). The aim here is to identify the decision-making criteria by which particular groups are (or, alternatively, are not) to be included as legitimate and interested parties in policy development, as well as their roles in the development and validation of those policies. The second is a case study of Cameroon which the World Bank has commended as exemplary in terms of participation.

The World Bank's *PRSP Sourcebook*

Chapter 7 ('Participation') of the Bank's *PRSP Sourcebook* addresses the questions 'What is participation and what role can it play in the PRSP?' The answer to the former is stated simply as 'the process by which stakeholders influence and share control over priority setting, policy making, resource allocations, and/or program implementation' (World Bank 2000: 237). Inclusion of a wide range of stakeholders is advocated, including poor and vulnerable groups, especially women. They are to be involved both as individuals and also through relevant institutions such as NGOs, membership organizations, private sector bodies, farmers' associations, unions, cooperatives, chambers of commerce and similar umbrella groups.

What the Bank has in mind here is something rather less than representative government, though this kind of broad inclusive language certainly has a flavour of it. The approach inevitably begs the question of how such rights of voice and representation are to be secured, legitimized and regulated, in order to ensure that 'participation' conforms to standards of good governance. The Bank's approach is somewhat deficient in relation to these three criteria. To an extent, this is explained (and perhaps justified) by reference to the need for a healthy flexibility: 'There is no blueprint for participation because it plays a role in many different contexts and for different purposes' (ibid., p. 237).

'Participation' is recognized to have no single meaning, but to be something that is crafted in response to particular national constraints. It is a process which is regarded as essentially nationally owned. At the same time, it is also one which is seen quite clearly as open to a degree of donor influence. Thus: 'The first step entails negotiation among the government, civil society and the World Bank and International Monetary Fund (IMF) staff to clarify and define participation and the role it can play in the poverty reduction strategy' (ibid.). It is accepted that the ultimate choices rest with 'the country', though the mechanism to convert this sentiment into a political force is left undefined: 'Countries chose their participatory process based on their starting point and their goals for the PRSP' (ibid., p. 242).

The 'country' here has something to do with government, though the two are not necessarily coterminous:

> Participatory processes should build as much as possible on existing governance and political systems ... Most countries have existing governance and political structures that extend from the local government structures to national Parliaments. However, the extent of discussion and debate about development strategies and development plans within existing governance structures varies considerably across countries. It depends largely on the transparency of the governance process. Strategies developed through a broader process involving different branches and levels of government tend to become institutionalised and lead to more sustainable poverty reduction (World Bank 2000: 238, 244)

A similar degree of fluidity is allowed in relation to civil society representation, characterized as 'civic engagement':

> Civic engagement at the local level improves the quality of data, especially from the poor and vulnerable. Because this can bring in the stakeholders who are most difficult to reach, it is vital that local participatory processes be publicized, with clear information on what will be the topic of discussion, when and where meetings will be held, and who is welcome ... Local-level civic engagement, especially with the poor, can be carried out in groups or

individually, provided the process is broadly representative of the community. (World Bank 2000: 246)

It is recommended that 'trusted facilitators' be involved, among other things, to personally invite (read 'select'?) participants. The criteria for such trust are not identified. Nor is it clear what is meant by the proposition that civic engagement need only be 'broadly representative' of the community. By what criteria will the validity of such representation be assessed? Is 'the community' anyway the appropriate unit for civic engagement? How broad is 'broad'?

The role of the wider publics, even when screened, is also seen as qualified: 'Also important is *public approval* reached through extensive consultation between civil society representatives and their *constituencies. Though non-binding*, this is vital for broadening ownership and making the PRSP *truly participatory*' (ibid., p. 241, my italics). There is an interesting use of language here. If 'non-binding consultations' are said to be 'truly participatory', then the concept appears not to be seen by the Bank as anything very substantial. But hints of a stronger language ('public approval' of governmental strategies by the 'constituents' of civil society organizations) obscures this qualification, and implies something much closer to the legitimacy of electoral politics.

Participatory governance and representative democracy These few quotations are enough to establish that what is under discussion here is a highly manipulated form of public consultation, in which stakeholder participation is achieved through a process of active selection, based upon subjective, and not necessarily openly articulated, standards of legitimacy and representation. This is clearly in the area of 'participation by invitation'. External agency (particularly that of Bank staffers) is crucial at every turn. Decisions as to what participation means in the particular national context would appear to be made by a cabal led by the host government and the World Bank. The links between participatory processes and public policy are thus viewed as qualified, and policy is not constrained in any substantive way.

All this may appear surprising, given the Bank's professed commitment to principles of national ownership and good governance. It sits rather oddly with the Bank's view that one of the major justifications for the participatory approach is precisely the additional increments to good governance which it offers, over and above the fact of representative government:

> Many governments argue that because they are democratically elected, they do not need to institute participatory processes for PRSP formulation ... Traditional democratic processes usually only allow citizens to make one

input in four or five years. Participatory processes allow citizens to actively participate in the governance of their country and their resources between electoral cycles, on a more regular basis. This not only empowers the public but also increases the overall ownership for development policies, thereby increasing their sustainability. (World Bank 2000: 253)

Thus put, participation appears as an entirely positive add-on to elective democracy. Its major benefits lie in the way it better informs the policy-makers as to the circumstances and interests of the publics they represent. To this extent, it is difficult to contest. The size of the benefits may vary, but one can hardly dispute the principle of always seeking better to inform the policy-makers. However, participatory processes are said not just to inform the administrative decisions of those in government, but also to increase the sense of ownership of the governed ('citizens', 'the public') and, ultimately, to empower them. These are rather more elevated claims.

It is beyond the scope of this chapter to digress into the philosophical foundations of democracy; but it is instructive to compare the forms of decision-making being promoted here with the fundamental characteristics of systems of representative government as conventionally understood. Conventional even in terms of the World Bank's rather proceduralist view of democracy. Before a system of government can be characterized as 'representative', a number of conditions must be met, among which the following would seem to be the most critical:

- That decision-making and government are derived from public opinion and are accountable to it; this accountability largely derives from periodic processes (usually electoral) by which the government 'tests its representativeness'.
- That public opinion is openly and freely expressed, through universal suffrage – the grant of an effective voice in decision-making to every citizen, on the understanding that the majority opinion prevails, and decisions, once made, will be publicly legitimated.
- That the body of representatives has firm and enduring rights to decide on policy and legislation, to accept or reject public impositions (e.g. taxes), to control the allocation of resources (the budget), and to question authority on behalf of the citizenry. (after Finer 1970: 63)

Now it is clear that these standards apply only peripherally, if at all, to the participatory processes by which poverty reduction strategies are to be devised, agreed, implemented and assessed. These are wanting in relation to at least five of the key characteristics set out above, viz.

- accountability of representation

- universality of voice
- public legitimation of decision-making
- representativeness subjected to periodic tests
- institutionalized questioning of authority

While some publics are to be given a voice, this is on a purely discretionary basis, as a condescension not a right. The voice which is granted is neither fundamental nor universal. It is granted by an imprecise and self-selected grouping, with unspecified and obscure links to sovereign authorities, and no public accountability of its own. Nor is there any underlying standard of 'justiciability' – it is not possible in this situation to establish a basis on which the 'right' of participation can be infringed and remedial action taken.

The governance link is crucial to the legitimacy of the PRSP process though, as presented in the Bank documents, it derives as much from the alleged limitations of representative democracy as from the manifest qualities of the participatory approach. And it arguably misrepresents the nature of electoral systems – a misrepresentation which serves at one and the same time to diminish the significance of institutionalized democratic processes and to inflate the virtues of discretionary ones.

We need to make a distinction here between democracy as 'events' (such as elections) and the 'underlying powers' to which such events refer. These powers are, in a sense, periodically 'condensed' into electoral events. The World Bank's justification for participatory processes largely rests upon the limitations of the individual events, but this perhaps undervalues the extent to which they are the instruments of a more enduring set of powers, albeit ones whose exercise is cyclical and indirect.

In such a context, slogans such as 'policies broadly representative of the community' need to be carefully unpicked. There are questions pertaining both to the extent of representation and to its strength. The institutions through which the relevant publics are to be addressed are ones with a high quota of discretion, of 'condescension without obligation'. The emphasis is very heavily on 'civil society' as the interface between the public and the state. Underlying this is an assumption that civil society organizations (NGOs, for example) have stable constituencies, and that they exist primarily to represent them.

The discretionary element inherent in this model of participation seems likely to create a markedly quiescent form of representation, for there are no entitlements. On the one hand, those who continue to be excluded under the discretionary arrangements have no legal right to demand representation. On the other, those who are included will be put under pressure to accept whatever they are offered, on the grounds that, as supplicants, they could have received very much less. Where participation is offered on a representative basis to institutions – as, for example, with NGOs, NGO umbrella bodies and federations – then one suspects that solidarity will often be compromised, especially where the operative function is misconstrued as delegated power. Organizations which function well as integrative arenas for debate and discussion may be less well placed to decide on policy priorities in the name of their alleged constituents. Under the terms of the offer, however, such limitations are likely to be interpreted more as lost opportunities on the part of the invited participants than inherent flaws in the incorporative model. All this calls seriously into question the extent to which, in such participatory processes, the questioning of authority can be said to be genuinely institutionalized.[4]

Proponents of the participatory approach would tend to justify the informality of these arrangements by reference both to the additionality element, and the quality of the product. In the former reference, the claim is that the gains are purely incremental – they do not detract from democratic rights where these exist, but merely complement and reinforce them. But this discounts their ability to stifle democratic policy development. There may be major benefits to be had by governments from the ability to claim that their preferred policies have been derived from an extensive process of public consultation, validated by the whole spectrum of civil society. The reassuring tone of the PRSPs so far submitted to the IMF Board even by non-democratic regimes is witness to these sanitizing effects.[5] A government which is able to assure its public that its policies represent not only its own interests but those of all its major stakeholders, including its international backers and the poor and marginal, is clearly provided with powerful symbols of public legitimacy. One which is able to back up those claims by sizeable indirect foreign aid flows which benefit significant sections of society (if not necessarily all the stakeholders originally consulted) is even better placed. There can be positive outcomes of a political nature whether or not the poor gain anything at all.

The claim of incrementalism can also be challenged on its own terms. Discretionary processes not only jar with electoral ones in terms of principle, but may also actively undermine them. This is to a degree acknowledged by the World Bank, but in a context in which what is needed is seen to be more and better discretion, not more and better democracy. Thus:

> [T]here are still issues to be resolved ... There is also a concern that broad country ownership over the PRSP process has not developed as hoped. Several factors contribute to this. First, weak attempts at participation can

> leave out key groups and detract from broad ownership. Second, if the Bank and Fund, or other IFIs play too large a role in formulating the PRSP and the participatory process, then the government and civil society will not own the process. Third, if the PRSP process does not build on existing political and/or participatory processes, stakeholders may feel that the process will not be sustainable and could be ineffective. Finally, expectations must be managed. There is a tendency in these large initiatives to raise the expectations of stakeholders who are consulted that participation will have a large and immediate impact. However, at the national level, this will not be the case. The PRSP process is a medium to long term process. ('Participation in PRSPs', World Bank website, February 2001)

The solution, therefore, lies in more and better of the same – stronger and more nuanced attempts at participation – not more genuinely representative forms of government. The need to build on existing political and/or participatory processes (note the 'and/or') derives not from principles of governance, but from lesser and more practical concerns such as sustainability and effectiveness.

As regards the product, there must be concerns as to the quality of both PRSPs and the strategies they define. Some of the papers are strong statements that appear to commit governments firmly to a plan of action. Time will tell if this is what they actually achieve. Others are administrative documents, to be admired more for the way in which hapless civil servants negotiate a politically hazardous terrain than for their ability to commit the political authorities to any substantive reforms. While weaker documents, PRSPs of this latter type may still have real value as levers to force an unpromising government to care about its poorer citizens. If oppressive governments can be made to claim they care, then this is at least a starting point. So far so good. But the strategies they describe are more problematic. In almost all cases, the quality of the poverty analysis is limited by its purely descriptive nature and technocratic tone. The depoliticization of the process means that few if any alternatives are offered, and even where they are, then the mechanisms for their prioritization are, by the very nature of the process, administrative. Most appear as checklists and compendia, with none of the vigour which is found in political manifestos. Nor do they have the ability to commit a political constituency to take actions which voters will later be able to judge at the ballot box for their courage and effectiveness.

It is arguably the very fact that the character of the whole process is participatory which is at the origin of this difficulty. The argument here would be that, because of their discretionary nature, because they are non-binding, they can never be 'truly participatory' however great the level of public approval appears to be. This view would contend that public ownership derives ultimately from robust and stable structures of public debate and contention, not from the sort of inclusiveness that discretionary participation is able to generate. A brief examination of a country case study (that of Cameroon) would tend to support this view.

The PRSP process in Cameroon

Cameroon was one of thirty-four African countries selected for debt relief under the enhanced HIPC Initiative. It successfully reached 'Decision Point' in October 2000, on acceptance of its interim PRSP by the IMF Board. It then entered the preparatory process leading to 'Completion Point' (CP), involving, inter alia, production of the full PRSP. However, acting under donor pressure, the Cameroon government accepted a situation in which HIPC expenditures in the initial three-year period to CP would be supervised and monitored by a specially constituted board. This was the 'Comité consultatif de suivi des dépenses PPTE' (CCS) which comprised state, donor and civil society representatives. This arrangement was unique in international terms.

Civil society representation on the CCS was selected in a variety of ways. Each confessional community was allowed a representative (the leader of the Islamic conference was subsequently elected vice-chair of the CCS, under the Minister of Finance). For the mainstream NGO community, selection was placed in the hands of a private management consulting firm, which invited applications from interested and eligible parties. After an initial screening for eligibility, the firm made a pre-selection of twenty-two NGOs. This was said to have been made on technical criteria, though the nature of these was not revealed. However, though not very transparently derived, the list was generally regarded as not unreasonable. Representatives of successful candidate organizations were then invited to participate in a national competition (*concours*). At a large gathering in the Palais de Congrès in Yaoundé, each made a presentation to its peers, indicating how it would approach the task of representing the NGO community on the consultative committee, and how it would feed back information to the membership. Each NGO was invited to score the others, and the two winning candidates were selected on the basis of the aggregate scores. The two NGOs in question have done their best to make sound technical judgements on matters brought to the CCS, and to keep their peers informed. However, they are not necessarily well qualified to function effectively at high policy levels, nor well enough funded to serve as a conduit to convey CCS decisions and PRSP deliberations to the broader civil society.

The GoC also organized a major programme of public consultation, on a province by province basis. In the words of the government:

> [In the spring of 2000] the first phase of participatory consultations was conducted in all the 58 divisions of the country, with 203 target groups representing all segments of the civil society and the different active forces of the population. In all, close to 10,000 persons – some 40% of them women – freely expressed their views during these consultations. The group discussions, which were completely open, were led by some fifteen teams of facilitators and rapporteurs drawn from Government Services and the civil society. Observers from the IMF, the World Bank and GTZ were also present. (Government of Cameroon 2002: 16–17)

Participants were asked to comment on the causes and consequences of poverty in Cameroon, and the means by which it might be reduced. In May 2000, a national workshop was organized in Yaoundé to present the results of the participatory consultations, with 'participants, the majority of whom were from the civil society'. A second phase of participatory consultations was then conducted in January 2002, involving 'about 6,000 people from different social backgrounds', as part of the PRSP preparation process. Again, this was followed by a national seminar to share findings.

This participatory process has been a source of some satisfaction to the government and is lauded by the Bank. It was certainly an innovation in its approach, and did bring together large numbers of people, many of whom would not normally be so involved. But it was arguably rather less open and 'participatory' than might at first appear. Participants included individuals, consultants, NGOs and other groupings in 'civil society' though the most activist organizations were often not invited. Interestingly, where national legislators participated in the deliberations, they did so only in their personal capacities. The participation in the national seminars differed somewhat from that in the divisional and provincial meetings. Organizations with a strong presence in the capital city were more in evidence than the purely locally-based ones, which often lacked the contacts and means to contribute effectively outside the local milieu.

As regards issues of quality, the debate was said to have involved frank discussions which did not shirk from the performance of government, including issues of corruption. Wide dissatisfaction was expressed with the government. Views on poverty were systematically collected, and are annexed to the current PRSP draft. These are generally unexceptional, involving long lists detailing what locals perceive as the causes and effects of poverty in Cameroon, very largely in the form of asset deficiencies. Little attempt would appear to have been made to analyse or systematize findings, beyond a basic sorting and classification. The government is certainly presented as partly culpable for the high levels of poverty in the country, though traditional culture is also given its share of blame by the participants. While not without interest, the unrefined state of the lists inevitably diminishes their operational worth.

The PRSP document is very much an administrative statement, and the political authorities are pledged to very little by way of firm policies. It has been criticized as seeking to be all things to all people (though the donors' interests figure more strongly than those of the NGOs, and other forms of civil society get only a cursory mention here and there).

An outstanding feature of the document is the prominence which it gives to the role of productive sectors in poverty alleviation. The forest sector has quite detailed coverage, and a strong link is made from the forest resource to the welfare of the poor, through harnessing the sector's local fiscal base to the structure of decentralized local government. This was a very positive development, possibly unique, though its inclusion arguably owed more to donor and activist pressure (supported by the PRSP technical team) than to the participatory consultations. Indeed, it must be doubted whether such a link would have been made at all had there been a 'truly national process'. The public were largely unaware of these provisions for local government funding (raised public awareness was not, one notes, a function of the participatory consultations), but even if they had been, the chances are that they would have lacked the political leverage to ensure that the legislative provision would be converted into reality.

The HIPC process in Cameroon has thus involved some interesting innovations. Public involvement has been quite broad. Important sectoral linkages have been made which may well have positive effects on rural poverty. Interesting projects have been funded. However, these may owe more to donor influence of an essentially conditional nature than to national participation. Indeed, there is little to suggest that participation of sectors of the national population has made any real difference at all. Though massive in scale, the public consultations were too broad and unfocused to exert real policy influence. And the NGO representation in PRSP implementation (through the CCS) has been most effective only in the interstices of a system under firm government control. And what these forms of representation have most notably failed to achieve, however, is any clarity about the decision-making processes which are being applied; arguably, priorities are being set very much in keeping with the established – and essentially authoritarian – styles of the Cameroon government. The acid test for the PRSP will be the future well-being of the 40 per cent of Cameroon's population currently living below the poverty line.

Conclusion

PRSPs are currently the main instrument for international concessional aid, and one which is expected to deliver not only sizeable welfare benefits, but also a new relationship between donor nations and recipients. Participation is a central pillar of the new philosophy, and important not only in its own right but also as a critical component of a process which is expected to deliver 'national ownership'.

The prescriptions which this chapter reviews would seem to fall some way short of this ideal. What is described here is not a process under unequivocal national ownership, but one in which positive participatory sentiments function as much to obscure as to reveal the nature of central control; more the co-optation of faddish language in the service of the status quo than a radical reform of political relationships.

It could be argued that this is what happens when powerful financial institutions hijack exciting new ideas. But it could equally well be suggested that the roots of this problem lie further back than this, in the very foundations of the participatory movement. They relate to the vanity of a movement which has sought to appropriate to itself rights over policy not just by criticizing the status quo (this is surely a legitimate function of dissent) but also by moralizing its own boundaries (cf. Francis 2001). Thus infused with moral sentiment, the movement has claimed its own mandate to decide both the nature of 'participation', and who has the authority to represent its authentic essence. The virtues of such discretionary and sub-democratic sentiments may be typical of the IFIs' approach to governance but, in the present context, they are justified and reinforced by reference to a corpus of quasi-independent theory and evidence. Such self-aggrandisement readily takes on a mythic quality: 'mythic' in the sense of proselytizing the cause, and in this way cutting off dissent (cf. Douglas 1966). International finance institutions which need to justify heavy streams of international funds are only too happy to be offered such myths on a plate, and to use their moralization to give specious academic legitimacy to institutional self-interest.

The proponents of the participatory approach seek to justify it by reference to its positive, incremental role. This chapter has suggested some grounds to challenge this view. At the end of the day, the failing of the approach risks being a failure not just to provide incremental gains to democracy, but an active undermining of one of its major purposes. It is the failure to uphold a vital characteristic of democratic functioning – limiting and holding in check the power of those who rule – which is at the heart of the case against the participatory movement in its present form. In this regard, the rejuvenation of the notion of participation represented by the

PRSP approach arguably represents not its coming of age as a legitimate and genuinely transformative approach to development but, rather, further proof of its continuing 'tyranny'.

Notes

1 They are a formal requirement for a country to reach HIPC 'Completion Point', which provides the trigger to long-term debt relief.

2 The 'core principles' of PRSPs are that they should be: country driven/led, and participatory; results-oriented; comprehensive; partnership-oriented; and oriented to offering a long-term perspective.

3 'Rentier' in the sense of depending heavily on external and 'unearned' rents, and producing an income stream largely disconnected from the economic activity in the society.

4 In a recent survey of the field, Stewart and Wang (2003: 22) suggest that PRSPs have achieved little in the way of increasing national ownership/ empowerment over programme design by national governments, and that where empowerment of civil society has occurred, it has often been limited to local and foreign NGOs which are 'not necessarily representative of society as a whole or the poor, in particular'.

5 One notes that the two PRSPs which are widely acclaimed as setting the standard for the class are Uganda and Vietnam. Neither of these is a multi-party democracy.

References

Bretton Woods Project (2002) *Blinding with Science or Encouraging Debate? How World Bank Analysis Determines PRSP Policies* (London: Bretton Woods Project with World Vision).

Brown, D. (1995) 'Seeking the Consensus: Populist Tendencies at the Interface between Research and Consultancy', *AERDD Working Papers*, 5 (Reading: University of Reading), p. 12.

— (1998) 'Professionalism, Participation, and the Public Good: Issues of Arbitration in Development Management and the Critique of the Neo-Populist Approach', in M. Minogue, C. Poldano and D. Hulme (eds), *Beyond the New Public Management: Changing Ideas and Practices in Governance* (Cheltenham: Edward Elgar).

Brown, D., M. Howes, K. Hussein, K. Longley and K. Swindell (2002) *Participation in Practice: Case Studies from the Gambia* (London: ODI).

Cooke, B. and U. Kothari (eds) (2001) *Participation: The New Tyranny?* (London: Zed Books).

Douglas, M. (1966) *Purity and Danger* (London: Penguin Books).

Finer, S. E. (1970) *Comparative Government* (London: Allen Lane).

Francis, P. (2001) 'Participatory Development at the World Bank: The Primacy of Process', in B. Cooke and U. Kothari (eds), *Participation: The New Tyranny?* (London: Zed Books), pp. 72–87.

Government of Cameroon (2003) *Poverty Reduction Strategy Paper* (translation of the French draft of December 2002) (Yaoundé: Government of Cameroon).

Stewart, F. and M. Wang (2003) 'Do PRSPs Empower Poor Countries and Disempower the World Bank, or is It the Other Way Round?', *Working Paper*, 108 (Oxford: Queen Elizabeth House).

World Bank (2000) *PRSP Sourcebook* (Washington, DC: World Bank).

16 | Beyond the technical fix? participation in donor approaches to rights-based development

JEREMY HOLLAND, MARY ANN BROCKLESBY AND CHARLES ABUGRE

During the past decade, the international development community has united behind a renewed focus on poverty reduction. This convergence is most powerfully reflected in the common objectives presented by the Millennium Development Goals (MDGs).[1] During this period there has also been some dramatic movement in the way that development agencies think about poverty. Poverty reduction during the early part of the 1990s was driven by a slavish adherence to the poverty line, with insufficient emphasis on identifying the underlying dimensions of poverty in any particular society or context. A decade later, discussion and thinking about poverty has moved on apace, with new dynamic and powerful analytical frameworks emerging among the international donor community a testament to this shift of thinking. These frameworks have evolved from work by Sen (1981, 1997) on entitlements and capabilities, from the food security literature of the 1980s (Devereux and Maxwell 2001) and later work on vulnerability (Swift 1989; Moser 1998). The frameworks share a conceptualization of poverty as multi-dimensional and complex and introduce a more dynamic and entitlements-focused analytical approach to poverty assessment.

Throughout the 1990s, debates about human rights and development increasingly converged. During the same period that development agencies embraced multi-dimensional analytical frameworks, human rights concerns developed from a first-generation 'negative' concern with protecting individual civil and political (CP) rights to a broader and more developmental concern with ensuring economic, social and cultural (ESC) rights linked to poverty reduction goals. Sen's (1999) characterization of Development as Freedom aptly captures the mutually reinforcing relationship between rights and development: without freedom there is no development; with freedom, development as a process of uplifting personal well-being is enhanced. Among development agencies, the UNDP (2000) has been instrumental in pushing the rights and entitlements agenda, now widely reflected in development agency discourse. The OECD Development Assistance Committee (DAC) Guidelines note the importance of a rights approach which links empowerment to international agreements on human political as well as economic, social and cultural rights, while a more recent UN inter-agency statement (United Nations 2003) of common understanding stresses the need for development cooperation to contribute to the development of the capacities of 'duty bearers' to meet their obligations and/or of rights holders to claim their rights.

This convergence of discourse – the developmental approach to rights and the dynamic approach to poverty – enables development agencies in principle to engage with what Moore and Putzel (1999) call the 'politics of poverty'. The rights discourse politicizes poverty analysis and refocuses attention on the institutions and processes that determine development outcomes. Continuing poverty reduction initiatives, however, do not tend to reflect this convergence of debates, with change continuing to be driven by 'political or bureaucratic imperative' (Norton et al. 2001: 19). Poverty is politically sensitive. Important factors explaining the absence of a rights focus in poverty and policy debates are the language of rights and the politicized nature of rights assessment and fulfilment. In this chapter, through a review of a continuing DFID initiative that seeks to operationalize its stated commitment to rights-based development, we will ask whether donor agencies, technocratically driven and politically constrained, can and should take on a more transformational role in facilitating participation and change.

Rights, participation and institutional change

In moving from poverty assessment to a more politicized rights-based assessment, the role of national institutions and the need for institutional analysis takes on an added significance. Not only does rights-based development politicize development but it builds in a strong action orientation linked to institutional accountability and transparency: 'people now have a claim or entitlement on other people or institutions which, if it is socially-accepted or legally-defined, gives people a minimum level of expected well-being' (Mohan and Holland 2001: 183).

Within this context, participation itself becomes politicized, echoing Gaventa and Valderrama's (1999) thesis on the evolution of community and political participation into what Lister (1998) describes as 'citizenship participation': 'Citizenship as participation can be seen as representing an expression of human agency in the political arena, broadly defined; citizenship as rights enables people to act as agents' (Lister 1998, cited in Gaventa and Valderrama 1999: 4).

Webster and Engberg-Pederson make a critical distinction between strategies of the poor to access directly assets and resources and those that seek to influence policy design and implementation in favour of re-distributive equity. This second type of strategy, they argue, has important implications both for the nature of participation and for the institutional basis of poverty and inequality: 'Here an important focus is upon effecting institutional change in terms of the formulation and implementation of policies ... The discussion of poverty reduction thereby becomes one of mobilisation, organisation, representation, and empowerment' (Webster and Engberg-Pederson 2002: 7).

The success of this qualitatively different type of participation, however, is contingent upon the opening up of 'political space' for engagement and change. Webster and Engberg-Pederson (ibid.) conceive of three elements of political space for participation by the poor:

- *institutional channels* through which policy formulation and implementation can be accessed, controlled or contested by the poor
- *political discourses* in which poverty and poverty reduction are significant issues
- *social and political practices* of the poor which may be a basis for influencing decision-making, agendas, policy and programme implementation, etc.

This conceptualization of the constitution of political space is given operational focus by Moser and Norton (2001) in their analysis of the 'channels of contestation' through which the poor can claim their rights in the context of a range of formal and informal 'rights regimes', each with its own institutional structures. They define a rights regime as a system of rights which derive from a particular regulatory order or source of authority. These can overlap, for example, through customary, religious and statutory law. Institutional structures are those that determine the definition, interpretation and implementation of key rights. The political process then defines the channels through which actors can contest claims and challenge institutional norms.

Rights-based development and 'genuine' participation

Recent debates have focused on what 'rights-based development' means for participatory principles and practice: 'The unquestioning acceptance of concepts such as the rights based approach does little to allow us to develop genuine participatory development, unless we are clear what we mean' (Pratt 2003: 1).

Does rights-based development get us closer to what Pratt calls 'genuine' participatory development? There are a number of well-rehearsed critiques of rights-based development which give significant pause for thought.

Critics have argued, for example, that rights-based development can be blindingly legalistic and removed from rights implementation. From a political perspective, critics have pointed out that international rights standards can reinforce the loss of national sovereignty experienced through debt leverage and expose the eroding capability of a fiscally-squeezed state as primary duty bearer. Others have argued from a cultural-relativist perspective that a normative and universal human rights discourse is insufficiently cognisant of cultural context, identity and particularities. Alternatively, critics have suggested that such international normative frameworks cannot in reality direct processes of contextually-derived social transformation. At best they are ephemeral to and at worst they can undermine important needs-based service delivery. At the very worst, they are simply a metaphor for a bundling of value systems with no operational use.

Potentially a way of addressing these concerns is by an operational focus on participation and empowerment for the progressive realization of rights. In effect this shifts implementation away from problematizing contexts and difference and situates them within an operational framework which seeks to reposition recipients of development goods and services as citizens claiming their rights. This focus bridges the gulf between rights in principle and development realities in two ways. First, it redefines the roles assigned to and the relationships between the state and other development actors. Specifically, this challenges the role consistently assigned to marginalized and subordinate people as clients or beneficiaries of development and offers instead possibilities of shaping different relationships predicated on the political right to participate in decision-making processes. Second, it addresses the tension between international norms and local understandings and interpretations of rights through participatory processes that are emic, interpretive and seek difference rather than standard experiences.

This can be linked to Lister's (1998) notion of citizenship as process wherein rights are not given unconditionally but contested, practised and secured. To act as a citizen involves fulfilling the potential that citizenship rights confer on the individual. In this sense, participation is the foundation of democratic practice: a fundamental right that helps to protect and guarantee all others and by doing so highlights the capacities people have to act as agents in their own development.

Operationalizing the discourse: participatory rights-based assessment

Rights-based development, it seems, provides an operational commitment to a qualitatively different form of participation, in which citizens exercise their right to participate in challenging and changing the institutions that govern their lives. If this is the case, then how might development agencies most effectively change their practice to make this approach work?

Certainly, elements of the donor community have arrived at a position of promoting *process* as the basis for rights-based development. For UNDP, rights are not an outcome of development but integral to the development process: 'human rights are not, as has sometimes been argued, a reward of development. Rather they are critical to achieving it' (UNDP 2000: iii).

The World Bank's *World Development Report, 2000/01* marked a shift in emphasis on 'empowerment' through enhanced political participation of poor people, prompting greater efforts to articulate and categorize the forms of relations between citizen voice and duty bearer/service provider responsiveness (IDS 2001).

DFID's Target Strategy Paper (DFID 2000) outlines its commitment to a rights-based approach to development[2] as the most effective means for achieving poverty reduction outcomes, measured by the Millennium Development Goals. Founded on values of active citizenship, democracy and accountability, and equality and non-discrimination, the Target Strategy Paper builds its strategy on the three core principles of *participation, inclusion* and *fulfilling obligation*. Participation is central to the DFID strategy and means ensuring that the voices of the poor are heard as active citizens rather than muted as passive beneficiaries. Recent studies, including the World Bank's series of Consultations with the Poor, have revealed that people, even those living under democratically elected governments, feel powerless, starved of information, unable to hold public duty bearers to account and lacking in influence over the key decisions that affect their lives. People's right to freedom of opinion and expression and their right to receive and impart information are widely threatened. DFID's position is that, through participation, poor people, and not just local elites, are empowered to claim all their human rights.

In seeking to operationalize its Target Strategy Paper, one way forwards for DFID was to develop an existing research instrument – the Participatory Poverty Assessment (PPA) – but with greater focus on rights assessment and fulfilment. The PPA is an instrument that brings together participation and multi-dimensional poverty analysis. The first generation of PPAs in the early 1990s emphasized information extraction for donor evaluation through participation, with a variable emphasis on entitlements. 'Second generation' PPAs emphasize more strongly the national ownership of process and findings, tied to policy processes such as the Poverty Reduction Strategy Paper (PRSP), while emerging 'third generation' PPAs stress greater local ownership, the 'scaling up' of participation (from its roots in community development and project cycles) through direct interaction between policy-makers and citizens and the need to identify political space for institutional change.

A focus on participatory rights-based assessment ties in closely with the evolving PPA and PRSP process, with its emphasis on institutional engagement and change and on local ownership. By bringing a more specific rights and entitlements analytical framework, however, a participatory rights-based assessment approach politicizes analysis, highlighting power relations and processes of exclusion and discrimination. Participatory rights-based assessments have the potential to identify both the institutional structures, or 'rights regimes' (Moser and Norton 2001) that define, interpret and implement rights as well as the political processes that define the channels through which citizens can contest their claims.

DFID is presently piloting participatory rights-based assessment in four different country and political space contexts. The authors work as part of a team of consultants assigned the task of testing the implementation of DFID's Target Strategy Paper in collaboration with DFID country programmes. The project aims to find ways in which DFID can put its focus on rights fulfilment into practice, by supporting governments, civil society and other social actors in understanding their rights and obligations and in creating the institutional change necessary to ensure participation, inclusion and obligation for all human rights for all people. The project aims to facilitate:

- people's own identification and assessment of their rights
- understanding and agreement between stakeholders of the obstacles poor people face in accessing those rights
- identification of actions to support governments and other duty bearers in the protection, promotion and realization of human rights
- institutional change and the opening up of new channels of institutional engagement between citizens and duty bearers towards these ends

The project is being piloted in partnership with DFID country desks in Malawi, Peru, Romania and Zambia. The process being followed in each country can be mechanistically broken down into phases of scoping, partnership building, identification, assessment and institutional change. The scoping process has focused on the institutional context for rights assessment in order to ensure that rights assessment is linked closely to institutional engagement (see Box overleaf). The project identifies institutional structures as those that determine the definition, interpretation and implementation of key rights. The political process is seen to define the channels through which actors can contest claims, thus giving the analysis

Scoping the institutional context for rights-based assessment

- Is a commitment to rights fairly broad-based within government? Is this reflected in a rights discourse operating at the national level (e.g. through the PRSP process)? Who are the primary and secondary stakeholders? How is that language understood by different stakeholders? What is the level of stakeholders' 'investment' in RBAs? What do they stand to gain/lose from engaging in RBAs?
- What is the constitutional framework with respect to rights? What in the mechanisms of the constitutional framework support people's rights in practice? Whose rights are supported? Is there particular mention of non-discrimination – e.g. on grounds of race, ethnicity, religion, age or disability?
- Where many different types of rights are recognized and in operation, is there a process by which tensions between these are acknowledged and negotiated?
- What is civil society understanding of the constitutional framework and legal process in-country in order to further their claims? What are the processes and mechanisms for stakeholder engagement in relation to rights? What are their strengths and weaknesses? To what extent do these mechanisms rely on 'outside' influence? Who is missing? What are the critical gaps in consultation and engagement that might be addressed in future?
- If engagement with rights is more isolated and mainstream, how do those championing rights engage with mainstream institutions?
- Which sectoral or thematic issues are linked with the rights discourse? Is there a public or private sector focus? Are there politically sensitive sectoral or thematic issues regarding rights fulfilment among specific stakeholders or more generally?
- How are rights issues portrayed in the media?
- What types of 'rights regime' (including international, national, religious, customary and tribal systems of rights) are in operation in relation to the sector or theme?
- What are the processes of policy change (relating to the allocation of resources, service delivery, regulatory frameworks and processes of governance) that influence rights and entitlements outcomes?

an operational focus. Stakeholder identification and partnership building is a key component of DFID process projects and is no less important in the context of this intervention. This has involved early identification and analysis of primary and secondary stakeholders and a time commitment to briefing and ownership-building with key stakeholders.

The political space and institutional vehicle identified in which to encourage participatory rights-based assessment is different in each country. In Malawi and Zambia the intervention is being integrated with broader sector interventions: an education sector support programme in Malawi with a focus on community participation in school management and a health sector HIV/AIDs programme in Zambia focusing on promoting reproductive rights and creating institutional changes in health delivery and accountability. In Romania the vehicle is a regional development programme, aiming for a participatory rights-based assessment to promote a shift from needs-based to rights-based regional development, while in Peru participatory rights-based assessment is being embedded in a human rights programme which disburses project funding and facilitates citizenship participation in local governance. While representing only a relatively limited range of policy, sector and programme contexts, these entry points would, it was hoped, provide useful lessons for piloting participatory rights-based assessment in different institutional and policy contexts.

The process of assessment will involve partnership with local actors with experience in participatory research and will employ a range of participatory methods. Identifying methods or tools for participatory rights assessment will build on an initial scoping of existing methods being used in the country and of the sources of information on rights. Many participatory methods in widespread use are those from the continually expanding Participatory Rural Appraisal (PRA) toolkit. These methods characteristically produce data that are qualitative and contextual although they can produce numbers that can be aggregated and compared across populations.

Ultimately, the participatory rights-based assessment process aims to challenge and transform existing institutions at different levels to improve the understanding and realization of human rights. This means, for example, providing the basis for change within the policies and practices of legal and administrative entities, challenging the conduct of public officials, addressing private sector practice in protecting individual freedoms in the workplace and transforming social institutions at the community and household level. If the process that DFID is encouraging works, then, it is argued, institutions will change.

Discussion: can donors drive institutional change?

While the case study reflects an increasing willingness among donors to engage with politicized processes, the twin association of the donor community with political-ideological conditionality and technical bureaucracy creates very real challenges for an institutional change agenda. Certainly, discussions encouraged by bilateral donors such as DFID, in the context of a shift from project funding to sector and direct budget support, indicate an increasing awareness of the need to identify policy and practice 'paces' as entry points (see, for example, Bevan 2000), reflecting an increasing concern with process over inputs and outputs. This is certainly not the first nor the last time that observers will call for contextual understanding and respect for (time-consuming) process over inputs and outputs. Recent debates over the implementation and monitoring of Poverty Reduction Strategy Papers (PRSPs) testify to this (Booth and Lucas 2001; McGee with Norton 2000).

Here DFID's experience with identifying political space for participatory rights-based assessment demonstrates that donor agencies can identify the institutional channels, poverty-focused political discourses and social and political practices of the poor (Webster and Engberg-Pederson 2002). Clearly, there are particular institutional channels and political discourses that are prioritized by donors in line with donor 'harmonization' around direct budget support, with a concentration on medium-term expenditure frameworks, sector-wide approaches and, in HIPC contexts, the PRSP process.

At the same time that these political spaces are being identified, however, the process part of the 'New Poverty Agenda' is being criticized as formulaic, functional and supply-driven (Booth and Lucas 2001). The current methodology for implementing the New Poverty Agenda – the PRSP – provides useful warnings here on the supply-driven and conditionality burdened cultivation of political space (Maxwell 2003). Caution here comes with a recognition that donor-driven discourses, institutional influence and forms of citizenship participation by the poor will not automatically become rapidly contextualized and owned. As critiques of the PRSP process have noted (Craig and Porter 2002), participation can rapidly become tokenistic, particularly where processes are ghettoized within a policy agenda that is largely non-negotiable under debt-laden conditionality (see Brown, this volume).

Above all, we need to be careful not to endow political space with a voluntaristic sense of participation in the face of anti-democratic forces that occupy such spaces. Political space is not power-neutral. The political and gendered dynamics of communities and locally constructed forms of social capital – Mosse's (2003) 'black box' between policy prescriptions and poverty reducing effects – may reproduce patterns of domination with spaces intended to strengthen marginalized voices being filled by gatekeepers, speaking of rather than with the people they represent (Cornwall 2002). We suggest that engagement with political spaces requires moving beyond a simple recognition of power differentials towards a more nuanced understanding of how its creation involves an interplay between social and power relations shaped through locally situated knowledge and practice. From this perspective, actors within the space are inherently politicized and politicizing. Political spaces are susceptible to human agency: every time a political space opens up or is created, the relationships engendered and the dynamics of the space will throw up different configurations and offer differing possibilities to challenge the status quo of existing power relations (McGee 2002). These are not fixed nor are they predictable and offer possibilities for multiple choices and alternatives to the dominant discourses and existing frames of reference within which decisions are made and policies formulated.[3]

The concept and practice of identifying and facilitating the expansion of political space for participation and rights fulfilment also has the potential to challenge successfully many of the 'tyrannical' attributes ascribed to participation. The epistemological essentializing and privileging of superior local knowledge vs demonic outside scientific rationalism and the construction of 'separate rationalities of ... insider and outsider' (Mohan 2001: 163) can be replaced by a less dualistic scenario in which discourses are multiple, competing and complex.[4] At the same time, concerns about the disempowering effect of localized participation and personal transformations (Mohan 2001)[5] can be replaced by higher and more structural levels of consciousness and action.

DFID's experience with participatory rights-based assessment, however, betrayed a technocratic instinct closely to manage 'invited' political space rather than identify and expand 'autonomous' political space.[6] Linked to this technocratic instinct is a tendency to treat participation as a technical method of project work rather than as a political methodology of empowerment. Paralleling Moser's (1989) distinction between *practical* and *strategic* gender needs, these responses lie on a continuum between interventions which work within existing structures and those which seek to transform those structures. For DFID and other donors the challenge is to recognize the importance of the transformative institutional foundations of rights-based approaches. This requires a close reading of local development processes and partnerships with local organizations, in part through building on existing forms of participation. Eyben's (2003) reflections, based on heading up the DFID Bolivia office, on the roles and responsibilities of the donor community map a normative position of reflexivity for donor staff which would allow them 'to work more comfortably and sensitively with the ambiguity, paradox and unanticipated outcomes that they encounter on a daily basis' with the goal of 'expanding real freedoms ... (in Sen's terms) ... of poor people in poor countries' (ibid., pp. iii–vii).

DFID's experience to date with participatory rights-based assessment has flagged that depoliticized technical approaches can be reinforced by a tendency to drive process with tools. The focus here moves to the relationship between the use of participatory research tools and institutional context for rights realization. Diagnostic tools are powerful and empowering as long as they are embedded in (and can therefore transform) political and institutional space. The flexible (rather than pre-packaged) use of participatory assessment tools was also recognized as important for the same reason. For bureaucrats sitting in donor agencies, it is important that the tools themselves are not seen as off-the-peg transformers.

However, we must also consider the possibility that these 'local' methods are anti-democratic or patriarchal according to the normative gaze of a team of outsiders. This point again reinforces the need to recognize the complexities of dialogue while moving away from binary ideas about methods and their appropriateness. Outsiders have a position as subjects while insiders are not privileged according to some patronizing and disempowering notion of cultural specificity. The dominant discourse has a dominant set of methods; the challenge is to validate alternative methods without essentializing them and so marginalizing them.

In operational terms, adoption of the metaphor of political space brings with it a responsibility to avoid 'originating the process ... (and) ... colonising social change' (Mohan 2001: 167). Mohan stresses that interventions need to be cognisant of the tradition of state, donor and NGO manipulation of civil society and use of the local 'as a political discourse that disempowers', from colonial indirect rule to the Apartheid system to attempts in Latin America to bureaucratize and control the organization of popular participation. The way to avoid this trap is to understand and engage with context. Cornwall (2002) calls for a 'greater understanding of the micro politics of participation as situated practice'. Contextual engagement, she argues, should force outside actors to 'frame their possibilities with reference to actual political, social, cultural and historical particularities'.

Here the shackling effects of donor bureaucratic systems on institutional engagement are being freed somewhat by signs of change in the way that development is 'managed' and 'delivered'. Management thinking in development has been influenced by new business school models which challenge the reductionist way in which managers in professional development tackle complex problems of political process. The tradition of project planning and evaluation in many development agencies has been driven and motivated by 'tyrannical' linear, input–output-driven tools such as the logical framework tool used by DFID or GTZ's ZOP tool and critiqued from within social development circles (Chambers 1997; Pasteur 2001; Davies 2002). Forms of engagement by development agencies are changing, with a move away from positivist linear management to a more post-modern adherence to flexible and adaptive learning. This is particularly evident in the monitoring and evaluation of development interventions (Estrella and Gaventa 1998). New management thinking promotes a shift from 'hard systems' to 'soft systems' methodologies (Checkland 1989) in which bureaucracies using information systems become 'learning organizations' that behave flexibly and improve outcomes by empowering people (Peters 1989; Senge 1992; Pasteur 2001).

This movement to a process approach in projects is coinciding with a major shift in thinking by development agencies on entry points for development assistance. As discussed earlier, bilateral and multilateral agencies are now beginning to work more closely together in engaging with 'upstream' sector and policy processes. The fact that this type of engagement is messier, more complex, less linear and less controllable merely serves to accelerate the perceived need for a process approach to management. That said, there is little let-up in the neo-liberal imperative that drives donor engagement. This is again aptly illustrated by the PRSP process, which has thrown up a number of concerns on the supply-driven and conditionality-burdened 'cultivation' of political space (Maxwell 2003; Craig and Porter 2002).

Conclusion: beyond technical fixes?

The new poverty reduction consensus, influenced as we have noted by more dynamic and process-based understandings of the causes of poverty, has moved the international development agency position considerably from that laid out by the World Bank in its 1990 *World Development Report*. This position, slavishly supported by a series of unmotivated Poverty Assessments during the 1990s, focused narrowly on economic growth as the engine of poverty reduction supported by investment in human capital. Criticisms of the World Bank's lack of attention on inequalities in the distribution of resources as a constraint on growth and poverty reduction (Tjonneland et al. 1998) have been replaced by an acknowledgement that there is a greater emphasis on distribution and inequality (Maxwell 2003). Critics of the 'cheap talk' of community empowerment have started to be swayed by a growing recognition of a rhetorical focus on material and political notions of empowerment (Moore 2001) backed by an operational focus on citizenship participation and institutional change.

For the UN, the World Bank and bilateral agencies such as DFID, 'empowerment' represents essentially a liberal concern with enabling people to make their own choices and in the case of the UNDP (2000) to claim their rights actively as citizens (Gaventa and Valderrama 1999). This brings with it an operational focus on building knowledge and capability to help people to know about their rights, so that they can defend or uphold them. It also forces donors to engage with context by understanding the (informal and formal) 'rights regimes' (Moser and Norton 2001) within which people live and by identifying and 'stretching' the political space in which individuals and groups can exercise their rights and participate in decisions that affect their lives.

Certainly, interventions such as DFID's continuing work on participatory rights-based assessment, create an opportunity for critics to denounce, as they have done in the past, the bureaucratic use of participation as 'technical management solutions to what are basically political issues' (Guijt and Shah 1998: 3). The tensions within DFID, as an institution with its own complex inter-subjective meanings, indicate that there remains a bureaucratic and technical *modus operandi* that acts as a brake on more politicized rights discourse. The complexities and messiness of relations between a DFID policy centre in London and increasingly autonomous DFID regional and country accounting offices often serve to strengthen these tensions. Yet whether or not this type of intervention is conceived of as a technical fix or a politicizing Trojan horse is probably not the most important question on which to conclude. There are two bigger questions that emerge from this discussion. The first is whether donors are able to play this role without directing political space from without. As purveyors of the New Poverty Agenda (Maxwell 2003), donors are signed up to a neo-liberal agenda that carries very clear notions of what empowerment means and which brings managerial and instrumental overtones to institutional change and learning, with participation becoming what Cornwall (2002: 11) describes as 'an instrument for managed intervention'.

The second and related question is whether they should be playing this role at all. When political space is identified and invitations extended by such powerful agents, how much distortion does this create? How much does it create strategic, dysfunctional or non-sustainable process and institutional outcomes? Gaventa and Valderamma's conceptualization of autonomously created spaces for citizenship participation seem suddenly distant and unattainable.[7] The answer, we argue, lies in reformulating inter-subjectivity to include donors as subjects and agents rather than as bureaucratic puppeteers. Donors have to recognize that they are not outside pulling strings but are politicized and part of the process. Taking this to its logical conclusion, the uncertainty and dynamism that characterizes the transition from rights assessment to rights fulfilment – whether they are called political spaces, knowledge battlefields or pure chaos – demand abandonment of positivist-based tools and modes of intervention. We believe it will take a radical, but achievable, shift in mindsets for donors to rise to this challenge.

Notes

1 The Millennium Development Goals were approved by the General Assembly of the United Nations in 2000. They represent a continuation of the International Development Targets codified by the Development Assistance Committee of the OECD in 1996.

2 See also Häusermann's (1998) background discussion paper.

3 This position fits well with perspectives on scaled-up participation and increasingly complex inter-linkages between actors from the local to the global (Edwards and Gaventa 2001).

4 Mohan's strategy for 'deepened empowerment' introduces his ideas on 'radical hybridity' in which the duality of powerless (but all-knowing) subjects vs well-established structures of power is replaced by complex, power-infused social institutions that operate in 'the inter-subjective worlds (where) meaning, knowledge and political action will emerge' (Mohan 2001: 164). These are non-consensual and non-normative, but are also non-exclusive. They describe a non-linear or 'fuzzy' social reality that flies in the face of the prevailing development thinking and practice (Chambers 1997).

5 Mohan (2001: 162) argues that 'the focus on the personal and local as the site of empowerment and knowledge circumscribes consciousness and action'.

6 See McGee (2002) for a discussion of the distinction between invited and autonomous political space.

7 This means in the first instance a shift in language from partnerships to alliances. As Bevan (2000: 15) points out, 'partners are stakeholders with different goals, aims and power'. Partnerships suggest functional, consensual and normative ways of working. Alliances accommodate difference.

References

Bevan, P. (2000) 'Programme Approaches: Spaces and Entry Points for Social Development', *SD SCOPE Paper*, 11, DFID.

Booth, D. and H. Lucas (2001) 'Good Practice in the Development of PRSP Indicators and Monitoring Systems', *ODI Working Paper*, 172 (July) (London: Overseas Development Institute).

Brock, K., A. Cornwall and J. Gaventa (2001) 'Power, Knowledge and Political Spaces in the Framing of Poverty Policy', *IDS Working Paper*, 143 (Brighton: Institute of Development Studies).

Chambers, R. (1997) *Whose Reality Counts? Putting the First Last* (London: IT Publications).

Checkland, P. (1989) 'Soft Systems Methodology', in *Human Systems Management*, 8: 273–89.

Cornwall, A. (2002) 'Making Spaces, Changing Places: Situating Participation in

Development', *IDS Working Paper*, 170 (Brighton: Institute of Development Studies).

Craig, D. and D. Porter (2002) 'Poverty Reduction Strategy Papers: A New Convergence', *World Development*, 31 (1): 53–69.

Davies, R. (2002) 'Improved Representations of Change Processes: Improved Theories of Change', Paper presented at the 5th Biennial Conference of the European Evaluation Society, Seville, October.

Devereux, S. and S. Maxwell (eds) (2001) *Food Security in Sub-Saharan Africa* (London: IT Development Group Publishing).

DFID (1997) *Evaluation of DFID Support for Poverty Reduction* (London: Department for International Development).

— (2000) *Realising Human Rights for Poor People* (London: Department for International Development).

Edwards, M. and J. Gaventa (eds) (2001) *Global Citizen Action* (Boulder, CO: Lynne Rienner).

Estrella, M. and J. Gaventa (1998) 'Who Counts Reality? Participatory Monitoring and Evaluation: A Literature Review', *IDS Working Paper*, 70 (Brighton: Institute of Development Studies).

Eyben, R. (2003) 'Donors as Political Actors: Fighting the Thirty Years War in Bolivia', *IDS Working Paper*, 183 (Brighton: Institute of Development Studies).

Gaventa, J., A. Shankland and J. Howard (eds) (2002) 'Making Rights Real: Exploring Citizenship, Participation and Accountability', *IDS Bulletin*, 33 (2) (Brighton: Institute of Development Studies).

Gaventa, J. and C. Valderrama, (1999) 'Participation, Citizenship and Local Governance', Background note for workshop, June.

Guijt, I. and M. Shah (1998) 'Waking up to Power, Conflict and Process', in I. Guijt and M. Shah (eds), *The Myth of Community: Gender Issues in Participatory Development* (London: IT Publications), pp. 1–23.

Häusermann, J. (1998) 'Rights and Humanity: A Human Rights Approach to Development, Rights and Humanity', Discussion Paper (London: Department for International Development).

IDS (2001) 'From Consultation to Influence: Bringing Citizen Voice and Client Focus into Service Delivery', *Consultancy Report*, March (Brighton: Institute of Development Studies).

Lister, R. (1998) 'Citizen in Action: Citizenship and Community Development in the Northern Ireland Context', *Community Development Journal*, 33 (3): 226–35.

McGee, R, (2002) 'Conclusion: Participatory Poverty Research: Opening Spaces for Change', in K. Brock and R. McGee (eds), *Knowing Poverty: Critical Reflections on Participatory Research and Policy* (London: Earthscan), pp. 189–205.

McGee, R. with A. Norton (2000) 'Participation in Poverty Reduction Strategies: A Synthesis of Experience with Participatory Approaches to Policy Design, Implementation and Monitoring', *IDS Working Paper*, 109 (Brighton: Institute of Development Studies).

Maxwell, S. (2003) 'Heaven or Hubris: Reflections on the New Poverty Agenda', *Development Policy Review*, 21 (1): 5–25.

Mohan, G. (2001) 'Beyond Participation: Strategies for Deeper Empowerment', in B. Cooke and U. Kothari (eds), *Participation: The New Tyranny?* (London: Zed Books).

Mohan, G. and J. Holland (2001) 'Human Rights and Development in Africa: Moral Intrusion or Empowering Opportunity', *Review of African Political Economy*, 88: 177–96.

Moore, M. (2001) 'Empowerment at Last?', *Journal of International Development*, 13: 321–9.

Moore, M. and J. Putzel (1999) 'Politics and Poverty: A Background Paper for the World Development Report 2000/1', mimeo (Brighton: Institute of Development Studies).

Moser, C. (1989) 'Gender Planning in the Third World: Meeting Practical and Strategic Gender Needs', *World Development*, 17 (11): 1799–825.

— (1998) 'The Asset–Vulnerability Framework: Reassessing Urban Poverty Reduction Strategies', *World Development*, 26 (1): 1–19.

Moser, C. and A. Norton (2001) 'To Claim Our Rights: Livelihood Security, Human Rights and Sustainable Development', Concept paper (London: Overseas Development Institute).

Mosse, D. (2003) 'Re-presenting Development: Reflections on the Ethnography of Aid Policy and Practice', Draft paper (London: School of Oriental and African Studies).

Norton, A., with B. Bird, K. Brock, M. Kakande and C. Turk (2001) *A Rough Guide to PPAs, Participatory Poverty Assessment: An Introduction to Theory and Practice* (London: Department for International Development).

Pasteur, K. (2001) 'Thinking about Logical Frameworks and Sustainable Livelihoods: A Short Critique and a Possible Way Forward', Unpublished paper (Brighton: Institute of Development Studies).

Peters, T. (1989) *Thriving on Chaos: Handbook for a Management Revolution* (London: Pan Books).

Pratt, B. (2003) 'Rights or Values?', *Ontrac*, 1–2 (Oxford: International NGO Training and Research Centre).

Sen, A. (1981) *Poverty and Famines: An Essay on Entitlement and Deprivation* (Oxford: Clarendon Press).

— (1997) 'Editorial: Human Capital and Human Capability', *World Development*, 25 (12): 1959–61.

— (1999) *Development as Freedom* (Oxford: Oxford University Press).

Senge, P. (1992) *The Fifth Discipline: The Art and Practice of the Learning Organisation* (London: Random House).

Sengupta, A. (2000) 'Realizing the Right to Development', *Development and Change*, 31: 553–78.

Shivji, I. (1989) *The Concept of Human Rights in Africa* (Dakar: Codesria).

Swift, J. (1989) 'Why are Rural People Vulnerable to Famine?', *IDS Bulletin*, 20 (2): 8–15.

Thin, N. (1998) *Social Development Policies, Results and Learning: Experiences from European Agencies* (London: Social Development Division, DFID).

Tjonneland, E. et al. (1998) *The World Bank and Poverty in Africa: A Critical Assessment of the Bank's Operational Strategies for Poverty Reduction*, Report for the Norwegian Ministry for Foreign Affairs, Oslo.

UNDP (2000) *Human Rights and Human Development (Human Development Report 2000)*, United Nations Development Programme (New York and Oxford: Oxford University Press).

United Nations (2003) 'The Human Rights Based Approach: Towards a Common Understanding Among the UN Agencies', Draft statement produced at the Second Inter-agency Workshop on Implementing a Human Rights Based Approach in the Context of UN Reform, Stamford, CT, 5–7 May.

Webster, N. and L. Engberg-Pederson (2002) *In the Name of the Poor: Contesting Political Space for Poverty Reduction* (London: Zed Books).

World Bank (2000) *World Development Report 2000–2001: Attacking Poverty* (Oxford: Oxford University Press).

SIX | Broader perspectives on 'from tyranny to transformation'

17 | The social embeddedness of agency and decision-making

FRANCES CLEAVER

In this volume Hickey and Mohan advocate the furthering of a radical political project based on the promotion of citizenship. This they see as necessary to overcome the perceived 'tyranny' of localized project-led approaches to participation and to provide the potential for transformation of inequitable relations at a number of levels. The citizenship approach, also elaborated by Gaventa, offers the possibility of multi-level approaches to participation; linking the micro-politics of community participation to good governance and the workings of the state. Linking this focus to a wider political project of social justice (Hickey and Mohan, Chapter 4) allows us to broaden thinking about participation away from a focus on projects and techniques towards the implicit possibilities of dealing with structural inequality through participatory governance and state action. This focus on tackling inequality structurally does not, however, involve abandoning the perceived importance of agency in participatory development. Indeed, active citizenship, the exercise of voice, the championing of interests and the advocacy of rights are seen as the very manifestation of agency, by individuals, their representatives and collectivities.

This approach offers some valuable insights, in advancing the more rigorous conceptualization of under-theorized participatory approaches, in embracing the complexities of a multi-level perspective and in tackling the need for structural change in the interests of transformation of inequality. In this short chapter, however, I will identify some conceptually problematic areas where caution is needed to avoid advancing a heady but ultimately unconvincing notion of participatory citizenship based on over-optimistic notions of agency and combined with romantic ideas about groups and institutions.

Citizenship, agency and culture

Theorists of agency tend to emphasize the positive possibilities of such purposive human action, the transformatory and emancipatory potential of agency-as-opposition (Giddens 1984; Long and Long 1992). Hickey and Mohan's concept of radical political citizenship builds on this trend; they see agency as a range of sociopolitical practices which allow people to *extend* their status and rights as members of particular political communities and thus *increase* their control over socioeconomic resources (Chapter 4). Through the exercise of such citizenship the 'room for manoeuvre' of the poor and marginalized can be increased.

In defining citizenship as the active manifestation of agency there is a danger of abstracted under-socialization. Agency cannot be exercised in a vacuum and it is the very minutiae of social life and relationships which shape the forms that citizenship can take. These may prove much more difficult to transform than public spaces and institutions of the state. Through an engagement with the chapters in Section III on 'Participation as Popular Agency' in particular, I identify three key factors which both enable and *constrain* the exercise of agency and therefore shape citizenship; moral understandings of action and the unconscious motivation of many acts, the complexity of both individual and collective identities and the (often unequal) interdependence involved in the exercise of rights and livelihood interests.

Henry, writing about Ethiopia in this volume, suggests that to be a good Gurage citizen involves active participation in family and community events. Experience from elsewhere in Africa shows us that such events are governed by ideas of moral behaviour, 'the right way of doing things'. Thus showing respect (to elders, or to the powerful), avoiding open conflict and furthering reconciliation are common moral principles within which relationships within families and communities are (at least nominally) conducted. But several of these moral understandings of the right way to behave are incompatible with a notion of active citizenship as proposed by Hickey and Mohan, despite their elaboration of 'ethnic citizenship'. The concept of active citizenship has equal citizens entering political debate informed by local moralities but none the less able to exercise open voice (or active resistance), operate transparently, freely confront perceived inequalities and to join together with similar citizens to overcome these. In writing elsewhere I have tried to illustrate how the moral norms of decision-making are deeply psychologically and socially embedded and often (at least partially) elude conscious scrutiny and discourse (Cleaver 2000, 2002). Moreover, agency is further limited by the role of habit in defining our actions – the importance of routine in reproducing everyday practices and societal structures (Bourdieu 1977; Douglas 1987). Decision-making processes and the exercise of agency within them, therefore, may be contradictory in their social effects; respectful attitudes, conflict avoidance and consensus decision-making can all serve to reinforce inequality despite securing functional outcomes.

The exercise of agency involves not just morality, but the mutuality and interdependence of people with multiple identities. Rights do not exist in a vacuum but are embedded in social relations; these very social relations may either enable or constrain the exercise of such agency. For example, evidence from Africa (Odgaard 2002) and India (Rao 2003) suggest the complexity of identities and relationships through which women's land rights are exercised. Women may claim rights to land as legal (and equal) citizens but also through their subject positions as daughters, wives and mothers, as members of a particular caste or ethnic group. To these women, living their lives within marriages and kin groups, exercising their legal and political rights to land may *not* be the preferred option; the costs of asserting such rights to their conjugal and family relations, to their status in the community, to their livelihood outcomes may mean that they prefer to secure (inequitable) access through social institutions. How, within a model of radicalized, political citizenship do we see a preference for exercising agency *within* inequitable relationships (as argued by Williams, this volume), rather than for overcoming or challenging them?

Chapters by Masaki and Henry in this volume strongly emphasize the livelihood interdependence of people in different power positions. Henry quotes the Gurage rural dwellers, operating within power relations in which they do the collective work while the urban elite offer leadership, as saying, 'We depend on our brothers in Addis for everything'. And while the landowning elite of Masaki's Nepalese village indeed need the lower-caste villagers as labourers of their land, the relationship is one of skewed interdependence as the labourers are unlikely to survive without the patronage of the landowners. Relations of interdependence do offer the possibility of negotiation (as shown by Masaki's case) but such interdependence exists alongside structural inequality and the exercise of agency by the poor can only be partial, intermittent and cumulatively ineffectual in these circumstances. Vincent warns against optimistically interpreting any signs of non-participation as resistance and this warning seems to encapsulate a problem we have with agency. We so want the active exercise of agency to lead to transformation that we even romanticize procrastination and deception as resistance. But the exercise of agency may well be passively a-social or actively anti-social (stealing, cheating, vandalism) and 'being social' may well involve securing livelihood stability at the cost of equality. To understand and further a project of radical citizenship, surely we need better understandings of what it means to be an acting subject in particular circumstances, and the complex constraints on the exercise of agency, particularly for the poor and marginalized. The chapters by Vincent, Henry and Masaki point to the need for analyses which combine an illumination of the varying *forms* of agency and decision-making with a rigorous and differentiated scrutiny of the *effects* of these on different actors.

Collective action, governance and institutionalizing participation

Despite much recent research showing the diversity of institutions through which individual and collective interests are pursued (Benjaminsen and Lund 2002), writings about participation still overwhelmingly focus on the legible, the bureaucratic, the public manifestations of decision-making. There is much talk now about 'new spaces' and 'new rules' through which expressions of emancipatory citizenship are to be articulated and promoted. Hickey and Mohan (Chapter 4) conceive citizenship being claimed 'from below' through groups, and being exercised through particular political communities. However, despite their efforts and those of Cornwall to resolve these issues, questions remain about how groups and communities are defined and delimited, how new spaces and new rules are socially authorized and legitimated, how far they can encapsulate the decision-making processes of everyday life, and to what extent are ideas about the development of fora for the exercise of citizenship informed by simple evolutionism.

Theorists of society and institutions suggest that we all have a need to naturalize human arrangements, to see even the most modern mechanisms of social organization, decision-making and resource allocations as having continuity with the past, with the world as we know it, with existing systems of authority and legitimation (Giddens 1984; Douglas 1987). Inevitably, then, 'old' sources of authority are used to legitimize new institutions, accepted norms of public discourse and decision-making shape people's voice and articulation in new spaces. So we see existing elites (chiefs, headmen, landowners, higher castes, the urban educated) playing prominent roles in new spaces, in representing and articulating the needs of the poor and marginalized. Such processes do not obviate all progressive change, but they do cast doubt on the potential for dramatic transformation, at least over shorter and more immediate timescales. Odgaard (2002) has well illustrated how both 'traditional' and 'modern' institutional channels are used by people to 'double safeguard' their rights, but how such institutions can also doubly disadvantage the marginalized and inarticulate. Here, Masaki has illustrated the double reinforcement of disadvantage through customary labour arrangements and modern (development induced) adaptations of these.

So how can a concept of politicized citizenship be worked through the multiplicity of channels within which (inequitable) norms are negotiated, reproduced, reinforced, through which authority is exercised and sanctions imposed? Hickey and Mohan suggest the need for collective decisions to be arrived at through a process of pragmatic reasoning, a micro-politics of consensus formation. This position assumes that most decision-making (and citizenship-shaping) takes place transparently, in public spaces. What does it mean, though, to be a good citizen at the waterpoint, or at the market, in negotiating collective labour arrangements, in managing resources at the point of use? Research shows us that it is at these intersections between private and public livelihood activity that many negotiations about resource allocation, sharing, compromise, conflict resolution and appropriate representation actually take place (Cleaver 2002). The more vibrant the associational life in a community, the more diverse the livelihoods and the inter-meshing of cultures, the less likely that 'participation' or 'citizenship' or 'collective action' manifests through any one channel.

Critics have highlighted the instrumental nature of many participatory initiatives, the focus on efficiency over empowerment, the use of participants as cheap labourers on public works. However, prominent in the accounts in this volume and elsewhere is the concern of poor people for very material development assistance, for the delivery of infrastructure, welfare provisions and effective government that will ease the burden of their lives. Surely 'empowerment' and 'transformation' require not just the opening up of participatory spaces to transparently debate citizenship, to hold the state to account and so on, but also the more prosaic transformation of everyday life: relief from the burden of queueing for and carrying water, of hand-tilling fields, of dependence on relations of patronage for daily subsistence, of the burden of care imposed by diseases caused by undernutrition, poor hygiene and frequent pregnancy. Poor people suffering such conditions have little chance of even being a good neighbour, never mind articulating their rights in public spaces, or becoming representatives of others similarly disadvantaged. Transforming the notion of participation into one of a radicalized and political citizenship, reliant on the open and transparent negotiation of rights, doesn't suddenly do away with the costs of participation. And the costs to the poorest, the most marginalized, those with most to gain from transformation, are the greatest. In the short term, the disadvantages to them of confronting unequal relations on which they depend, may simply outweigh the costs of acquiescence. In advocating participatory citizenship as a route to transformation, we may simply perpetuate the pervasive myth of the endless resourcefulness of the poor (Gonzalez de la Rocha 2003).

Many writings on participation are implicitly underpinned by evolutionary concepts. It is assumed that the practice of participation is unilinear and cumulative; that spaces for participation can be progressively strengthened, that the exercise of agency and voice in one forum has knock-on and cumulative effects in others (although see Cornwall and Kelly, this volume). But institutions don't work like that. People's behaviour isn't so consistent and, as shown by Masaki's case, where structural inequalities are great, the exercise of oppositional agency is intermittent and partial. Processes of empowerment and transformation can be reversed, development discourse used regressively (e.g. Upperman 2000). One-off ad hoc manifestations of collective action and solidarity (as in Vincent's case) can be read two ways; as evidence of the potential for building something more durable, or as illustration of the crippling constraints which preclude frequent, regularized participation for the public good. In considering the time–space dimensions of participation we should be concerned with the possibility of stoppages and reversals in the transformatory direction, and also with the inherent limitations of ad hoc, infrequent collective action.

Conclusion: the partiality of agency, the inequality of structure

In normative attempts to find transformatory prospects in the politics of participation and representation, we tend to look at social processes and highlight the potential of the bits that we like: the transformation rather than the tyranny, the solidarity rather than the conflict, articulation rather than mutedness, the enablement of agency rather than the constraint of structure. However, the nature of these social processes is that the duality is inherent to them, and cannot be done away with. In thinking through participation, we do ourselves no favours in wishing away the potentially negative aspects of representation. Our challenge is to use an understanding of the dynamic nature of such duality to identify opportunities for change. However, we have to reconcile ourselves to these only ever being partial, intermittent, involving winners and losers, not entirely controllable or predictable. Recognizing the limits of the makeability of social life is as important to achieving something in development as over-optimistic faith in the possibilities of participatory politics.

References

Benjaminsen T. and C. Lund (eds) (2002) 'Securing Land Rights in Africa', *European Journal of Development Research*, 14 (2).

Bourdieu, P. (1977) *Outline of a Theory of Practice* (Cambridge: Cambridge University Press).

Cleaver, F. (2000) 'Moral Ecological Rationality, Institutions and the Management of Common Property Resources', *Development and Change*, 31: 361–83.

— (2002) 'Reinventing Institutions: Bricolage and the Social Embeddedness of Natural Resource Management', *European Journal of Development Research*, 14 (2): 11–30.

Douglas, M. (1987) *How Institutions Think* (London: Routledge and Kegan Paul).

Giddens, A. (1984) *The Constitution of Society: Outline of the Theory of Structuration* (Cambridge: Polity Press).

Gonzalez de la Rocha, M. (2003) 'The Construction of the Myth of Survival',

Paper given at workshop on Gender Myths and Feminist Fables: Repositioning Gender in Development Policy and Practice, Institute of Development Studies, University of Sussex, 2–4 July.

Long, N. and A. Long (1992) *Battlefields of Knowledge: The Interlocking of Theory and Practice in Social Research and Development* (London: Routledge).

Odgaard, R. (2002) 'Scrambling for Land in Tanzania: Processes of Formalisation and Legitimisation of Land Rights', *European Journal of Development Research*, 14 (2): 71–88.

Rao, N. (2003) 'Only Women Can and Will Represent Women's Interests: The Case of Land Rights', Paper given at workshop on Gender Myths and Feminist Fables: Repositioning Gender in Development Policy and Practice, Institute of Development Studies, University of Sussex, 2–4 July.

Upperman, E. (2000) 'Gender Relations in a Traditional Irrigation Scheme in Northern Tanzania', in C. Creighton and C. K. Omari (eds), *Gender, Family and Work in Tanzania* (Aldershot: Ashgate), ch. 12.

18 | Theorizing participation and institutional change: ethnography and political economy

ANTHONY BEBBINGTON

The tense interface between theory and practice, thought and action, has never been far from the surface in discussions of participatory development. Participation helps unite people who share commitments to more equitable and humane forms of social and political economic organization but who differ greatly on strategy: some are more reformist, others are deeply sceptical that reform can make much difference; some are more forgiving of people who work, live and seek reform within dominant institutions that otherwise tend to impose agendas and so foster exclusion, while others see Machiavellian intent everywhere they look; some see the need to theorize strategy carefully, others view such abstraction as a tyranny that obstructs change-oriented action and once again privileges elite forms of knowledge. And as David Brown reminds us, moralizing stances are everywhere, even among those who feel they are above such holier-than-thou position-taking.

The chapters I was asked to review for this short commentary[1] touch on and in their own ways reflect each of these tensions and while each walks its own tightrope, they all ultimately assume positions. While there are differences, the positions taken are generally sceptical of reform, doubtful of 'external' efforts to foster participation, and pro-theory. I want to focus the second part of my comment on this matter of theory (and the comment will make clear that I place myself in the camp that sees the importance of theorizing strategy). I want to begin, though, with a reflection about how these discussions compare with those of just a decade ago (a reflection located more on the reformist, forgiving side of the tensions I have just noted).

A few years back, and on the morning after I had given a talk that had more or less bombed, a kind (and brilliant) colleague simply and supportively said to me, 'You do what you can.'[2] Reflecting on the themes of the essays in this collection, it seems evident that the frontier of what can be done around participatory development and social change has expanded enormously, opening up many more options and possibilities to those seeking to foster social and institutional change through participatory processes. This can be too easily forgotten in the heat of dissatisfaction with PRSPs and a World Bank in which many still, clearly, resist more transformative approaches to development (though if you think this is bad, wait until we get the Bush-selected president of the World Bank). Yet the change is important. Less than ten years ago social development professionals in the World Bank were struggling to make the case for participatory project design and management visible within the institution, and the idea of fostering participation in the background work that went into the design of Country Assistance Strategies[3] was far more tenuous and ambitious (Aronson 1995). Today participatory policy formulation in the form of PRSPs is a requirement, and Bank publications (internally contested as they were: Kanbur 2001; Wade 2001) speak of the need to democratize public institutions (World Bank 2000). A decade ago, the UK government's Overseas Development Administration seemed clunky and conservative in comparison to other European bilaterals. Today it speaks of human rights and rights-based approaches that *necessarily* politicize discussions of development and poverty (as Holland et al. note). Of course, oceans can and do divide what is said and what is done – but what is said still matters, and has much bearing on what *can* be done. The frontier of the *do-able* has changed.

It might be that this is not a good thing – that these new pronouncements on participation allow these international and bilateral agencies to colonize even more deeply national institutions and political processes, and have the effect of undermining representative democracy as Brown suggests might be the case in his chapter. It might also be that these pronouncements are mostly hot air – how can there really be participation in PRSPs if they all end up looking similar (as Bill Cooke [forthcoming] has suggested)? Is what is going on here mostly a discursive strategy to facilitate the management of a global transition to deep-seated neo-liberalism (cf. Cammack 2002)? These are important and troubling questions and these chapters pose them (and others) effectively.

Even if these are – or might one day be – the *effects* of such scaled-up, ostensible commitments to participatory policy and to such apparent openness to more politicized discussions of poverty and exclusion, I doubt such effects were the *intent* of those who committed their lives, careers and often families to fostering such changes.[4] While critiques that PRSPs and PPAs merely deepen the power of external agencies and foster 'highly manipulated' (Brown) forms of participation may serve important advocacy purposes, they skate over a crucial analytical question in their urge to stake out criticism. Namely, how did such apparently progressive agendas emerge within these bureaucracies in the first place; how was it possible to promote such new languages and arguments within these institutions; and then, how were these languages and initiatives reworked and captured, both within these institutions and within the countries in which they operate (Bebbington et al. forthcoming)?

These questions are genuinely important for those concerned to understand and foster institutional change, and are questions about which too little is known (even if far more is asserted). They mean that not only ought development agencies fostering participation become far more self-reflexive in the ways Holland et al. very rightly suggest; these agencies, and their internal processes, need to become objects of inquiry. Only by understanding how spaces that are won are then lost will it be possible to win spaces that are more resilient to capture by conservative forces.

And this is my segue into development theory. This collection – particularly Part II on 'Rethinking Participation' – argues convincingly that theory is an important tool for guarding against such capture, for understanding how and where it might occur, and for thinking through strategies that are less easily captured and distorted. There are many pointers to elements of such theory in these papers. On the wider canvas, and in line with a series of recent interventions on development theory, Hickey and Mohan suggest that the distinction between development as a process of structural change in society (as in the development of capitalism) and development as deliberate intervention (as in development projects) offers one framework within which to understand the nature, potential and likely effects of participatory interventions. Such frameworks, which understand participation in the context of actually existing capitalisms, are essential if the underlying normative interest is that participatory processes lead to forms of social transformation. If this is indeed the goal, then frameworks used to understand, but also to strategize, participation must have a well-developed structuralist and political economic dimension. Without this they lack the tools to understand 'what the fight is really about' or to understand the factors that will determine whether the fight is won or lost.

There is evidently a risk that approaches that emphasize political economy in such ways will indulge 'negative academics' (cf. Chambers 1983; Moore 1999) – negativity of the type that argues that the effects, and even intent, of participatory approaches is to do little more than soften the harsh blows of neo-liberalism, and in the process to stabilize neo-liberalism and the governing power of international financial institutions.[5] But this does not have to be the tack of such analyses. The point of framing not just participation, but also the sites from which it is advocated and promoted, in relationship to structural context is to be realistic about what is more and less possible, and also – and this is more important still – to be clearer about the obstacles to social transformation and increased levels of meaningful social inclusion. It means that participation events – in projects, research cycles, planning processes etc. – should never again be considered without considering the 'immanent' conditions under which they occur. This seems to me a most important conclusion.[6]

These are bigger picture frameworks. At the micro-scale, there is much to Cornwall's suggestion that ethnographies of participation as practised could have great value in illuminating the workings of power in development interventions, and the ways in which it fosters exclusion/inclusion in the spaces in which participation occurs. The suggestion here – consistent with the well established body of (largely but not always post-structuralist) writing on resistance and the micro-foundations of power – is that it is critical to understand how power operates in order to understand how spaces for change open and close, and how the intentions and effects of action converge and diverge. However, there is also a refreshing humanist edge to her argument (and to that of Holland et al.) – namely that such ethnographic engagement with participation in practice can also throw light on how surprises emerge, on how personal transformations occur, and on how people matter to the course taken by participatory interventions. Theorizing such surprise is difficult, but it does at least imply that much more needs to be known about what happens to certain people (and why) when they become involved in the participation game. While we should still theorize, we ought to do so humbly.

If the theoretical arguments of Hickey, Mohan and Cornwall are read together, the implication is that theorizing participatory development *necessarily* requires an engagement with practices that pose awkward questions about attitudes and behaviours (Chambers's messages still resonate), unexpected outcomes, and normative commitments. Meanwhile, practising participation *necessarily* requires engagement with theories that pose difficult questions and challenges, that force the practitioner never to lose site of the wider picture – a picture in which questions of capitalist development, state formation, the constitution of civil society and social differentiation all loom large and that demand that the practitioner be clear on the fights that need to be picked. These are important challenges for they suggest the importance of particular types of partnerships in both research and practice, and they suggest that, at least in development studies, theory workers and practice workers ought never to lose touch. This is a critical message in these days when the dynamics and values that dominate academic assessment push academics away from practice, and when the pressure to demonstrate poverty impact leaves governmental and non-governmental development organizations even less inclined to support, or even have any great belief in, research.

In these ways, the arguments of these chapters can be viewed as rehearsing once again the positions explored and argued in David Booth's (1994) collection on rethinking social development, particularly regarding the interaction of theory and practice, structure and agency. This time, though, the exercise is more specific – it is one of rethinking participation. The focus, I think, helps sharpen the message and means that this collection has also gone much further than did Booth's project in bringing researchers and practitioners together. This is very welcome. The problem, perhaps, is that they seem to come together in an atmosphere of great scepticism – more so, surprisingly, than in the Booth collection. This perhaps is a measure of the gravity of the legitimacy crisis of development institutions and interventions. I think it is an open question as to whether these chapters do anything to offset that crisis.

Notes

1 I was asked to review Chapters 1 (Hickey and Mohan), 4 (Hickey and Mohan), 5 (Cornwall), 15 (Brown) and 16 (Holland et al.).

2 This was the literary theorist, Eduardo Cadava, of Princeton.

3 CASs are the documents that guide World Bank activities in a particular country.

4 These commitments are not to be sneered at, nor easily explained away in terms of the salaries many such people are paid.

5 Such insinuations are clearly present in some of the chapters in this volume.

6 It is also one that finds antecedents within earlier discussions of participation, agency and populism (e.g. Booth 1994; Bebbington 1994).

References

Aronson, D. (1995) *Participation in Country Economic and Sector Work*, Social Development Paper, 6 (Washington, DC: World Bank).

Bebbington, A. (1994) 'Knowledge, Practice, Organization. Theory and Relevance in Indigenous Agricultural Development', in D. Booth (ed.), *Rethinking Social Development: Theory, Research and Practice* (Harlow: Longmans).

Bebbington, A., S. Guggenheim, E. Olson and M. Woolcock (forthcoming) 'Exploring Social Capital Debates at the World Bank', *Journal of Development Studies*.

Booth, D. (ed.) (1994) *Rethinking Social Development: Theory, Research and Practice* (Harlow: Longmans).

Cammack, P. (2002) 'Attacking the Poor', *New Left Review*, 2 (13): 125–34.

Chambers, R. (1983) *Rural Development. Putting the Last First* (Harlow: Longmans).

Cooke, B. (forthcoming) 'The Managing of the (Third) World', *Organization*.

Kanbur, R. (2001) 'Economic Policy, Distribution and Poverty: The Nature of Disagreements', *World Development*, 29 (6): 1083–94.

Moore, M. (1999) 'Politics against Poverty? Global Pessimism and National Optimism', *IDS Bulletin*, 30 (2): 33–46.

Wade, R. (2001) 'Making the World Development Report 2000: Attacking Poverty', *World Development*, 29 (8): 1435–41.

World Bank (2000) *Attacking Poverty: World Development Report 2000/2001* (Washington, DC: World Bank).

Contributors

Charles Abugre (CDS, University of Wales Swansea) is an NGO practitioner, researcher and consultant with a background in social development and governance. He established two leading NGOs in Ghana in the early 1980s and was active in the establishment of the African Regional Secretariat of the Third World Network, which links African Civil Society Organizations in addressing global policy issues.

Anthony Bebbington (IDPM, University of Manchester) is Professor of Development Studies at the Institute for Development Policy and Management. His interests are in rural development and livelihoods, non-governmental organizations, social movements and indigenous organizations and policy processes within development bureaucracies. He has worked extensively throughout Latin America, Indonesia, Nepal, Uganda and Sierra Leone. Recent publications have appeared in *Journal of Development Studies*, *World Development*, *Progress in Development Studies*, *Journal of International Development, and Tijdschrift voor Economische et Sociale Geografie.*

Mary Ann Brocklesby (CDS, University of Wales Swansea) is a social scientist with a research and advisory focus on poverty alleviation strategies, gender, social policy, governance and participatory monitoring and evaluation. Her recent advisory work has focused on providing guidance on analytical and methodological frameworks for poverty analysis.

David Brown (ODI, London) is a Research Fellow of the Overseas Development Institute in London. His research work focuses on the governance dimensions of forest resource exploitation in the tropics, particularly in relation to national policy and international aid instruments. His critical writings on the theme of participation include: 'Professionalism, Participation, and the Public Good: Issues of Arbitration in Development Management and the Critique of the Neo-populist Approach', in M. Minogue et al. (eds), *Beyond the New Public Management* (1998); and the edited volume *Participation in Practice: Case Studies.*

Frances Cleaver (University of Bradford) is a senior lecturer at the Bradford Centre for International Development. Her research interests include the social analysis of institutions and collective arrangements for the management of natural resources in Africa, the theory and practice of participatory approaches in development and gender approaches to water policy.

Bill Cooke (Manchester School of Management, UMIST) was editor with Uma Kothari of *Participation: The New Tyranny?* (2001). A former management consultant, he researches and teaches the history and problems of participatory methodologies in the workplace and in other social arenas. Recent work has looked at participation's roots as a form of colonial administration, at the uses of participation by the World Bank, and at managerialism as a Cold War phenomenon. He is now a management academic based at the University of Manchester.

Andrea Cornwall (IDS, University of Sussex) is a Fellow in participation in development at the Institute of Development Studies, Sussex. A social anthropologist by training, her work focuses on historical, ethnographic and conceptual dimensions of participation in development. She is co-editor of *Realizing Rights: Transforming Approaches to Sexual and Reproductive Wellbeing* (2002) and *Pathways to Participation: Practitioners' Reflections on Participatory Rural Appraisal* (2003).

Glauco Regis Florisbelo (CTA-ZM, Brazil) is a staff member of CTA-ZM (Centro de Tecnologias Alternatives – Zona da Mata; Centre for Alternative Technologies of the Zona da Mata), Brazil. He worked on participatory municipal planning in the municipality of Tombos for three years before taking over the coordination of all the municipal planning work in CTA-ZM.

John Gaventa (IDS, University of Sussex) is a political sociologist based at the Institute of Development Studies, University of Sussex. He also serves as Director of the Development Research Centre on Citizenship, Participation and Accountability and of LogoLink, a programme on citizen participation and local governance. He has worked in both North and South, and has written widely on issues of power, participation and citizenship. He is best known for his book *Power and Powerlessness: Quiescence and Rebellion in an Appalachian Valley* (1980) and most recently co-edited (with Michael Edwards) *Global Citizen Action* (2002). He holds a DPhil from Oxford University.

Irene Guijt (Learning by Design and Wageningen University, the Netherlands) is a freelance adviser and researcher, operating under the company name 'Learning by Design', who focuses on learning processes and systems (including monitoring and evaluation) in rural development and natural resource management, particularly where this involves collective action. She is completing her PhD on the contribution of monitoring to trigger learning. Key publications include *Participatory Learning and Action: A Trainer's Guide* and (as co-editor), *The Myth of Community: Gender Issues in Participatory Development.*

Leroi Henry (DPP, Open University) is Research Fellow at the Development Policy and Practice group at the Open University. His research interests include the relationships between ethnicity and African development, processes of legitimacy in indigenous development associations and the role of the African diaspora in development.

Sam Hickey (IDPM, University of Manchester) is a lecturer and researcher in international development at the Institute for Development Policy and Management, University of Manchester. His research focuses on participation and citizenship, NGOs and social movements, the links between politics and poverty reduction, and the use of political analysis in development. He is currently co-editing a forthcoming *World Development* special issue entitled 'The Politics of Poverty Reduction: Who Represents the Poorest?'.

Jeremy Holland (CDS, University of Wales Swansea) is a social development researcher, lecturer and consultant. He has a background in urban development, poverty and policy analysis and rights-based approaches, with a methodological emphasis on participatory and combined methods. He is the joint editor of *Whose Voice?* (1998) and *Who Changes?* (1998).

Ute Kelly (University of Bradford) is a research fellow at the Department of Peace Studies, University of Bradford. She is interested in the theory and practice of participation, dialogue and debate, particularly in situations of conflict and/or inequality. Previous articles have been published in *Review of International Studies* and *Peace Review*.

Katsuhiko Masaki (Seisen University, Tokyo) is an assistant professor at the Department of Studies on Global Citizenship of Seisen University in Tokyo, Japan. He holds a PhD from the Institute of Development Studies (IDS) at the University of Sussex, Brighton, UK. His research interests include nuanced approaches to power analysis, and discursive interplays in the policy process in such areas as participation, decentralization, and conflict resolution.

Diana Mitlin (IIED, London and IDPM, University of Manchester) is an economist working as a senior research associate at the International Institute for Environment (IIED) and a senior Research Fellow at the Institute for Development Policy and Management (University of Manchester). Diana is presently researching urban poverty including poverty reduction programmes, particularly the contribution of NGOs and grassroots organizations to pro-poor urban development. Her contribution in this collection draws on a long history of collaborative learning and research with members of Shack/Slum Dwellers International (SDI), an international network of national federations of homeless and landless people. Work on this has been published in *Community Development*, *Environment and Urbanization*, and *International Planning Studies.*

Giles Mohan (DPP, Open University) is a lecturer in development studies at the Open University. His research interests have centred on the politics of localism, particularly issues of decentralization, participation and civil society. More recently he has focused on breaking out of the local by examining the role of migration and diasporas in development. Empirical work on Ghanaians in the UK was funded by the Open University and so far has appeared in the *Journal of International Development.* He has been associated with Village AiD for eight years, has researched their programmes, and is currently on the Board of Trustees.

Susan Vincent (St Francis Xavier University, Canada) is a social anthropologist in the Department of Sociology and Anthropology, St Francis Xavier University, Canada. She has carried out research in the Peruvian community of Matachico since 1984.

Mark Waddington (formerly of Village AiD, UK) was Village AiD's Africa Programme Coordinator for eight years. He is currently using this experience base in supporting several small UK-based INGOs in areas of programme design, partnership management and fund-raising. However, Mark's main focus is now on managing a campaign in South Yorkshire that will challenge negative perceptions of older people, while raising funds for social housing and care provision for them.

Glyn Williams (King's College, University of London) is a lecturer in the Department of Geography, King's College London. For the last ten years he has conducted fieldwork in eastern India, investigating issues of poverty, development and political change. He is currently completing a co-authored book (with Stuart Corbridge, Manoj Srivastava and René Véron) on these issues, provisionally titled *Seeing the State: How Poor People Experience Local Government in India.*

Index

Page references in *italics* refer to boxes and tables. An 'n' after a page reference refers to a note.